Generative Adversarial Networks Projects

Build next-generation generative models using TensorFlow and Keras

Kailash Ahirwar

BIRMINGHAM - MUMBAI

Generative Adversarial Networks Projects

Commissioning Editor: Sunith Shetty
Acquisition Editor: Aman Singh
Content Development Editor: Snehal Kolte
Technical Editor: Dharmendra Yadav
Copy Editor: Safis Editing
Language Support Editor: Mary McGowan
Project Coordinator: Manthan Patel
Proofreader: Safis Editing
Indexer: Mariammal Chettiyar
Graphics: Jisha Chirayil
Production Coordinator: Shraddha Falebhai

First published: January 2019

Production reference: 1310119

Published by Packt Publishing Ltd.
Livery Place
35 Livery Street
Birmingham
B3 2PB, UK.

ISBN 978-1-78913-667-8

www.packtpub.com

`mapt.io`

Mapt is an online digital library that gives you full access to over 5,000 books and videos, as well as industry leading tools to help you plan your personal development and advance your career. For more information, please visit our website.

Why subscribe?

- Spend less time learning and more time coding with practical eBooks and Videos from over 4,000 industry professionals

- Improve your learning with Skill Plans built especially for you

- Get a free eBook or video every month

- Mapt is fully searchable

- Copy and paste, print, and bookmark content

Packt.com

Did you know that Packt offers eBook versions of every book published, with PDF and ePub files available? You can upgrade to the eBook version at `www.packt.com` and as a print book customer, you are entitled to a discount on the eBook copy. Get in touch with us at `customercare@packtpub.com` for more details.

At `www.packt.com`, you can also read a collection of free technical articles, sign up for a range of free newsletters, and receive exclusive discounts and offers on Packt books and eBooks.

Contributors

About the author

Kailash Ahirwar is a machine learning and deep learning enthusiast. He has worked in many areas of **Artificial Intelligence (AI)**, ranging from natural language processing and computer vision to generative modeling using GANs. He is a co-founder and CTO of Mate Labs. He uses GANs to build different models, such as turning paintings into photos and controlling deep image synthesis with texture patches.

He is super optimistic about AGI and believes that AI is going to be the workhorse of human evolution.

This book wouldn't have been possible without the help of my family. They supported me and encouraged me during this journey. I would like to thank Rahul Vishwakarma and the whole team at Mate Labs for their support. Also, a big thanks to Ruby Mohan, Neethu Daniel, Abhishek Kumar, Tanay Agarwal, Amara Anand Kumar, and others for their valuable inputs.

About the reviewer

Jalaj Thanaki is an experienced data scientist with a demonstrated history of working in the information technology, publishing, and finance industries. She is author of *Python Natural Language Processing* and *Machine Learning Solutions*, by Packt Publishing.

Her research interest lies in natural language processing, machine learning, deep learning, and big data analytics. Besides being a data scientist, Jalaj is also a social activist, traveler, and nature lover.

Packt is searching for authors like you

If you're interested in becoming an author for Packt, please visit authors.packtpub.com and apply today. We have worked with thousands of developers and tech professionals, just like you, to help them share their insight with the global tech community. You can make a general application, apply for a specific hot topic that we are recruiting an author for, or submit your own idea.

Table of Contents

Preface

Generative Adversarial Networks (GANs) have the potential to build next-generation models, as they can mimic any distribution of data. Major research and development work is being undertaken in this field because it is one of the most rapidly growing areas of **machine learning (ML)**. This book will test unsupervised techniques of training neural networks as you build eight end-to-end projects in the GAN domain.

Generative Adversarial Network Projects begins by covering the concepts, tools, and libraries that you will use to build efficient projects. You will also use a variety of datasets in the different projects in the book. With every chapter, the level of complexity and operations advances, helping you get to grips with the GAN domain.

You will cover popular approaches such as 3D-GAN, DCGAN, StackGAN, and CycleGAN, and you'll understand the architecture and functioning of generative models through their practical implementation.

By the end of this book, you will be ready to build, train, and optimize your own end-to-end GAN models at work or in your projects.

Who this book is for

If you're a data scientist, ML developer, deep learning practitioner, or AI enthusiast looking for a project guide to test your knowledge and expertise in building real-world GANs models, this book is for you.

What this book covers

Chapter 1, *Introduction to Generative Adversarial Networks*, starts with the concepts of GANs. Readers will learn what a discriminator is, what a generator is, and what Game Theory is. The next few topics will cover the architecture of a generator, the architecture of a discriminator, objective functions for generators and discriminators, training algorithms for GANs, Kullback–Leibler and Jensen–Shannon Divergence, evaluation matrices for GANs, different problems with GANs, the problems of vanishing and exploding gradients, Nash equilibrium, batch normalization, and regularization in GANs.

Chapter 2, *3D-GAN – Generating Shapes Using GANs*, starts with a short introduction to 3D-GANs and various architectural details. In this chapter, we will train a 3D-GAN to generate real-world 3D shapes. We write code for collecting a 3D Shapenet dataset, cleaning it, and making it training ready. Then, we will write code for a 3D-GAN with the Keras deep learning library.

Chapter 3, *Face Aging Using Conditional GAN*, introduces Conditional Generative Adversarial Networks (cGANs) and Age-cGAN to the readers. We will learn different steps in data preparation, such as downloading, cleaning, and formatting data. We will be using the IMDb Wiki Images dataset. We will write code for an Age-cGAN using the Keras framework. Next, we will train the network on the IMDb Wiki Images dataset. Finally, we will generate images using our trained model with age as our conditional argument, and our trained model will generate images for a person's face at different ages.

Chapter 4, *Generating Anime Characters Using DCGANs*, starts with an introduction to DCGANs. We will learn different steps in data preparation, such as gathering the anime characters dataset, cleaning the dataset, and preparing it for training. We will cover the Keras implementation of a DCGAN inside a Jupyter Notebook. Next, we will learn different ways to train the DCGAN and choose different hyper-parameters for it. Finally, we will generate anime characters using our trained model. Also, we will discuss practical applications of DCGANs.

Chapter 5, *Using SRGANs to Generate Photo-Realistic Images*, explains how to train an SRGAN to generate photo-realistic images. The first step in the training process is to gather the dataset, followed by cleaning it and formatting it for training. Readers will learn where to gather the dataset from, how to clean it, and how to get it into a format that is ready for training.

Chapter 6, *StackGAN – Text to Photo-Realistic Image Synthesis*, this chapter will start with an introduction to StackGAN. Data collection and data preparation are important steps, and we will learn the process of gathering the dataset, cleaning the dataset, and formatting it ready for training. We will write the code for a StackGAN in Keras inside a Jupyter Notebook. Next, we will train the network on the CUB dataset. Finally, after we finish training the model, we will generate photo-realistic images from the text descriptions. We will discuss different industry applications of StackGANs and how to deploy them in production.

Chapter 7, *CycleGAN – Turn Paintings into Photos*, explains how to train a CycleGAN to turn paintings into photos. We will start with an introduction to CycleGANs and look at their different applications. We will cover different data gathering, data cleaning, and data formatting techniques. Next, we will write the Keras implementation of the CycleGAN and get a detailed explanation of the code in Jupyter Notebook. We will train the CycleGAN on the dataset that we have prepared. We will test our trained model to turn paintings into photos. Finally, we look at practical applications of CycleGANs.

Chapter 8, *Conditional GAN – Image-to-Image Translation Using Conditional Adversarial Networks*, covers how to train a conditional GAN for image-to-image translation. We will start with an introduction to conditional GANs and different data preparation techniques, such as data gathering, data cleaning, and data formatting. Next, we will write the code for the conditional GAN in Keras inside Jupyter Notebook. Next, we learn how to train the conditional GAN on the dataset that we have prepared. We will explore different hyper-parameters for training. Finally, we will test the conditional GAN and will discuss different use cases of image-to-image translation in real-world applications.

Chapter 9, *Predicting the Future of GANs*, is the final chapter. After covering the fundamentals of GANs and going through six projects, this chapter will give readers a glimpse into the future of GANs. Here, we will look at how, in the last 3-4 years, the adoption of GANs has been phenomenal and how well the industry has accepted it. I will also discuss my personal views on the future of GANs.

To get the most out of this book

Familiarity with deep learning and Keras and some prior knowledge TensorFlow is required. Experience of coding in Python 3 will be useful.

Download the example code files

You can download the example code files for this book from your account at www.packt.com. If you purchased this book elsewhere, you can visit www.packt.com/support and register to have the files emailed directly to you.

You can download the code files by following these steps:

1. Log in or register at www.packt.com.
2. Select the **SUPPORT** tab.
3. Click on **Code Downloads & Errata**.
4. Enter the name of the book in the **Search** box and follow the onscreen instructions.

Once the file is downloaded, please make sure that you unzip or extract the folder using the latest version of:

- WinRAR/7-Zip for Windows
- Zipeg/iZip/UnRarX for Mac
- 7-Zip/PeaZip for Linux

The code bundle for the book is also hosted on GitHub at https://github.com/PacktPublishing/Generative-Adversarial-Networks-Projects. In case there's an update to the code, it will be updated on the existing GitHub repository.

We also have other code bundles from our rich catalog of books and videos available at https://github.com/PacktPublishing/. Check them out!

Conventions used

There are a number of text conventions used throughout this book.

CodeInText: Indicates code words in text, database table names, folder names, filenames, file extensions, pathnames, dummy URLs, user input, and Twitter handles. Here is an example: "Use the loadmat() function from scipy to retrieve the voxels."

A block of code is set as follows:

```
import scipy.io as io
voxels = io.loadmat("path to .mat file")['instance']
```

Any command-line input or output is written as follows:

```
pip install -r requirements.txt
```

Bold: Indicates a new term, an important word, or words that you see onscreen.

Warnings or important notes appear like this.

 Tips and tricks appear like this.

Get in touch

Feedback from our readers is always welcome.

General feedback: If you have questions about any aspect of this book, mention the book title in the subject of your message and email us at customercare@packtpub.com.

Errata: Although we have taken every care to ensure the accuracy of our content, mistakes do happen. If you have found a mistake in this book, we would be grateful if you would report this to us. Please visit www.packt.com/submit-errata, selecting your book, clicking on the Errata Submission Form link, and entering the details.

Piracy: If you come across any illegal copies of our works in any form on the Internet, we would be grateful if you would provide us with the location address or website name. Please contact us at copyright@packt.com with a link to the material.

If you are interested in becoming an author: If there is a topic that you have expertise in and you are interested in either writing or contributing to a book, please visit authors.packtpub.com.

Reviews

Please leave a review. Once you have read and used this book, why not leave a review on the site that you purchased it from? Potential readers can then see and use your unbiased opinion to make purchase decisions, we at Packt can understand what you think about our products, and our authors can see your feedback on their book. Thank you!

For more information about Packt, please visit packt.com.

Introduction to Generative Adversarial Networks

1

In this chapter, we will look at **Generative Adversarial Networks (GANs)**. They are a type of deep neural network architecture that uses unsupervised machine learning to generate data. They were introduced in 2014, in a paper by Ian Goodfellow, Yoshua Bengio, and Aaron Courville, which can be found at the following link: `https://arxiv.org/pdf/1406.2661`. GANs have many applications, including image generation and drug development.

This chapter will introduce you to the core components of GANs. It will take you through how each component works and the important concepts and technology behind GANs. It will also give you a brief overview of the benefits and drawbacks of using GANs and an insight into certain real-world applications.

The chapter will cover all of these points by exploring the following topics:

- What is a GAN?
- The architecture of a GAN
- Important concepts related to GANs
- Different varieties of GANs
- Advantages and disadvantages of GANs
- Practical applications of GANs

What is a GAN?

A GAN is a deep neural network architecture made up of two networks, a generator network and a discriminator network. Through multiple cycles of generation and discrimination, both networks train each other, while simultaneously trying to outwit each other.

What is a generator network?

A generator network uses existing data to generate new data. It can, for example, use existing images to generate new images. The generator's primary goal is to generate data (such as images, video, audio, or text) from a randomly generated vector of numbers, called a **latent space**. While creating a generator network, we need to specify the goal of the network. This might be image generation, text generation, audio generation, video generation, and so on.

What is a discriminator network?

The discriminator network tries to differentiate between the real data and the data generated by the generator network. The discriminator network tries to put the incoming data into predefined categories. It can either perform multi-class classification or binary classification. Generally, in GANs binary classification is performed.

Training through adversarial play in GANs

In a GAN, the networks are trained through adversarial play: both networks compete against each other. As an example, let's assume that we want the GAN to create forgeries of artworks:

1. The first network, the generator, has never seen the real artwork but is trying to create an artwork that looks like the real thing.
2. The second network, the discriminator, tries to identify whether an artwork is real or fake.
3. The generator, in turn, tries to fool the discriminator into thinking that its fakes are the real deal by creating more realistic artwork over multiple iterations.
4. The discriminator tries to outwit the generator by continuing to refine its own criteria for determining a fake.
5. They guide each other by providing feedback from the successful changes they make in their own process in each iteration. This process is the training of the GAN.
6. Ultimately, the discriminator trains the generator to the point at which it can no longer determine which artwork is real and which is fake.

In this game, both networks are trained simultaneously. When we reach a stage at which the discriminator is unable to distinguish between real and fake artworks, the network attains a state known as **Nash equilibrium**. This will be discussed later on in this chapter.

Practical applications of GANs

GANs have some fairly useful practical applications, which include the following:

- **Image generation**: Generative networks can be used to generate realistic images after being trained on sample images. For example, if we want to generate new images of dogs, we can train a GAN on thousands of samples of images of dogs. Once the training has finished, the generator network will be able to generate new images that are different from the images in the training set. Image generation is used in marketing, logo generation, entertainment, social media, and so on. In the next chapter, we will be generating faces of anime characters.

- **Text-to-image synthesis**: Generating images from text descriptions is an interesting use case of GANs. This can be helpful in the film industry, as a GAN is capable of generating new data based on some text that you have made up. In the comic industry, it is possible to automatically generate sequences of a story.

- **Face aging**: This can be very useful for both the entertainment and surveillance industries. It is particularly useful for face verification because it means that a company doesn't need to change their security systems as people get older. An age-cGAN network can generate images at different ages, which can then be used to train a robust model for face verification.

- **Image-to-image translation**: Image-to-image translation can be used to convert images taken in the day to images taken at night, to convert sketches to paintings, to style images to look like Picasso or Van Gogh paintings, to convert aerial images to satellite images automatically, and to convert images of horses to images of zebras. These use cases are ground-breaking because they can save us time.

- **Video synthesis**: GANs can also be used to generate videos. They can generate content in less time than if we were to create content manually. They can enhance the productivity of movie creators and also empower hobbyists who want to make creative videos in their free time.

- **High-resolution image generation**: If you have pictures taken from a low-resolution camera, GANs can help you generate high-resolution images without losing any essential details. This can be useful on websites.

- **Completing missing parts of images**: If you have an image that has some missing parts, GANs can help you to recover these sections.

The detailed architecture of a GAN

The architecture of a GAN has two basic elements: the generator network and the discriminator network. Each network can be any neural network, such as an **Artificial Neural Network (ANN)**, a **Convolutional Neural Network (CNN)**, a **Recurrent Neural Network (RNN)**, or a **Long Short Term Memory (LSTM)**. The discriminator has to have fully connected layers with a classifier at the end.

Let's take a closer look at the components of the architecture of a GAN. In this example, we will imagine that we are creating a dummy GAN.

The architecture of the generator

The generator network in our dummy GAN is a simple feed-forward neural network with five layers: an input layer, three hidden layers, and an output layer. Let's take a closer look at the configuration of the generator (dummy) network:

Layer #	Layer name	Configuration
1	Input layer	`input_shape=(batch_size, 100),` `output_shape=(batch_size, 100)`
2	Dense layer	`neurons=500, input_shape=(batch_size, 100),` `output_shape=(batch_size, 500)`
3	Dense layer	`neurons=500, input_shape=(batch_size, 500),` `output_shape=(batch_size, 500)`
4	Dense layer	`neurons=784, input_shape=(batch_size, 500),` `output_shape=(batch_size, 784)`
5	Reshape layer	`input_shape=(batch_size, 784),` `output_shape=(batch_size, 28, 28)`

The preceding table shows the configurations of the hidden layers, and also the input and output layers in the network.

The following diagram shows the flow of tensors and the input and output shapes of the tensors for each layer in the generator network:

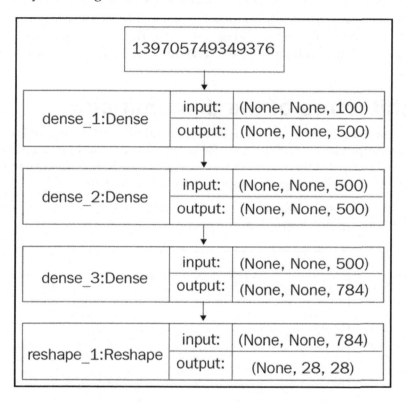

The architecture of the generator network.

Let's discuss how this feed-forward neural network processes information during forward propagation of the data:

- The input layer takes a 100-dimensional vector sampled from a Gaussian (normal) distribution and passes the tensor to the first hidden layer without any modifications.
- The three hidden layers are dense layers with 500, 500, and 784 units, respectively. The first hidden layer (a dense layer) converts a tensor of a shape of (`batch_size, 100`) to a tensor of a shape of (`batch_size, 500`).

- The second dense layer generates a tensor of a shape of (`batch_size, 500`).
- The third hidden layer generates a tensor of a shape of (`batch_size, 784`).
- In the last output layer, this tensor is reshaped from a shape of (`batch_size, 784`) to a shape of (`batch_size, 28, 28`). This means that our network will generate a batch of images, where one image will have a shape of (28, 28).

The architecture of the discriminator

The discriminator in our GAN is a feed-forward neural network with five layers, including an input and an output layer, and three dense layers. The discriminator network is a classifier and is slightly different from the generator network. It processes an image and outputs a probability of the image belonging to a particular class.

The following diagram shows the flow of tensors and the input and output shapes of the tensors for each layer in the discriminator network:

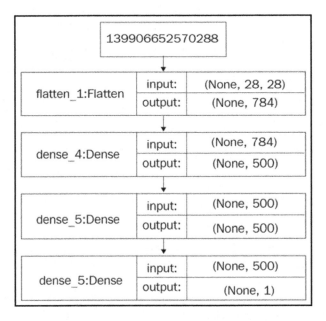

The architecture of the discriminator network

Let's discuss how the discriminator processes data in forward propagation during the training of the network:

1. Initially, it receives an input of a shape of 28x28.
2. The input layer takes the input tensor, which is a tensor with a shape of (`batch_sizex28x28`), and passes it to the first hidden layer without any modifications.
3. Next, the flattening layer flattens the tensor to a 784-dimensional vector, which gets passed to the first hidden (dense) layer. The first and second hidden layers modify this to a 500-dimensional vector.
4. The last layer is the output layer, which is again a dense layer, with one unit (a neuron) and sigmoid as the activation function. It outputs a single value, either a 0 or a 1. A value of 0 indicates that the provided image is fake, while a value of 1 indicates that the provided image is real.

Important concepts related to GANs

Now that we have understood the architecture of GANs, let's take a look at a brief overview of a few important concepts. We will first look at KL divergence. It is very important to understand JS divergence, which is an important measure to assess the quality of the models. We will then look at the Nash equilibrium, which is a state that we try to achieve during training. Finally, we will look closer at objective functions, which are very important to understand in order to implement GANs well.

Kullback-Leibler divergence

Kullback-Leibler divergence (KL divergence), also known as **relative entropy**, is a method used to identify the similarity between two probability distributions. It measures how one probability distribution p diverges from a second expected probability distribution q.

The equation used to calculate the KL divergence between two probability distributions $p(x)$ and $q(x)$ is as follows:

$$D_{KL}(p||q) = \int_x p(x) log \frac{p(x)}{q(x)} dx$$

The KL divergence will be zero, or minimum, when $p(x)$ is equal to $q(x)$ at every other point.

Due to the asymmetric nature of KL divergence, we shouldn't use it to measure the distance between two probability distributions. It is therefore should not be used as a distance metric.

Jensen-Shannon divergence

The **Jensen-Shannon** divergence (also called the **information radius (IRaD)** or the **total divergence to the average**) is another measure of similarity between two probability distributions. It is based on KL divergence. Unlike KL divergence, however, JS divergence is symmetric in nature and can be used to measure the distance between two probability distributions. If we take the square root of the Jensen-Shannon divergence, we get the Jensen-Shannon distance, so it is therefore a distance metric.

The following equation represents the Jensen-Shannon divergence between two probability distributions, p and q:

$$D_{JS}(p\|q) = \frac{1}{2}D_{KL}(p\|\frac{p+q}{2}) + \frac{1}{2}D_{KL}(q\|\frac{p+q}{2})$$

In the preceding equation, $(p+q)$ is the midpoint measure, while D_{KL} is the Kullback-Leibler divergence.

Now that we have learned about the KL divergence and the Jenson-Shannon divergence, let's discuss the Nash equilibrium for GANs.

Nash equilibrium

The Nash equilibrium describes a particular state in game theory. This state can be achieved in a non-cooperative game in which each player tries to pick the best possible strategy to gain the best possible outcome for themselves, based on what they expect the other players to do. Eventually, all the players reach a point at which they have all picked the best possible strategy for themselves based on the decisions made by the other players. At this point in the game, they would gain no benefit from changing their strategy. This state is the Nash equilibrium.

A famous example of how the Nash equilibrium can be reached is with the Prisoner's Dilemma. In this example, two criminals (A and B) have been arrested for committing a crime. Both have been placed in separate cells with no way of communicating with each other. The prosecutor only has enough evidence to convict them for a smaller offense and not the principal crime, which would see them go to jail for a long time. To get a conviction, the prosecutor gives them an offer:

- If A and B both implicate each other in the principal crime, they both serve 2 years in jail.
- If A implicates B but B remains silent, A will be set free and B will serve 3 years in jail (and vice versa).
- If A and B both keep quiet, they both serve only 1 year in jail on the lesser charge.

From these three scenarios, it is obvious that the best possible outcome for A and B is to keep quiet and serve 1 year in jail. However, the risk of keeping quiet is 3 years as neither A nor B have any way of knowing that the other will also keep quiet. Thus, they would reach a state where their actual optimum strategy would be to confess as it is the choice that provides the highest reward and lowest penalty. When this state has been reached, neither criminal would gain any advantage by changing their strategy; thus, they would have reached a Nash equilibrium.

Objective functions

To create a generator network that generates images that are similar to real images, we try to increase the similarity of the data generated by the generator to real data. To measure the similarity, we use objective functions. Both networks have their own objective functions and during the training, they try to minimize their respective objective functions. The following equation represents the final objective function for GANs:

$$\min_{G} \max_{D} V(D, G) = \mathbb{E}_{\boldsymbol{x} \sim p_{\text{data}}(\boldsymbol{x})}[\log D(\boldsymbol{x})] + \mathbb{E}_{\boldsymbol{z} \sim p_{\boldsymbol{z}}(\boldsymbol{z})}[\log(1 - D(G(\boldsymbol{z})))].$$

In the preceding equation, $D(x)$ is the discriminator model, $G(z)$ is the generator model, P_z is the real data distribution, P_z is the distribution of the data generated by the generator, and E is the expected output.

During training, **D** (the **Discriminator**) wants to maximize the whole output and G (the Generator) wants to minimize it, thereby training a GAN to reach to an equilibrium between the generator and discriminator network. When it reaches an equilibrium, we say that the model has converged. This equilibrium is the Nash equilibrium. Once the training is complete, we get a generator model that is capable of generating realistic-looking images.

Scoring algorithms

Calculating the accuracy of a GAN is simple. The objective function for GANs is not a specific function, such as mean squared error or cross-entropy. GANs learn objective functions during training. There are many scoring algorithms proposed by researchers to measure how well a model fits. Let's look at some scoring algorithms in detail.

The inception score

The inception score is the most widely used scoring algorithm for GANs. It uses a pre-trained inception V3 network (trained on Imagenet) to extract the features of both generated and real images. It was proposed by Shane Barrat and Rishi Sharma in their paper, *A Note on the Inception Score* (https://arxiv.org/pdf/1801.01973.pdf). The inception score, or IS for short, measure the quality and the diversity of the generated images. Let's look at the equation for *IS*:

$$\text{IS}(G) = \exp\left(\mathbb{E}_{\mathbf{x} \sim p_g} D_{KL}(\, p(y|\mathbf{x}) \, \| \, p(y) \,) \right),$$

In the preceding equation, notation x represents a sample, sampled from a distribution. p_g and $x \sim p_g$ represent the same concept. $p(y|x)$ is the conditional class distribution, and $p(y)$ is the marginal class distribution.

To calculate the inception score, perform the following steps:

1. Start by sampling N number of images generated by the model, denoted as (x^i)
2. Then, construct the marginal class distribution, using the following equation:

$$p(y) = \int_x p(\, y \mid x)p_g(x)$$

3. Then, calculate the KL divergence and the expected improvement, using the following equation:

$$IS(G) = \exp\left(\mathbb{E}_{\mathbf{x} \sim p_g} \, D_{KL}(\, p(y|\mathbf{x}) \, \| \, p(y) \,) \right),$$

4. Finally, calculate the exponential of the result to give us the inception score.

The quality of the model is good if it has a high inception score. Even though this is an important measure, it has certain problems. For example, it shows a good level of accuracy even when the model generates one image per class, which means the model lacks diversity. To resolve this problem, other performance measures were proposed. We will look at one of these in the following section.

The Fréchet inception distance

To overcome the various shortcomings of the inception Score, the **Fréchlet Inception Distance (FID)** was proposed by Martin Heusel and others in their paper, *GANs Trained by a Two Time-Scale Update Rule Converge to a Local Nash Equilibrium* (https://arxiv.org/pdf/1706.08500.pdf).

The equation to calculate the FID score is as follows:

$$FID = \|\mu_r - \mu_g\|^2 + T_r(\Sigma_r + \Sigma_g - 2(\Sigma_r \Sigma_g)^{1/2})$$

The preceding equation represents the FID score between the real images, *x*, and the generated images, *g*. To calculate the FID score, we use the Inception network to extract the feature maps from an intermediate layer in the Inception network. Then, we model a multivariate Gaussian distribution, which learns the distribution of the feature maps. This multivariate Gaussian distribution has a mean of μ and a covariance of Σ, which we use to calculate the FID score. The lower the FID score, the better the model, and the more able it is to generate more diverse images with higher quality. A perfect generative model will have an FID score of zero. The advantage of using the FID score over the Inception score is that it is robust to noise and that it can easily measure the diversity of the images.

The TensorFlow implementation of FID can be found at the following link: https://www.tensorflow.org/api_docs/python/tf/contrib/gan/eval/frechet_classifier_distance
There are more scoring algorithms available that have been recently proposed by researchers in academia and industry. We won't be covering all of these here. Before reading any further, take a look at another scoring algorithm called the Mode Score, information about which can be found at the following link: https://arxiv.org/pdf/1612.02136.pdf.

Variants of GANs

There are currently thousands of different GANs available and this number is increasing at a phenomenal rate. In this section, we will explore six popular GAN architectures, which we will cover in more detail in the subsequent chapters of this book.

Deep convolutional generative adversarial networks

Alec Radford, Luke Metz, and Soumith Chintala proposed **deep convolutional GANs (DCGANs)** in a paper titled *Unsupervised Representation Learning with Deep Convolutional Generative Adversarial Networks*, which is available at the following link: https://arxiv.org/pdf/1511.06434.pdf. Vanilla GANs don't usually have **convolutional neural networks (CNNs)** in their networks. This was proposed for the first time with the introduction of DCGANs. We will learn how to generate anime character faces using DCGANs in Chapter 3, *Face Aging Using Conditional GANs*.

StackGANs

StackGANs were proposed by Han Zhang, Tao Xu, Hongsheng Li, and others in their paper titled *StackGAN: Text to Photo-Realistic Image Synthesis with Stacked Generative Adversarial Networks*, which is available at the following link: `https://arxiv.org/pdf/1612.03242.pdf`. They used StackGANs to explore text-to-image synthesis with impressive results. A StackGAN is a pair of networks that generate realistic looking images when provided with a text description. We will learn how to generate realistic looking images from text descriptions using a StackGAN in `Chapter 6`, *StackGAN – Text to Photo-Realistic Image Synthesis.*

CycleGANs

CycleGANs were proposed by Jun-Yan Zhu, Taesung Park, Phillip Isola, and Alexei A. Efros in a paper titled *Unpaired Image-to-Image Translation using Cycle-Consistent Adversarial Networks*, which is available at the following link: `https://arxiv.org/pdf/1703.10593`. CycleGANs have some really interesting potential uses, such as converting photos to paintings and vice versa, converting a picture taken in summer to a photo taken in winter and vice versa, or converting pictures of horses to pictures of zebras and vice versa. We will learn how to turn paintings into photos using a CycleGAN in `Chapter 7`, *CycleGAN - Turn Paintings into Photos.*

3D-GANs

3D-GANs were proposed by Jiajun Wu, Chengkai Zhang, Tianfan Xue, William T. Freeman, and Joshua B. Tenenbaum in their paper titled *Learning a Probabilistic Latent Space of Object Shapes via 3D Generative-Adversarial Modeling*, which is available at the following link: `https://arxiv.org/pdf/1610.07584`. Generating 3D models of objects has many use cases in manufacturing and the 3D modeling industry. A 3D-GAN network is able to generate new 3D models of different objects, once trained on 3D models of objects. We will learn how to generate 3D models of objects using a 3D-GAN in `Chapter 2`, *3D-GAN - Generating Shapes Using* GAN.

Age-cGANs

Face aging with Conditional GANs was proposed by Grigory Antipov, Moez Baccouche, and Jean-Luc Dugelay in their paper titled *Face Aging with Conditional Generative Adversarial Networks*, which is available at the following link: https://arxiv.org/pdf/1702.01983. pdf. Face aging has many industry use cases, including cross-age face recognition, finding lost children, and in entertainment. We will learn how to train a conditional GAN to generate a face given a target age in Chapter 3, *Face Aging Using Conditional GAN*.

pix2pix

The pix2pix network was introduced by Phillip Isola, Jun-Yan Zhu, Tinghui Zhou, and Alexei A. Efros in their paper titled *Image-to-Image Translation with Conditional Adversarial Networks*, which is available at the following link: https://arxiv.org/abs/1611.07004. The pix2pix network has similar use cases to the CycleGAN network. It can convert building labels to pictures of buildings (we will see a similar example in the pix2pix chapter), black and white images to color images, images taken in the day to night images, sketches to photos, and aerial images to map-like images.

 For a list of all the GANs in existence, refer to *The GAN Zoo*, an article by Avinash Hindupur available at https://github.com/hindupuravinash/the-gan-zoo.

Advantages of GANs

GANs have certain advantages over other methods of supervised or unsupervised learning:

- **GANs are an unsupervised learning method**: Acquiring labeled data is a manual process that takes a lot of time. GANs don't require labeled data; they can be trained using unlabeled data as they learn the internal representations of the data.
- **GANs generate data**: One of the best things about GANs is that they generate data that is similar to real data. Because of this, they have many different uses in the real world. They can generate images, text, audio, and video that is indistinguishable from real data. Images generated by GANs have applications in marketing, e-commerce, games, advertisements, and many other industries.

- **GANs learn density distributions of data**: GANs learn the internal representations of data. As mentioned earlier, GANs can learn messy and complicated distributions of data. This can be used for many machine learning problems.
- **The trained discriminator is a classifier**: After training, we get a discriminator and a generator. The discriminator network is a classifier and can be used to classify objects.

Problems with training GANs

As with any technology, there are some problems associated with GANs. These problems are generally to do with the training process and include mode collapse, internal covariate shifts, and vanishing gradients. Let's look at these in more detail.

Mode collapse

Mode collapse is a problem that refers to a situation in which the generator network generates samples that have little variety or when a model starts generating the same images. Sometimes, a probability distribution is multimodal and very complex in nature. This means that it might contain data from different observations and that it might have multiple peaks for different sub-graphs of samples. Sometimes, GANs fail to model a multimodal probability distribution of data and suffer from mode collapse. A situation in which all the generated samples are virtually identical is known as complete collapse.

There are many methods that we can use to overcome the mode collapse problem. These include the following:

- By training multiple models (GANs) for different modes

- By training GANs with diverse samples of data

Vanishing gradients

During backpropagation, gradient flows backward, from the final layer to the first layer. As it flows backward, it gets increasingly smaller. Sometimes, the gradient is so small that the initial layers learn very slowly or stop learning completely. In this case, the gradient doesn't change the weight values of the initial layers at all, so the training of the initial layers in the network is effectively stopped. This is known as the **vanishing gradients** problem.

This problem gets worse if we train a bigger network with gradient-based optimization methods. Gradient-based optimization methods optimize a parameter's value by calculating the change in the network's output when we change the parameter's value by a small amount. If a change in the parameter's value causes a small change in the network's output, the weight change will be very small, so the network stops learning.

This is also a problem when we use activation functions, such as Sigmoid and Tanh. Sigmoid activation functions restrict values to a range of between 0 and 1, converting large values of x to approximately 1 and small or negative values of x to approximately zero. The Tanh activation function squashes input values to a range between -1 and 1, converting large input values to approximately 1 and small values to approximately minus 1. When we apply backpropagation, we use the chain rule of differentiation, which has a multiplying effect. As we reach the initial layers of the network, the gradient (the error) decreases exponentially, causing the vanishing gradients problem.

To overcome this problem, we can use activation functions such as ReLU, LeakyReLU, and PReLU. The gradients of these activation functions don't saturate during backpropagation, causing efficient training of neural networks. Another solution is to use batch normalization, which normalizes inputs to the hidden layers of the networks.

Internal covariate shift

An internal covariate shift occurs when there is a change in the input distribution to our network. When the input distribution changes, hidden layers try to learn to adapt to the new distribution. This slows down the training process. If a process slows down, it takes a long time to converge to a global minimum. This problem occurs when the statistical distribution of the input to the networks is drastically different from the input that it has seen before. Batch normalization and other normalization techniques can solve this problem. We will explore these in the following sections.

Solving stability problems when training GANs

Training stability is one of the biggest problems that occur concerning GANs. For some datasets, GANs never converge due to this type of problem. In this section, we will look at some solutions that we can use to improve the stability of GANs.

Feature matching

During the training of GANs, we maximize the objective function of the discriminator network and minimize the objective function of the generator network. This objective function has some serious flaws. For example, it doesn't take into account the statistics of the generated data and the real data.

Feature matching is a technique that was proposed by Tim Salimans, Ian Goodfellow, and others in their paper titled *Improved Techniques for Training GANs*, to improve the convergence of the GANs by introducing a new objective function. The new objective function for the generator network encourages it to generate data, with statistics, that is similar to the real data.

To apply feature mapping, the network doesn't ask the discriminator to provide binary labels. Instead, the discriminator network provides activations or feature maps of the input data, extracted from an intermediate layer in the discriminator network. From a training perspective, we train the discriminator network to learn the important statistics of the real data; hence, the objective is that it should be capable of discriminating the real data from the fake data by learning those discriminative features.

To understand this approach mathematically, let's take a look at the different notations first:

- $f(x)$: The activation or feature maps for the real data from an intermediate layer in the discriminator network
- $f(G(z))$: The activation/feature maps for the data generated by the generator network from an intermediate layer in the discriminator network

This new objective function can be represented as follows:

$$||\mathbb{E}_{x \sim p_{\text{data}}} \mathbf{f}(x) - \mathbb{E}_{z \sim p_z(z)} \mathbf{f}(G(z))||_2^2.$$

Using this objective function can achieve better results, but there is still no guarantee of convergence.

Mini-batch discrimination

Mini-batch discrimination is another approach to stabilize the training of GANs. It was proposed by Ian Goodfellow and others in *Improved Techniques for Training GANs*, which is available at `https://arxiv.org/pdf/1606.03498.pdf`. To understand this approach, let's first look in detail at the problem. While training GANs, when we pass the independent inputs to the discriminator network, the coordination between the gradients might be missing, and this prevents the discriminator network from learning how to differentiate between various images generated by the generator network. This is mode collapse, a problem we looked at earlier. To tackle this problem, we can use mini-batch discrimination. The following diagram illustrates the process very well:

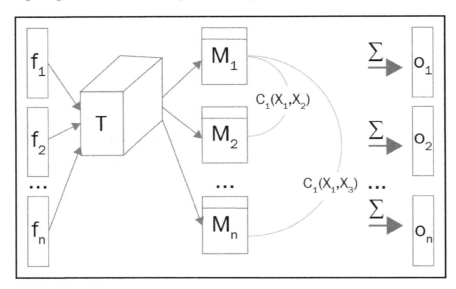

Mini-batch discrimination is a multi-step process. Perform the following steps to add mini-batch discrimination to your network:

1. Extract the feature maps for the sample and multiply them by a tensor, $T \in R^{A \times B \times C}$, generating a matrix, $M_i \in R^{A \times B}$.

2. Then, calculate the L1 distance between the rows of the matrix M_i using the following equation:

$$c_b(x_i, x_j) = exp(-||M_{i,b} - M_{j,b}||_{L1}) \in \mathbb{R}$$

3. Then, calculate the summation of all distances for a particular example, x_i:

$$o(x_i)_b = \sum_{j=1}^{n} c_b(x_i, x_j) \in \mathbb{R}$$

3. Then, concatenate $o(x_i)$ with $f(x_i)$ and feed it to the next layer of the network:

$$o(x_i) = [o(x_i)_1, o(x_i)_2, \ldots, o(x_i)_B] \in \mathbb{R}^B$$

$$o(X) \in \mathbb{R}^{n \times B}$$

To understand this approach mathematically, let's take a closer look at the various notions:

- $f(x_i)$: The activation or feature maps for ith sample from an intermediate layer in the discriminator network
- $T \in R^{A \times B \times C}$: A three-dimensional tensor, which we multiply by $f(x_i)$
- $M_i \in R^{A \times B}$: The matrix generated when we multiply the tensor T and $f(x_i)$
- $o(x_i)$: The output after taking the sum of all distances for a particular example, x_i

Mini-batch discrimination helps prevent mode collapse and improves the chances of training stability.

Historical averaging

Historical averaging is an approach that takes the average of the parameters in the past and adds this to the respective cost functions of the generator and the discriminator network. It was proposed by Ian Goodfellow and others in a paper mentioned previously, *Improved Techniques for Training GANs*.

The historical average can be denoted as follows:

$$\left\| \theta - \frac{1}{t} \sum_{i=1}^{t} \theta[i] \right\|^2$$

In the preceding equation, $\theta[i]$ is the value of parameters at a particular time, i. This approach can improve the training stability of GANs too.

One-sided label smoothing

Earlier, label/target values for a classifier were 0 or 1; 0 for fake images and 1 for real images. Because of this, GANs were prone to adversarial examples, which are inputs to a neural network that result in an incorrect output from the network. Label smoothing is an approach to provide smoothed labels to the discriminator network. This means we can have decimal values such as 0.9 (true), 0.8 (true), 0.1 (fake), or 0.2 (fake), instead of labeling every example as either 1 (true) or 0 (fake). We smooth the target values (label values) of the real images as well as of the fake images. Label smoothing can reduce the risk of adversarial examples in GANs. To apply label smoothing, assign the labels 0.9, 0.8, and 0.7, and 0.1, 0.2, and 0.3, to the images. To find out more about label smoothing, refer to the following paper: https://arxiv.org/pdf/1606.03498.pdf.

Batch normalization

Batch normalization is a technique that normalizes the feature vectors to have no mean or unit variance. It is used to stabilize learning and to deal with poor weight initialization problems. It is a pre-processing step that we apply to the hidden layers of the network and it helps us to reduce internal covariate shift.

Batch normalization was introduced by Ioffe and Szegedy in their 2015 paper, *Batch Normalization: Accelerating Deep Network Training by Reducing Internal Covariate Shift*. This can be found at the following link: https://arxiv.org/pdf/1502.03167.pdf.

The benefits of batch normalization are as follows:

- **Reduces the internal covariate shift**: Batch normalization helps us to reduce the internal covariate shift by normalizing values.
- **Faster training**: Networks will be trained faster if the values are sampled from a normal/Gaussian distribution. Batch normalization helps to whiten the values to the internal layers of our network. The overall training is faster, but each iteration slows down due to the fact that extra calculations are involved.
- **Higher accuracy**: Batch normalization provides better accuracy.
- **Higher learning rate**: Generally, when we train neural networks, we use a lower learning rate, which takes a long time to converge the network. With batch normalization, we can use higher learning rates, making our network reach the global minimum faster.
- **Reduces the need for dropout**: When we use dropout, we compromise some of the essential information in the internal layers of the network. Batch normalization acts as a regularizer, meaning we can train the network without a dropout layer.

In batch normalization, we apply normalization to all the hidden layers, rather than applying it only to the input layer.

Instance normalization

As mentioned in the previous section, batch normalization normalizes a batch of samples by utilizing information from this batch only. Instance normalization is a slightly different approach. In instance normalization, we normalize each feature map by utilizing information from that feature map only. Instance normalization was introduced by Dmitry Ulyanov and Andrea Vedaldi in the paper titled *Instance Normalization: The Missing Ingredient for Fast Stylization*, which is available at the following link: `https://arxiv.org/pdf/1607.08022.pdf`.

Summary

In this chapter, we learned about what a GAN is and which components constitute a standard GAN architecture. We also explored the various kinds of GANs that are available. After establishing the basic concepts of GANs, we moved on to looking at the underlying concepts that go into the construction and functioning of GANs. We learned about the advantages and disadvantages of GANs, as well as the solutions that help overcome those disadvantages. Finally, we learned about the various practical applications of GANs.

Using the fundamental knowledge of GANs in this chapter, we will now move on to the next chapter, where we will learn to generate various shapes using GANs.

3D-GAN - Generating Shapes Using GANs

2

A 3D-GAN is a GAN architecture for 3D shape generation. 3D shape generation is typically a complex problem, due to the complexities involved in processing 3D images. A 3D-GAN is a solution that can generate realistic and varied 3D shapes and was introduced by Jiajun Wu, Chengkai Zhang, Tianfan Xue, and others in the paper titled *Learning a Probabilistic Latent Space of Object Shapes via 3D Generative-Adversarial Modeling*. This paper is available at `http://3dgan.csail.mit.edu/papers/3dgan_nips.pdf`. In this chapter, we will implement a 3D-GAN using the Keras framework.

We will cover the following topics:

- Introduction to the basics of 3D-GANs
- Setting up the project
- Preparing the data
- A Keras implementation of a 3D-GAN
- Training the 3D-GAN
- Hyperparameter optimization
- Practical applications of 3D-GANs

Introduction to 3D-GANs

3D Generative Adversarial Networks (3D-GANs) is a variant of GANs, just like StackGANs, CycleGANs, and **Super-Resolution Generative Adversarial Networks (SRGANs)**. Similar to a vanilla GAN, it has a generator and a discriminator model. Both of the networks use 3D convolutional layers, instead of using 2D convolutions. If provided with enough data, it can learn to generate 3D shapes with good visual quality.

Let's understand 3D convolutions before looking closer at the 3D-GAN network.

3D convolutions

In short, 3D convolution operations apply a 3D filter to the input data along the three directions, which are x, y, and z. This operation creates a stacked list of 3D feature maps. The shape of the output is similar to the shape of a cube or a cuboid. The following image illustrates a 3D convolution operation. The highlighted part of the left cube is the input data. The kernel is in the middle, with a shape of (3, 3, 3). The block on the right-hand is the output of the convolution operation:

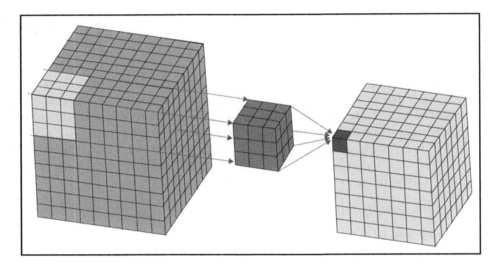

Now that we have a basic understanding of 3D convolutions, let's continue looking at the architecture of a 3D-GAN.

The architecture of a 3D-GAN

Both of the networks in a 3D-GAN are deep convolutional neural networks. The generator network is, as usual, an upsampling network. It upsamples a noise vector (a vector from probabilistic latent space) to generate a 3D image with a shape that is similar to the input image in terms of its length, breadth, height, and channels. The discriminator network is a downsampling network. Using a series of 3D convolution operations and a dense layer, it identifies whether the input data provided to it is real or fake.

In the next two sections, we will go through the architecture of the generator and the discriminator network.

The architecture of the generator network

The generator network contains five volumetric, fully convolutional layers with the following configuration:

- **Convolutional layers**: 5
- **Filters**: 512, 256, 128, 64, 1
- **Kernel size**: 4 x 4 x 4, 4 x 4 x 4, 4 x 4 x 4, 4 x 4 x 4, 4 x 4 x 4
- **Strides**: 1, 2, 2, 2, 2 or (1, 1), (2, 2), (2, 2), (2, 2), (2, 2)
- **Batch normalization**: Yes, Yes, Yes, Yes, No
- **Activations**: ReLU, ReLU, ReLU, ReLU, Sigmoid
- **Pooling layers**: No, No, No, No, No
- **Linear layers**: No, No, No, No, No

The input and output of the network are as follows:

- **Input**: A 200-dimensional vector sampled from a probabilistic latent space
- **Output**: A 3D image with a shape of `64x64x64`

The architecture of the generator can be seen in the following image:

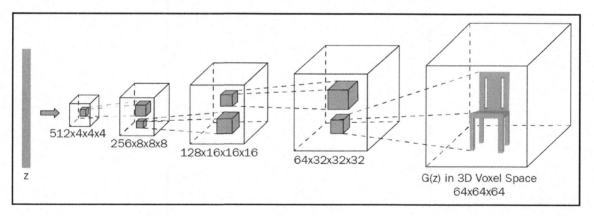

The flow of the tensors and the input and output shapes of the tensors for each layer in the discriminator network are shown in the following diagram. This will give you a better understanding of the network:

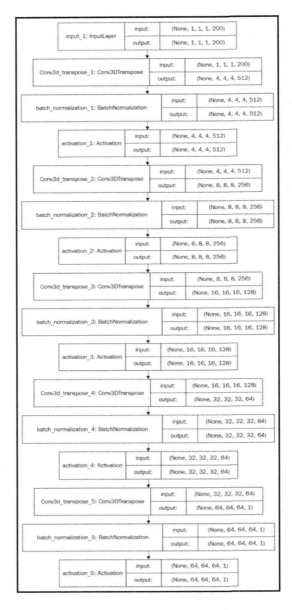

A fully convolutional network is a network without fully connected dense layers at the end of the network. Instead, it just consists of convolutional layers and can be end-to-end trained, like a convolutional network with fully connected layers. There are no pooling layers in a generator network.

The architecture of the discriminator network

The discriminator network contains five volumetric convolutional layers with the following configuration:

- **3D convolutional layers**: 5
- **Channels**: 64, 128, 256, 512, 1
- **Kernel sizes**: 4, 4, 4, 4, 4
- **Strides**: 2, 2, 2, 2, 1
- **Activations**: Leaky ReLU, Leaky ReLU, Leaky ReLU, Leaky ReLU, Sigmoid
- **Batch normalization**: Yes, Yes, Yes, Yes, None
- **Pooling layers**: No, No, No, No, No
- **Linear layers**: No, No, No, No, No

The input and output of the network are as follows:

- **Input**: A 3D image with shape (64, 64, 64)
- **Output**: The probability of the input data belonging to either the real or the fake class

The flow of the tensors and the input and output shapes of the tensors for each layer in the discriminator network are shown in the following diagram. This will provide you with a better understanding of the discriminator network:

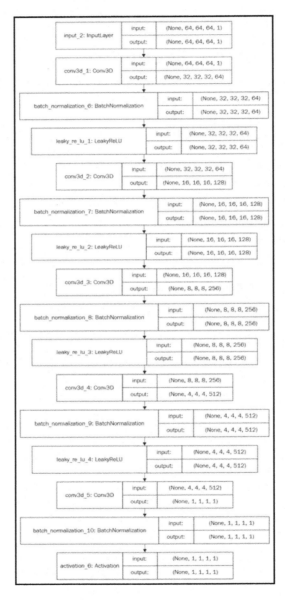

The discriminator network mostly mirrors the generator network. An important difference is that it uses LeakyReLU instead of ReLU as the activation function. Also, the sigmoid layer at the end of the network is for binary classification and predicts whether the provided image is real or fake. The last layer has no normalization layer, but the other layers use batch normalization to regularize the input.

Objective function

The objective function is the main method for training a 3D-GAN. It provides loss values, which are used to calculate gradients and then to update the weight values. The adversarial loss function for a 3D-GAN is as follows:

$$L_{3D-GAN} = logD(x) + log(1 - D(G(z)))$$

Here, $log(D(x))$ is the binary cross-entropy loss or classification loss, $log(1-D(G(z)))$ is the adversarial loss, z is the latent vector from probabilistic space $p(z)$, $D(x)$ is the output from the discriminator network, and $G(z)$ is the output from the generator network.

Training 3D-GANs

Training a 3D-GAN is similar to training a vanilla GAN. The steps involved in the training of a 3D-GAN are as follows:

1. Sample a 200-dimensional noise vector from a Gaussian (normal) distribution.
2. Generate a fake image using the generator model.
3. Train the generator network on real images (sampled from real data) and on the fake images generated by the generator network.
4. Use the adversarial model to train the generator model. Don't train the discriminator model.
5. Repeat these steps for a specified number of epochs.

We will explore these steps in detail in a later section. Let's move on to setting up a project.

Setting up a project

The source code for the project is available on GitHub at the following link: `https://github.com/PacktPublishing/Generative-Adversarial-Networks-Projects`.

Run the following commands to set up the project:

1. Start by navigating to the parent directory, as follows:

   ```
   cd Generative-Adversarial-Networks-Projects
   ```

2. Next, change directory from the current directory to the `Chapter02` directory:

   ```
   cd Chapter02
   ```

3. Next, create a Python virtual environment for this project:

   ```
   virtualenv venv
   ```

4. After that, activate the virtual environment:

   ```
   source venv/bin/activate
   ```

5. Finally, install all the requirements that are indicated in the `requirements.txt` file:

   ```
   pip install -r requirements.txt
   ```

We have now successfully set up the project. For more information, refer to the `README.md` file included with the code repository.

Preparing the data

In this chapter, we will use the 3D ShapeNets dataset, available at `http://3dshapenets.cs.princeton.edu/3DShapeNetsCode.zip`. It was released by Wu and Song et al. and consists of properly annotated 3D shapes for 40 object categories. We will use the volumetric data available in the directory, which we will discuss in more detail later on in this chapter. In the next few sections, we will download, extract, and explore the dataset.

The 3D ShapeNets dataset is for academic use only. If you intend to use the dataset for commercial purposes, request permission from the authors of the paper, who can be reached at the following email address: shurans@cs.princeton.edu.

Download and extract the dataset

Run the following commands to download and extract the dataset:

1. Start by downloading 3DShapeNets using the following link:

   wget http://3dshapenets.cs.princeton.edu/3DShapeNetsCode.zip

2. After you have downloaded the file, run the following command to extract the files to an appropriate directory:

   unzip 3DShapeNetsCode.zip

We have now successfully downloaded and extracted the dataset. It contains images in the .mat (MATLAB) format. Every other image is a 3D image. In the next few sections, we will learn about voxels, which are points in 3D space.

Exploring the dataset

To understand the dataset, we need to visualize the 3D images. In the next few sections, we will first look in more detail at what a voxel is. Then, we will load and visualize a 3D image.

What is a voxel?

A **volume pixel** or voxel is a point in three-dimensional space. A voxel defines a position with three coordinates in x, y, and z directions. A voxel is a fundamental unit for representing 3D images. They are mostly used in CAT scans, X-rays, and MRIs to create an accurate 3D model of the human body and other 3D objects. To work with 3D images, it is very important to understand voxels as these are what 3D images are made of. The following diagram is included to give you an understanding of what a voxel in a 3D image looks like:

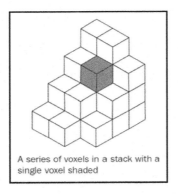

A series of voxels in a stack with a
single voxel shaded

A series of voxels in a 3D image. The shaded region is a single voxel.

The preceding image is a stacked representation of voxels. The gray-colored cuboid represents one voxel. Now you understand what a voxel is, let's load and visualize 3D images in the next section.

Loading and visualizing a 3D image

The 3D ShapeNets dataset contains **Computer-aided design (CAD)** models of different object categories, which are in the `.mat` file format. We will convert these `.mat` files to NumPy ndarrays. We will also visualize a 3D image to get a visual understanding of the dataset.

Execute the following code to load a 3D image from a `.mat` file:

1. Use the `loadmat()` function from `scipy` to retrieve the `voxels`. The code is as follows:

```
import scipy.io as io
voxels = io.loadmat("path to .mat file")['instance']
```

2. The shape of the loaded 3D image is `30x30x30`. Our network requires images of shape `64x64x64`. We will use NumPy's `pad()` method to increase the size of the 3D image to `32x32x32`:

```
import numpy as np
voxels = np.pad(voxels, (1, 1), 'constant', constant_values=(0, 0))
```

The `pad()` method takes four parameters, which are the ndarray of the actual voxels, the number of values that need to be padded to the edges of each axes, the mode values (`constant`), and the `constant_values` that are to be padded.

3. Then, use the `zoom()` function from the `scipy.ndimage` module to convert the 3D image to a 3D image with dimensions of `64x64x64`.

```
import scipy.ndimage as nd
voxels = nd.zoom(voxels, (2, 2, 2), mode='constant', order=0)
```

Our network requires images to be shaped `64x64x64`, which is why we converted our 3D images to this shape.

Visualizing a 3D image

Let's visualize a 3D image using matplotlib, as shown in the following code:

1. Start by creating a matplotlib figure and adding a subplot to it:

```
fig = plt.figure()
ax = fig.gca(projection='3d')
ax.set_aspect('equal')
```

2. Next, add `voxels` to the plot:

```
ax.voxels(voxels, edgecolor="red")
```

3. Next, show the figure and save it as an image, so that we can visualize and understand it later:

```
plt.show()
plt.savefig(file_path)
```

The first screenshot represents an aircraft in a 3D plane:

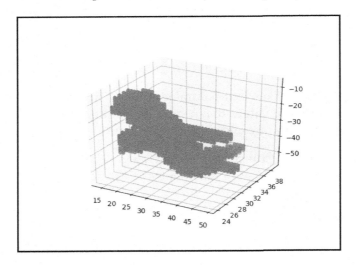

The second screenshot represents a table in a 3D plane:

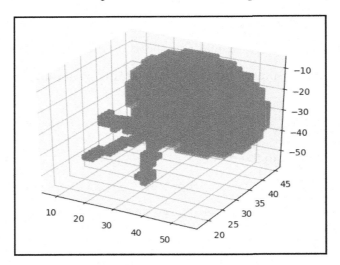

The third screenshot represents a chair in a 3D plane:

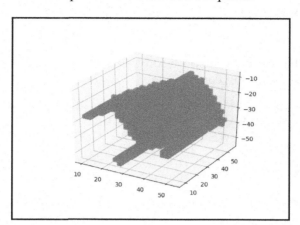

We have successfully downloaded, extracted, and explored the dataset. We have also looked at how to use voxels. In the next section, we will implement a 3D-GAN in the Keras framework.

A Keras implementation of a 3D-GAN

In this section, we will implement the generator network and the discriminator network in the Keras framework. We need to create two Keras models. Both of the networks will have their own separate weights values. Let's start with the generator network.

The generator network

To implement the generator network, we need to create a Keras model and add the neural network layers. The steps required to implement the generator network are as follows:

1. Start by specifying the values for different hyperparameters:

```
z_size = 200
gen_filters = [512, 256, 128, 64, 1]
gen_kernel_sizes = [4, 4, 4, 4, 4]
gen_strides = [1, 2, 2, 2, 2]
gen_input_shape = (1, 1, 1, z_size)
gen_activations = ['relu', 'relu', 'relu', 'relu', 'sigmoid']
gen_convolutional_blocks = 5
```

2. Next, create an input layer to allow the network to take input. The input to the generator network is a vector sampled from a probabilistic latent space:

```
input_layer = Input(shape=gen_input_shape)
```

3. Then, add the first 3D transpose convolution (or 3D deconvolution) block, as shown in the following code:

```
# First 3D transpose convolution( or 3D deconvolution) block
a = Deconv3D(filters=gen_filters[0],
             kernel_size=gen_kernel_sizes[0],
             strides=gen_strides[0])(input_layer)
a = BatchNormalization()(a, training=True)
a = Activation(activation=gen_activations[0])(a)
```

4. Next, add four more 3D transpose convolutions (or 3D deconvolution) blocks, shown as follows:

```
# Next 4 3D transpose convolution( or 3D deconvolution) blocks
for i in range(gen_convolutional_blocks - 1):
    a = Deconv3D(filters=gen_filters[i + 1],
                 kernel_size=gen_kernel_sizes[i + 1],
                 strides=gen_strides[i + 1], padding='same')(a)
    a = BatchNormalization()(a, training=True)
    a = Activation(activation=gen_activations[i + 1])(a)
```

5. Then, create a Keras model and specify the inputs and the outputs for the generator network:

```
model = Model(inputs=input_layer, outputs=a)
```

6. Wrap the entire code for the generator network inside a function called `build_generator()`:

```
def build_generator():
    """
    Create a Generator Model with hyperparameters values defined as
    follows
    :return: Generator network
    """
    z_size = 200
    gen_filters = [512, 256, 128, 64, 1]
    gen_kernel_sizes = [4, 4, 4, 4, 4]
    gen_strides = [1, 2, 2, 2, 2]
    gen_input_shape = (1, 1, 1, z_size)
    gen_activations = ['relu', 'relu', 'relu', 'relu', 'sigmoid']
    gen_convolutional_blocks = 5
```

```
input_layer = Input(shape=gen_input_shape)

# First 3D transpose convolution(or 3D deconvolution) block
a = Deconv3D(filters=gen_filters[0],
kernel_size=gen_kernel_sizes[0],
strides=gen_strides[0])(input_layer)
a = BatchNormalization()(a, training=True)
a = Activation(activation='relu')(a)

# Next 4 3D transpose convolution(or 3D deconvolution) blocks
for i in range(gen_convolutional_blocks - 1):
a = Deconv3D(filters=gen_filters[i + 1],
kernel_size=gen_kernel_sizes[i + 1],
strides=gen_strides[i + 1], padding='same')(a)
a = BatchNormalization()(a, training=True)
a = Activation(activation=gen_activations[i + 1])(a)

gen_model = Model(inputs=input_layer, outputs=a)

gen_model.summary()
return gen_model
```

We have successfully created a Keras model for the generator network. Next, create a Keras model for the discriminator network.

The discriminator network

Similarly, to implement the discriminator network, we need to create a Keras model and add the neural network layers to it. The steps required to implement the discriminator network are as follows:

1. Start by specifying the values for different hyperparameters:

```
dis_input_shape = (64, 64, 64, 1)
dis_filters = [64, 128, 256, 512, 1]
dis_kernel_sizes = [4, 4, 4, 4, 4]
dis_strides = [2, 2, 2, 2, 1]
dis_paddings = ['same', 'same', 'same', 'same', 'valid']
dis_alphas = [0.2, 0.2, 0.2, 0.2, 0.2]
dis_activations = ['leaky_relu', 'leaky_relu', 'leaky_relu',
'leaky_relu', 'sigmoid']
dis_convolutional_blocks = 5
```

2. Next, create an input layer to allow the network to take input. The input to the discriminator network is a 3D image that has a shape of 64x64x64x1:

```
dis_input_layer = Input(shape=dis_input_shape)
```

3. Then, add the first 3D convolution block, shown as follows:

```
# The first 3D Convolution block
a = Conv3D(filters=dis_filters[0],
           kernel_size=dis_kernel_sizes[0],
           strides=dis_strides[0],
           padding=dis_paddings[0])(dis_input_layer)
a = BatchNormalization()(a, training=True)
a = LeakyReLU(alphas[0])(a)
```

4. After that, add four more 3D convolution blocks, shown as follows:

```
# The next 4 3D Convolutional Blocks
for i in range(dis_convolutional_blocks - 1):
    a = Conv3D(filters=dis_filters[i + 1],
               kernel_size=dis_kernel_sizes[i + 1],
               strides=dis_strides[i + 1],
               padding=dis_paddings[i + 1])(a)
    a = BatchNormalization()(a, training=True)
    if dis_activations[i + 1] == 'leaky_relu':
        a = LeakyReLU(dis_alphas[i + 1])(a)
    elif dis_activations[i + 1] == 'sigmoid':
        a = Activation(activation='sigmoid')(a)
```

5. Next, create a Keras model and specify the inputs and the outputs for the discriminator network:

```
dis_model = Model(inputs=dis_input_layer, outputs=a)
```

6. Wrap the complete code for the discriminator network inside a function, given as follows:

```
def build_discriminator():
    """
    Create a Discriminator Model using hyperparameters values
defined as follows
    :return: Discriminator network
    """

    dis_input_shape = (64, 64, 64, 1)
    dis_filters = [64, 128, 256, 512, 1]
    dis_kernel_sizes = [4, 4, 4, 4, 4]
    dis_strides = [2, 2, 2, 2, 1]
```

```
dis_paddings = ['same', 'same', 'same', 'same', 'valid']
dis_alphas = [0.2, 0.2, 0.2, 0.2, 0.2]
dis_activations = ['leaky_relu', 'leaky_relu', 'leaky_relu',
                   'leaky_relu', 'sigmoid']
dis_convolutional_blocks = 5

dis_input_layer = Input(shape=dis_input_shape)

# The first 3D Convolutional block
a = Conv3D(filters=dis_filters[0],
           kernel_size=dis_kernel_sizes[0],
           strides=dis_strides[0],
           padding=dis_paddings[0])(dis_input_layer)
a = BatchNormalization()(a, training=True)
a = LeakyReLU(dis_alphas[0])(a)

# Next 4 3D Convolutional Blocks
for i in range(dis_convolutional_blocks - 1):
    a = Conv3D(filters=dis_filters[i + 1],
               kernel_size=dis_kernel_sizes[i + 1],
               strides=dis_strides[i + 1],
               padding=dis_paddings[i + 1])(a)
    a = BatchNormalization()(a, training=True)
    if dis_activations[i + 1] == 'leaky_relu':
        a = LeakyReLU(dis_alphas[i + 1])(a)
    elif dis_activations[i + 1] == 'sigmoid':
        a = Activation(activation='sigmoid')(a)

dis_model = Model(inputs=dis_input_layer, outputs=a)
print(dis_model.summary())
return dis_model
```

In this section, we created a Keras model for the discriminator network. We are now ready to train a 3D-GAN.

Training a 3D-GAN

Training a 3D-GAN is similar to training a vanilla GAN. We first train the discriminator network on both the generated images and the real images but freeze the generator network. Then, we train the generator network but freeze the discriminator network. We repeat this process for a specified number of epochs. During one iteration, we train both of the networks in a sequence. Training a 3D-GAN is an end-to-end training process. Let's work on these steps one by one.

Training the networks

To train the 3D-GAN, perform the following steps:

1. Start by specifying the values for the different hyperparameters required for the training, shown as follows:

```
gen_learning_rate = 0.0025
dis_learning_rate = 0.00001
beta = 0.5
batch_size = 32
z_size = 200
DIR_PATH = 'Path to the 3DShapenets dataset directory'
generated_volumes_dir = 'generated_volumes'
log_dir = 'logs'
```

2. Next, create and compile both of the networks, shown as follows:

```
# Create instances
generator = build_generator()
discriminator = build_discriminator()

# Specify optimizer
gen_optimizer = Adam(lr=gen_learning_rate, beta_1=beta)
dis_optimizer = Adam(lr=dis_learning_rate, beta_1=0.9)

# Compile networks
generator.compile(loss="binary_crossentropy", optimizer="adam")
discriminator.compile(loss='binary_crossentropy',
optimizer=dis_optimizer)
```

We are using the Adam optimizer as the optimization algorithm and binary_crossentropy as the loss function. The hyperparameter values for the Adam optimizer are specified in the first step.

3. Then, create and compile the adversarial model:

```
discriminator.trainable = False
adversarial_model = Sequential()
adversarial_model.add(generator)
adversarial_model.add(discriminator)
adversarial_model.compile(loss="binary_crossentropy",
optimizer=Adam(lr=gen_learning_rate, beta_1=beta))
```

4. After that, extract and load all the `airplane` images for training:

```
def getVoxelsFromMat(path, cube_len=64):
    voxels = io.loadmat(path)['instance']
    voxels = np.pad(voxels, (1, 1), 'constant', constant_values=(0,
0))
    if cube_len != 32 and cube_len == 64:
        voxels = nd.zoom(voxels, (2, 2, 2), mode='constant',
order=0)
    return voxels

def get3ImagesForACategory(obj='airplane', train=True, cube_len=64,
obj_ratio=1.0):
    obj_path = DIR_PATH + obj + '/30/'
    obj_path += 'train/' if train else 'test/'
    fileList = [f for f in os.listdir(obj_path) if
f.endswith('.mat')]
    fileList = fileList[0:int(obj_ratio * len(fileList))]
    volumeBatch = np.asarray([getVoxelsFromMat(obj_path + f,
cube_len) for f in fileList], dtype=np.bool)
    return volumeBatch

volumes = get3ImagesForACategory(obj='airplane', train=True,
obj_ratio=1.0)
volumes = volumes[..., np.newaxis].astype(np.float)
```

5. Next, add a `TensorBoard` callback and add the `generator` and `discriminator` networks:

```
tensorboard = TensorBoard(log_dir="{}/{}".format(log_dir,
time.time()))
tensorboard.set_model(generator)
tensorboard.set_model(discriminator)
```

6. Add a loop, which will run for a specified number of epochs:

```
for epoch in range(epochs):
    print("Epoch:", epoch)

    # Create two lists to store losses
    gen_losses = []
    dis_losses = []
```

7. Add another loop inside the first loop to run for a specified number of batches:

```
number_of_batches = int(volumes.shape[0] / batch_size)
print("Number of batches:", number_of_batches)
for index in range(number_of_batches):
    print("Batch:", index + 1)
```

8. Next, sample a batch of images from the set of real images and a batch of noise vectors from the Gaussian Normal distribution. The shape of a noise vector should be `(1, 1, 1, 200)`:

```
z_sample = np.random.normal(0, 0.33, size=[batch_size, 1, 1, 1,
                            z_size]).astype(np.float32)
volumes_batch = volumes[index * batch_size:(index + 1) *
batch_size,
                            :, :, :]
```

9. Generate fake images using the generator network. Pass it a batch of noise vectors from `z_sample` and generate a batch of fake images:

```
gen_volumes = generator.predict(z_sample,verbose=3)
```

10. Next, train the discriminator network on the fake images generated by the generator and a batch of real images from the set of real images. Also, make the discriminator trainable:

```
# Make the discriminator network trainable
discriminator.trainable = True
# Create fake and real labels
labels_real = np.reshape([1] * batch_size, (-1, 1, 1, 1, 1))
labels_fake = np.reshape([0] * batch_size, (-1, 1, 1, 1, 1))
# Train the discriminator network
loss_real = discriminator.train_on_batch(volumes_batch,
                                         labels_real)
loss_fake = discriminator.train_on_batch(gen_volumes,
                                         labels_fake)
# Calculate total discriminator loss
d_loss = 0.5 * (loss_real + loss_fake)
```

The preceding piece of code trains the discriminator network and calculates the total discriminator loss.

11. Train the adversarial model containing both the `generator` and the `discriminator` network:

```
z = np.random.normal(0, 0.33, size=[batch_size, 1, 1, 1,
z_size]).astype(np.float32)

        # Train the adversarial model
        g_loss = adversarial_model.train_on_batch(z, np.reshape([1]
* batch_size, (-1, 1, 1, 1, 1)))
```

Also, add losses to their respective lists as follows:

```
gen_losses.append(g_loss)
dis_losses.append(d_loss)
```

12. Generate and save the 3D images after every second epoch:

```
if index % 10 == 0:
        z_sample2 = np.random.normal(0, 0.33, size=[batch_size, 1, 1,
1, z_size]).astype(np.float32)
        generated_volumes = generator.predict(z_sample2, verbose=3)
        for i, generated_volume in enumerate(generated_volumes[:5]):
            voxels = np.squeeze(generated_volume)
            voxels[voxels < 0.5] = 0.
            voxels[voxels >= 0.5] = 1.
            saveFromVoxels(voxels, "results/img_{}_{}_{}".format(epoch,
index, i))
```

13. After each epoch, save the average losses to `tensorboard`:

```
# Save losses to Tensorboard
write_log(tensorboard, 'g_loss', np.mean(gen_losses), epoch)
write_log(tensorboard, 'd_loss', np.mean(dis_losses), epoch)
```

My advice is to train it for 100 epochs to find the problems in the code. Once you have solved those problems, you can then train the network over the course of 100,000 epochs.

Saving the models

After training is complete, save the learned weights of the generator and the discriminator models by adding the following code:

```
"""
Save models
"""
generator.save_weights(os.path.join(generated_volumes_dir,
"generator_weights.h5"))
discriminator.save_weights(os.path.join(generated_volumes_dir,
"discriminator_weights.h5"))
```

Testing the models

To test the networks, create the `generator` and the `discriminator` networks. Then, load the learned weights. Finally, use the `predict()` method to generate predictions:

```
# Create models
generator = build_generator()
discriminator = build_discriminator()

# Load model weights
generator.load_weights(os.path.join(generated_volumes_dir,
"generator_weights.h5"), True)
discriminator.load_weights(os.path.join(generated_volumes_dir,
"discriminator_weights.h5"), True)

# Generate 3D images
z_sample = np.random.normal(0, 0.33, size=[batch_size, 1, 1, 1,
z_size]).astype(np.float32)
generated_volumes = generator.predict(z_sample, verbose=3)
```

In this section, we have successfully trained the generator and the discriminator of the 3D-GAN. In the next section, we will explore hyperparameter tuning and various hyperparameter optimization options.

Visualizing losses

To visualize the losses for the training, start the `tensorboard` server, as follows:

```
tensorboard --logdir=logs
```

Now, open `localhost:6006` in your browser. The **SCALARS** section of TensorBoard contains plots for both losses:

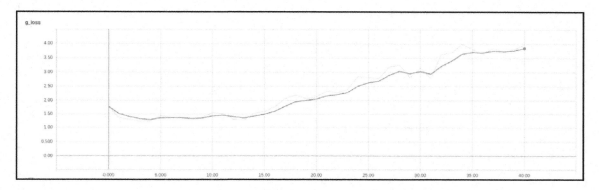

Loss plot for the generator network

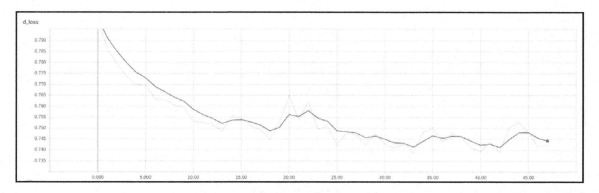

Loss plot for the discriminator network

These plots will help you to decide whether to continue or stop the training. If the losses are not decreasing anymore, you can stop the training, as there is no chance of improvement. If the losses keep increasing, you must stop the training. Play with the hyperparameters and select a set of hyperparameters that you think might provide better results. If the losses are decreasing gradually, keep training the model.

Visualizing graphs

The **GRAPHS** section of TensorBoard contains the graphs for both networks. If the networks are not performing well, these graphs can help you to debug the networks. They also show the flow of tensors and different operations inside each graph:

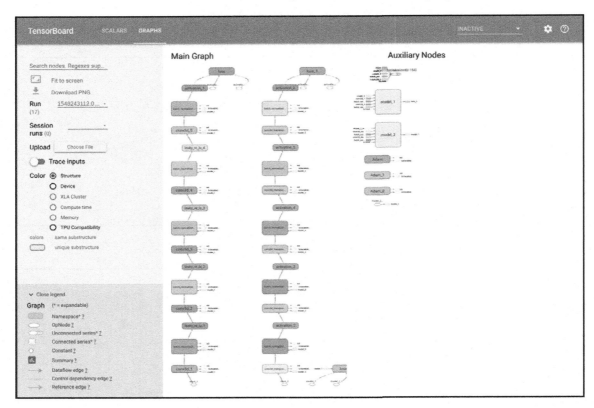

Hyperparameter optimization

The model that we trained might not be a perfect model, but we can optimize the hyperparameters to improve it. There are many hyperparameters in a 3D-GAN that can be optimized. These include the following:

- **Batch size**: Experiment with values of 8, 16, 32, 54, or 128 for the batch size.
- **The number of epochs**: Experiment with 100 epochs and gradually increase it to 1,000-5,000.

- **Learning rate**: This is the most important hyperparameter. Experiment with 0.1, 0.001, 0.0001, and other small learning rates.
- **Activation functions in different layers of the generator and the discriminator network**: Experiment with sigmoid, tanh, ReLU, LeakyReLU, ELU, SeLU, and other activation functions.
- **The optimization algorithm**: Experiment with Adam, SGD, Adadelta, RMSProp, and other optimizers available in the Keras framework.
- **Loss functions**: Binary cross entropy is the loss function best suited for a 3D-GAN.
- **The number of layers in both of the networks**: Experiment with different numbers in the network depending on the amount of training data available. You can make your network deep if you have enough data available to train it with.

We can also carry out automatic hyperparameter optimization by using libraries such as Hyperopt (`https://github.com/hyperopt/hyperopt`) or Hyperas (`https://github.com/maxpumperla/hyperas`) to select the best set of hyperparameters.

Practical applications of 3D-GANs

3D-GANs can potentially be used in a wide variety of industries, as follows:

- **Manufacturing**: 3D-GANs can be a creative tool to help create prototypes quickly. They can come up with creative ideas and can help in simulating and visualizing 3D models.
- **3D printing**: 3D images generated by 3D-GANs can be used to print objects in 3D printing. The manual process of creating 3D models is very lengthy.
- **Design processes**: 3D generated models can provide a good estimate of the eventual outcome of a particular process. They can show us what is going to get built.
- **New samples**: Similar to other GANs, 3D-GANs can generate images to train a supervised model.

Summary

In this chapter, we have explored 3D-GANs. We started with an introduction to a 3D-GAN and covered the architecture and the configurations of the generator and the discriminator. Then, we went through the different steps required to set up a project. We also looked at how to prepare the dataset. Finally, we implemented a 3D-GAN in the Keras framework and trained it on our dataset. We also explored different hyperparameter options. We concluded the chapter by exploring the practical applications of 3D-GANs.

In the next chapter, we will learn how to perform face aging using **Conditional Generative Adversarial Networks** (cGANs).

Face Aging Using Conditional GAN

3

Conditional GANs (cGANs) are an extension of the GAN model. They allow for the generation of images that have certain conditions or attributes and have proved to be better than vanilla GANs as a result. In this chapter, we will implement a cGAN that, once trained, can perform automatic face aging. The cGAN network that we will implement was first introduced by Grigory Antipov, Moez Baccouche, and Jean-Luc Dugelay, in their paper titled *Face Aging With Conditional Generative Adversarial Networks*, which can be found at the following link: https://arxiv.org/pdf/1702.01983.pdf.

In this chapter, we will cover the following topics:

- Introducing cGANs for face aging
- Setting up the project
- Preparing the data
- A Keras implementation of a cGAN
- Training a cGAN
- Evaluation and hyperparameter tuning
- Practical applications of face aging

Introducing cGANs for face aging

So far, we have implemented different GAN networks for different use cases. Conditional GANs extend the idea of vanilla GANs and allow us to control the output of the generator network. Face aging is all about changing the age of a person's face without changing their identity. In most other models (including GANs), the appearance or identity of a person is lost by 50% because facial expressions and facial accessories, such as sunglasses or beards, are not taken into account. Age-cGANs consider all of these attributes. In this section, we will explore cGANs for face aging.

Understanding cGANs

cGANs are a type of GAN that are conditioned on some extra information. We feed the extra information y to the generator as an additional input layer. In vanilla GANs, there is no control over the category of the generated images. When we add a condition y to the generator, we can generate images of a specific category, using y, which might be any kind of data, such as a class label or integer data. Vanilla GANs can learn only one category and it is extremely difficult to architect GANs for multiple categories. A cGAN, however, can be used to generate multi-modal models with different conditions for different categories.

The architecture of a cGAN is shown in the following diagram:

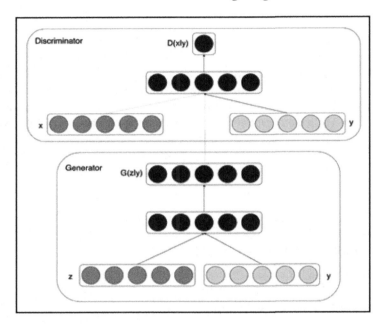

The training objective function for cGANs can be expressed as follows:

$$\min_{G} \max_{D} V(D, G) = \mathbb{E}_{\boldsymbol{x} \sim p_{\text{data}}(\boldsymbol{x})}[\log D(\boldsymbol{x}|\boldsymbol{y})] + \mathbb{E}_{\boldsymbol{z} \sim p_z(\boldsymbol{z})}[\log(1 - D(G(\boldsymbol{z}|\boldsymbol{y})))].$$

Here, G is the generator network and D is the discriminator network. The loss for the discriminator is $log D(x|y)$ and the loss for the generator is $log(1 - D(G(z|y)))$. We can say the $G(z|y)$ is modeling the distribution of our data given z and y. Here, z is a prior noise distribution of a dimension of 100 drawn from a normal distribution.

The architecture of the Age-cGAN

The architecture of a cGAN for face aging is slightly more complicated. The Age-cGan consists of four networks: an encoder, the FaceNet, a generator network, and a discriminator network. With the encoder, we learn the inverse mapping of input face images and the age condition with the latent vector z_0. FaceNet is a face recognition network that learns the difference between an input image x and a $\tilde{x}$ reconstructed image . We have a generator network, which takes a hidden representation consisting of a face image and a condition vector and generates an image. The discriminator network is to discriminate between the real images and the fake images.

The problem with cGANs is that they can't learn the task of inverse mapping an input image x with attributes y to a latent vector z. The solution to this problem is to use an encoder network. We can train an encoder network to approximate the inverse mapping of the input images x. In this section, we will explore the networks involved in Age-cGAN.

The encoder network

The primary goal of the encoder network is to generate a latent vector of the provided images. Basically, it takes an image of a dimension of (64, 64, 3) and converts it into a 100-dimensional vector. The encoder network is a deep convolutional neural network. The network contains four convolutional blocks and two dense layers. Each convolutional block contains a convolutional layer, a batch normalization layer, and an activation function. In each convolutional block, each convolutional layer is followed by a batch normalization layer, except the first convolutional layer. The configuration of the encoder network will be covered in the *Keras implementation of Age-cGAN* section.

The generator network

The primary goal of the generator is to generate an image of a dimension of (64, 64, 3). It takes a 100-dimensional latent vector and some extra information, y, and tries to generate realistic images. The generator network is a deep convolutional neural network too. It is made up of dense, upsampling, and convolutional layers. It takes two input values: a noise vector and a conditioning value. The conditioning value is the additional information provided to the network. For the Age-cGAN, this will be the age. The configuration of the generator network will be covered in the *Keras implementation of Age-cGAN* section.

The discriminator network

The primary goal of the discriminator network is to identify whether the provided image is fake or real. It does this by passing the image through a series of downsampling layers and some classification layers. In other words, it predicts whether the image is real or fake. Like the other networks, the discriminator network is another deep convolutional network. It contains several convolutional blocks. Each convolutional block contains a convolutional layer, a batch normalization layer, and an activation function, apart from the first convolutional block, which doesn't have the batch normalization layer. The configuration of the discriminator network will be covered in the *Keras implementation of Age-cGAN* section.

Face recognition network

The primary goal of the face recognition network is to recognize a person's identity in a given image. For our task, we will be using the pre-trained Inception-ResNet-2 model without fully connected layers. Keras has a pretty good library of pre-trained models. For experimentation purposes, you can use other networks, such as Inception or ResNet-50, as well. To learn more about Inception-ResNet-2, visit the link https://arxiv.org/pdf/1602. 07261.pdf. The pre-trained Inception-ResNet-2 network, once provided with an image, returns the corresponding embedding. The extracted embeddings for the real image and the reconstructed image can be calculated by calculating the Euclidean distance of the embeddings. More on the face recognition network will be covered in the *Keras implementation of Age-cGAN* section.

Stages of the Age-cGAN

The Age-cGAN has multiple stages of training. As mentioned in the previous section, the Age-cGAN has four networks, which get trained in three stages. The training of the Age-cGAN is made up of three stages:

1. **Conditional GAN training:** In this stage, we train the generator network and the discriminator network.
2. **Initial latent vector approximation:** In this stage, we train the encoder network.
3. **Latent vector optimization:** In this stage, we optimize both the encoder and the generator network.

The following screenshot shows the stages in the Age-cGAN:

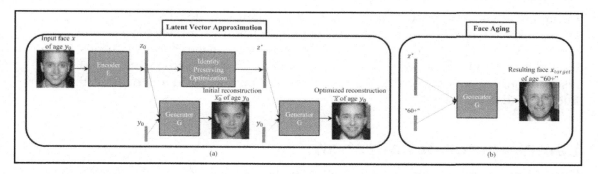

Stages in the Age-cGAN

Source: Face Aging with Conditional Generative Adversarial Networks, https://arxiv.org/pdf/1702.01983.pdf

We will cover all the stages of the Age-cGAN in the following sections.

Conditional GAN training

In this stage, we train the generator network and the discriminator network. Once trained, the generator network can generate blurred images of a face. This stage is similar to training a vanilla GAN, in which we train both networks simultaneously.

The training objective function

The training objective function for the training of cGANs can be represented as follows:

$$\min_{\theta_G} \max_{\theta_G} v(\theta_G, \theta_D) = \mathbf{E}_{x,y \sim p_{data}}[\log D(x, y)]$$
$$+ \mathbf{E}_{z \sim p_z(z), \tilde{y} \sim p_y}[\log(1 - D(G(z, \tilde{y}), \tilde{y}))] \tag{1}$$

Training a cGAN network involves optimizing the function, $v(\theta_G, \theta_D)$. Training a cGAN can be thought of as a minimax game, in which both the generator and the discriminator are trained simultaneously. In the preceding equation, θ_G represents the parameters of the generator network, θ_D represents the parameters of G and D, $log D(x, y)$ is the loss for the discriminator model, $log(1 - D(G(z, \tilde{y}), \tilde{y}))$ is the loss for the generator model, and p_{data} is the distribution of all possible images.

Initial latent vector approximation

Initial latent vector approximation is a method to approximate a latent vector to optimize the reconstruction of face images. To approximate a latent vector, we have an encoder network. We train the encoder network on the generated images and real images. Once trained, the encoder network will start generating latent vectors from the learned distribution. The training objective function for training the encoder network is the Euclidean distance loss.

Latent vector optimization

During latent vector optimization, we optimize the encoder network and the generator network simultaneously. The equation we use for latent vector optimization is as follows:

$$z^*{}_{IP} = \underset{z}{\arg\min} \, \|FR(x) - FR(\bar{x})\|_{L_2}$$

FR is the face recognition network. This equation indicates that the Euclidean distance between the real image and the reconstructed images should be minimal. In this stage, we try to minimize the distance to maximize identity preservation.

Setting up the project

If you haven't already cloned the repository with the complete code for all the chapters, clone the repository now. The cloned repository has a directory called Chapter03, which contains the entire code for this chapter. Execute the following commands to set up the project:

1. Start by navigating to the parent directory, as follows:

   ```
   cd Generative-Adversarial-Networks-Projects
   ```

2. Now, change the directory from the current directory to Chapter03:

   ```
   cd Chapter03
   ```

3. Next, create a Python virtual environment for this project:

   ```
   virtualenv venv
   virtualenv venv -p python3 # Create a virtual environment using
   python3 interpreter
   ```

```
virtualenv venv -p python2 # Create a virtual environment using
python2 interpreter
```

We will be using this newly created virtual environment for this project. Each chapter has its own separate virtual environment.

4. Next, activate the newly created virtual environment:

```
source venv/bin/activate
```

After you activate the virtual environment, all further commands will be executed in this virtual environment.

5. Next, install all the libraries given in the requirements.txt file by executing the following command:

```
pip install -r requirements.txt
```

You can refer to the README.md file for further instructions on how to set up the project. Very often, developers face the problem of mismatching dependencies. Creating a separate virtual environment for each project will take care of this problem.

In this section, we have successfully set up the project and installed the required dependencies. In the next section, we will work on the dataset.

Preparing the data

In this chapter, we will be using the Wiki-Cropped dataset, which contains more than 64, 328 images of various people's faces. The authors have also made a dataset available that contains only the cropped faces, so we don't need to crop faces.

The authors of the paper titled *Deep expectation of real and apparent age from a single image without facial landmarks,* which is available at https://www.vision.ee.ethz.ch/en/publications/papers/articles/eth_biwi_01299.pdf, have scraped these images from Wikipedia and made them available for academic purposes. If you intend to use the dataset for commercial purposes, contact the authors at rrothe@vision.ee.ethz.ch.

You can manually download the dataset from the following link and place all the compressed files in the directory inside the Age-cGAN project at https://data.vision.ee.ethz.ch/cvl/rrothe/imdb-wiki/

Perform the following steps to download and extract the dataset.

Downloading the dataset

To download the dataset that contains only the cropped faces, execute the following commands:

```
# Before download the dataset move to data directory
cd data

# Wikipedia : Download faces only
wget
https://data.vision.ee.ethz.ch/cvl/rrothe/imdb-wiki/static/wiki_crop.tar
```

Extracting the dataset

After downloading the dataset, extract the files in the data folder manually, or execute the following commands to extract the files:

```
# Move to data directory
cd data

# Extract wiki_crop.tar
tar -xvf wiki_crop.tar
```

The `wiki_crop.tar` file contains 62,328 images and a `wiki.mat` file that holds all the labels. The `scipy.io` library has a method called `loadmat`, which is a really handy method to load `.mat` files in Python. Use the following code to load extracted `.mat` files:

```python
def load_data(wiki_dir, dataset='wiki'):
    # Load the wiki.mat file
    meta = loadmat(os.path.join(wiki_dir, "{}.mat".format(dataset)))

    # Load the list of all files
    full_path = meta[dataset][0, 0]["full_path"][0]

    # List of Matlab serial date numbers
    dob = meta[dataset][0, 0]["dob"][0]

    # List of years when photo was taken
    photo_taken = meta[dataset][0, 0]["photo_taken"][0]  # year

    # Calculate age for all dobs
    age = [calculate_age(photo_taken[i], dob[i]) for i in range(len(dob))]
```

```
# Create a list of tuples containing a pair of an image path and age
images = []
age_list = []
for index, image_path in enumerate(full_path):
    images.append(image_path[0])
    age_list.append(age[index])

# Return a list of all images and respective age
return images, age_list
```

The `photo_taken` variable is a list of years and `dob` is Matlab's serial date number for the corresponding photo in the list. We can calculate the age of the person from the serial date number and the year the photo was taken. Use the following code to calculate the age:

```
def calculate_age(taken, dob):
    birth = datetime.fromordinal(max(int(dob) - 366, 1))

    # assume the photo was taken in the middle of the year
    if birth.month < 7:
        return taken - birth.year
    else:
        return taken - birth.year - 1
```

We have now successfully downloaded and extracted the dataset. In the next section, let's work on the Keras implementation of an Age-cGAN.

A Keras implementation of an Age-cGAN

Like vanilla GANs, the implementation of cGANs is straightforward. Keras provides enough flexibility to code complex generative adversarial networks. In this section, we will implement the generator network, the discriminator network, and the encoder network used in cGANs. Let's start by implementing the encoder network.

Before starting to write the implementations, create a Python file called `main.py` and import the essential modules, as follows:

```
import math
import os
import time
from datetime import datetime

import matplotlib.pyplot as plt
import numpy as np
import tensorflow as tf
from keras import Input, Model
```

```
from keras.applications import InceptionResNetV2
from keras.callbacks import TensorBoard
from keras.layers import Conv2D, Flatten, Dense, BatchNormalization,
Reshape, concatenate, LeakyReLU, Lambda, \
    K, Conv2DTranspose, Activation, UpSampling2D, Dropout
from keras.optimizers import Adam
from keras.utils import to_categorical
from keras_preprocessing import image
from scipy.io import loadmat
```

The encoder network

The encoder network is a **convolutional neural network (CNN)** that encodes an image (x) to a latent vector (z) or a latent vector representation. Let's start by implementing the encoder network in the Keras framework.

Perform the following steps to implement the encoder network:

1. Start by creating an input layer:

   ```
   input_layer = Input(shape=(64, 64, 3))
   ```

2. Next, add the first convolution block, which contains a 2D convolution layer with an activation function with the following configurations:
   - **Filters**: 32
   - **Kernel size**: 5
   - **Strides**: 2
   - **Padding**: same
   - **Activation**: LeakyReLU with alpha equal to 0.2:

   ```
   # 1st Convolutional Block
   enc = Conv2D(filters=32, kernel_size=5, strides=2,
   padding='same')(input_layer)
   enc = LeakyReLU(alpha=0.2)(enc)
   ```

3. Next, add three more convolution blocks, each one of which contains a 2-D convolution layer followed by a batch normalization layer and an activation function, with the following configurations:
   - **Filters**: 64, 128, 256
   - **Kernel size**: 5, 5, 5
   - **Strides**: 2, 2, 2
   - **Padding**: same, same, same

- **Batch normalization**: Each convolutional layer is followed by a batch normalization layer
- **Activations**: `LealyReLU, LeakyReLU, LeakyReLU` with `alpha` equal to `0.2`:

```
# 2nd Convolutional Block
enc = Conv2D(filters=64, kernel_size=5, strides=2,
padding='same')(enc)
enc = BatchNormalization()(enc)
enc = LeakyReLU(alpha=0.2)(enc)

# 3rd Convolutional Block
enc = Conv2D(filters=128, kernel_size=5, strides=2,
padding='same')(enc)
enc = BatchNormalization()(enc)
enc = LeakyReLU(alpha=0.2)(enc)

# 4th Convolutional Block
enc = Conv2D(filters=256, kernel_size=5, strides=2,
padding='same')(enc)
enc = BatchNormalization()(enc)
enc = LeakyReLU(alpha=0.2)(enc)
```

4. Next, flatten the output from the last convolution block, as follows:

```
# Flatten layer
enc = Flatten()(enc)
```

Converting an *n*-dimensional tensor to a one-dimensional tensor (array) is called **flattening**.

5. Next, add a dense (fully-connected) layer followed by a batch normalization layer and an activation function, with the following configurations:
   - **Units (nodes)**: 2,096
   - **Batch normalization**: Yes
   - **Activation**: `LeakyReLU` with `alpha` equal to `0.2`:

```
# 1st Fully Connected Layer
enc = Dense(4096)(enc)
enc = BatchNormalization()(enc)
enc = LeakyReLU(alpha=0.2)(enc)
```

6. Next, add the second dense (fully-connected) layer with the following configuration:
    - **Units (nodes)**: 100
    - **Activation**: None:

```
# Second Fully Connected Layer
enc = Dense(100)(enc)
```

7. Finally, create a Keras model and specify the inputs and outputs for the encoder network:

```
# Create a model
model = Model(inputs=[input_layer], outputs=[enc])
```

The entire code for the encoder network is shown here:

```
def build_encoder():
    """
    Encoder Network
    :return: Encoder model
    """
    input_layer = Input(shape=(64, 64, 3))

    # 1st Convolutional Block
    enc = Conv2D(filters=32, kernel_size=5, strides=2,
padding='same')(input_layer)
    enc = LeakyReLU(alpha=0.2)(enc)

    # 2nd Convolutional Block
    enc = Conv2D(filters=64, kernel_size=5, strides=2, padding='same')(enc)
    enc = BatchNormalization()(enc)
    enc = LeakyReLU(alpha=0.2)(enc)

    # 3rd Convolutional Block
    enc = Conv2D(filters=128, kernel_size=5, strides=2,
padding='same')(enc)
    enc = BatchNormalization()(enc)
    enc = LeakyReLU(alpha=0.2)(enc)

    # 4th Convolutional Block
    enc = Conv2D(filters=256, kernel_size=5, strides=2,
padding='same')(enc)
    enc = BatchNormalization()(enc)
    enc = LeakyReLU(alpha=0.2)(enc)

    # Flatten layer
    enc = Flatten()(enc)
```

```
# 1st Fully Connected Layer
enc = Dense(4096)(enc)
enc = BatchNormalization()(enc)
enc = LeakyReLU(alpha=0.2)(enc)

# Second Fully Connected Layer
enc = Dense(100)(enc)

# Create a model
model = Model(inputs=[input_layer], outputs=[enc])
return model
```

We have now successfully created a Keras model for the encoder network. Next, create a Keras model for the generator network.

The generator network

The generator network is a CNN that takes a 100-dimensional vector z and generates an image with a dimension of (64, 64, 3). Let's implement the generator network in the Keras framework.

Perform the following steps to implement the generator network:

1. Start by creating the two input layers to the generator network:

   ```
   latent_dims = 100
   num_classes = 6

   # Input layer for vector z
   input_z_noise = Input(shape=(latent_dims, ))

   # Input layer for conditioning variable
   input_label = Input(shape=(num_classes, ))
   ```

2. Next, concatenate the inputs along the channel dimension, as shown here:

   ```
   x = concatenate([input_z_noise, input_label])
   ```

   The preceding step will generate a concatenated tensor.

3. Next, add a dense (fully connected) block with the following configurations:
   - **Units (nodes):** 2,048
   - **Input dimension:** 106
   - **Activation:** LeakyReLU with alpha equal to 0.2

- **Dropout**: 0.2:

```
x = Dense(2048, input_dim=latent_dims+num_classes)(x)
x = LeakyReLU(alpha=0.2)(x)
x = Dropout(0.2)(x)
```

4. Next, add the second dense (fully-connected) block with the following configurations:
   - **Units (nodes)**: 16,384
   - **Batch normalization**: Yes
   - **Activation**: LeakyReLU with alpha equal to 0.2
   - **Dropout**: 0.2:

```
x = Dense(256 * 8 * 8)(x)
x = BatchNormalization()(x)
x = LeakyReLU(alpha=0.2)(x)
x = Dropout(0.2)(x)
```

5. Next, reshape the output from the last dense layer to a three-dimensional tensor with a dimension of (8, 8, 256):

```
x = Reshape((8, 8, 256))(x)
```

This layer will generate a tensor of a dimension of (batch_size, 8, 8, 256).

6. Next, add an upsampling block that contains an upsampling layer followed by a 2-D convolution layer and a batch normalization layer with the following configurations:
   - **Upsampling size**: (2, 2)
   - **Filters**: 128
   - **Kernel size**: 5
   - **Padding**: same
   - **Batch normalization**: Yes, with momentum equal to 0.8
   - **Activation**: LeakyReLU with alpha equal to 0.2:

```
x = UpSampling2D(size=(2, 2))(x)
x = Conv2D(filters=128, kernel_size=5, padding='same')(x)
x = BatchNormalization(momentum=0.8)(x)
x = LeakyReLU(alpha=0.2)(x)
```

Upsampling2D is the process of repeating the rows a specified number of times *x* and repeating the columns a specified number of times *y*, respectively.

7. Next, add another Upsampling block (similar to the previous layer), as shown in the following code. The configuration is similar to the previous block, except that the number of filters used in the convolution layer is 128:

```
x = UpSampling2D(size=(2, 2))(x)
x = Conv2D(filters=64, kernel_size=5, padding='same')(x)
x = BatchNormalization(momentum=0.8)(x)
x = LeakyReLU(alpha=0.2)(x)
```

8. Next, add the last Upsampling block. The configuration is similar to the previous layer, except for the the fact that there are three filters used in the convolution layer and batch normalization is not used:

```
x = UpSampling2D(size=(2, 2))(x)
x = Conv2D(filters=3, kernel_size=5, padding='same')(x)
x = Activation('tanh')(x)
```

9. Finally, create a Keras model and specify the inputs and the outputs for the generator network:

```
model = Model(inputs=[input_z_noise, input_label], outputs=[x])
```

The entire code for the generator network is shown here:

```
def build_generator():
    """
    Create a Generator Model with hyperparameters values defined as follows
    :return: Generator model
    """
    latent_dims = 100
    num_classes = 6

    input_z_noise = Input(shape=(latent_dims,))
    input_label = Input(shape=(num_classes,))

    x = concatenate([input_z_noise, input_label])

    x = Dense(2048, input_dim=latent_dims + num_classes)(x)
    x = LeakyReLU(alpha=0.2)(x)
    x = Dropout(0.2)(x)

    x = Dense(256 * 8 * 8)(x)
```

```
x = BatchNormalization()(x)
x = LeakyReLU(alpha=0.2)(x)
x = Dropout(0.2)(x)

x = Reshape((8, 8, 256))(x)

x = UpSampling2D(size=(2, 2))(x)
x = Conv2D(filters=128, kernel_size=5, padding='same')(x)
x = BatchNormalization(momentum=0.8)(x)
x = LeakyReLU(alpha=0.2)(x)

x = UpSampling2D(size=(2, 2))(x)
x = Conv2D(filters=64, kernel_size=5, padding='same')(x)
x = BatchNormalization(momentum=0.8)(x)
x = LeakyReLU(alpha=0.2)(x)

x = UpSampling2D(size=(2, 2))(x)
x = Conv2D(filters=3, kernel_size=5, padding='same')(x)
x = Activation('tanh')(x)

model = Model(inputs=[input_z_noise, input_label], outputs=[x])
return model
```

We have now successfully created the generator network. We will next write the code for the discriminator network.

The discriminator network

The discriminator network is a CNN. Let's implement the discriminator network in the Keras framework.

Perform the following steps to implement the discriminator network:

1. Start by creating two input layers, as our discriminator network will process two inputs:

```
# Specify hyperparameters
# Input image shape
input_shape = (64, 64, 3)
# Input conditioning variable shape
label_shape = (6,)

# Two input layers
image_input = Input(shape=input_shape)
label_input = Input(shape=label_shape)
```

2. Next, add a 2-D convolution block (Conv2D + Activation function) with the following configuration:
    - **Filters** = 64
    - **Kernel size**: 3
    - **Strides**: 2
    - **Padding**: same
    - **Activation**: LeakyReLU with alpha equal to 0.2:

```
x = Conv2D(64, kernel_size=3, strides=2,
padding='same')(image_input)
x = LeakyReLU(alpha=0.2)(x)
```

3. Next, expand label_input so that it has a shape of (32, 32, 6):

```
label_input1 = Lambda(expand_label_input)(label_input)
```

The expand_label_input function is as follows:

```
# The expand_label_input function
def expand_label_input(x):
    x = K.expand_dims(x, axis=1)
    x = K.expand_dims(x, axis=1)
    x = K.tile(x, [1, 32, 32, 1])
    return x
```

The preceding function will transform a tensor with a dimension of (6,) to a tensor with a dimension of (32, 32, 6).

4. Next, concatenate the transformed label tensor and the output of the last convolution layer along the channel dimension, as shown here:

```
x = concatenate([x, label_input1], axis=3)
```

5. Add a convolution block (2D convolution layer + batch normalization + activation function) with the following configuration:
    - **Filters**: 128
    - **Kernel size**: 3
    - **Strides**: 2
    - **Padding**: same
    - **Batch normalization**: Yes

- **Activation**: LeakyReLU with alpha equal to 0.2:

```
x = Conv2D(128, kernel_size=3, strides=2, padding='same')(x)
x = BatchNormalization()(x)
x = LeakyReLU(alpha=0.2)(x)
```

6. Next, add two more convolution blocks, as follows:

```
x = Conv2D(256, kernel_size=3, strides=2, padding='same')(x)
x = BatchNormalization()(x)
x = LeakyReLU(alpha=0.2)(x)

x = Conv2D(512, kernel_size=3, strides=2, padding='same')(x)
x = BatchNormalization()(x)
x = LeakyReLU(alpha=0.2)(x)
```

7. Next, add a flatten layer:

```
x = Flatten()(x)
```

8. Next, add a dense layer (classification layer) that outputs a probability:

```
x = Dense(1, activation='sigmoid')(x)
```

9. Finally, create a Keras model and specify the inputs and outputs for the discriminator network:

```
model = Model(inputs=[image_input, label_input], outputs=[x])
```

The entire code for the discriminator network looks as follows:

```
def build_discriminator():
    """
    Create a Discriminator Model with hyperparameters values defined as
follows
    :return: Discriminator model
    """
    input_shape = (64, 64, 3)
    label_shape = (6,)
    image_input = Input(shape=input_shape)
    label_input = Input(shape=label_shape)

    x = Conv2D(64, kernel_size=3, strides=2, padding='same')(image_input)
    x = LeakyReLU(alpha=0.2)(x)

    label_input1 = Lambda(expand_label_input)(label_input)
    x = concatenate([x, label_input1], axis=3)
```

```
x = Conv2D(128, kernel_size=3, strides=2, padding='same')(x)
x = BatchNormalization()(x)
x = LeakyReLU(alpha=0.2)(x)

x = Conv2D(256, kernel_size=3, strides=2, padding='same')(x)
x = BatchNormalization()(x)
x = LeakyReLU(alpha=0.2)(x)

x = Conv2D(512, kernel_size=3, strides=2, padding='same')(x)
x = BatchNormalization()(x)
x = LeakyReLU(alpha=0.2)(x)

x = Flatten()(x)
x = Dense(1, activation='sigmoid')(x)

model = Model(inputs=[image_input, label_input], outputs=[x])
return model
```

We have now successfully created the encoder, the generator, and the discriminator networks. In the next section, we will assemble everything and train the network.

Training the cGAN

Training the cGAN for face aging is a three-step process:

1. Training the cGAN
2. Initial latent vector approximation
3. Latent vector optimization

We will cover these steps one by one in the following sections.

Training the cGAN

This is the first step of the training process. In this step, we train the generator and the discriminator networks. Perform the following steps:

1. Start by specifying the parameters required for the training:

    ```
    # Define hyperparameters
    data_dir = "/path/to/dataset/directory/"
    wiki_dir = os.path.join(data_dir, "wiki_crop")
    epochs = 500
    batch_size = 128
    ```

```
image_shape = (64, 64, 3)
z_shape = 100
TRAIN_GAN = True
TRAIN_ENCODER = False
TRAIN_GAN_WITH_FR = False
fr_image_shape = (192, 192, 3)
```

2. Next, define the optimizers for the training. We will use the `Adam` optimizer, which is available in Keras. Initialize the optimizers, as shown in the following code:

```
# Define optimizers
# Optimizer for the discriminator network
dis_optimizer = Adam(lr=0.0002, beta_1=0.5, beta_2=0.999,
epsilon=10e-8)

# Optimizer for the generator network
gen_optimizer = Adam(lr=0.0002, beta_1=0.5, beta_2=0.999,
epsilon=10e-8)

# Optimizer for the adversarial network
adversarial_optimizer = Adam(lr=0.0002, beta_1=0.5, beta_2=0.999,
epsilon=10e-8)
```

Use a learning rate equal to `0.0002`, a `beta_1` value equal to `0.5`, a `beta_2` value equal to `0.999`, and an epsilon value equal to `10e-8` for all optimizers.

3. Next, load and compile the generator and the discriminator networks. In Keras, we must compile the networks before we train the networks:

```
# Build and compile the discriminator network
discriminator = build_discriminator()
discriminator.compile(loss=['binary_crossentropy'],
optimizer=dis_optimizer)

# Build and compile the generator network
generator = build_generator1()
generator.compile(loss=['binary_crossentropy'],
optimizer=gen_optimizer)
```

To compile the networks, use `binary_crossentropy` as the loss function.

4. Next, build and compile the adversarial model, as follows:

```
# Build and compile the adversarial model
discriminator.trainable = False
input_z_noise = Input(shape=(100,))
input_label = Input(shape=(6,))
recons_images = generator([input_z_noise, input_label])
valid = discriminator([recons_images, input_label])
adversarial_model = Model(inputs=[input_z_noise, input_label],
outputs=[valid])
adversarial_model.compile(loss=['binary_crossentropy'],
optimizer=gen_optimizer)
```

To compile the adversarial model, use `binary_crossentropy` as the loss function and `gen_optimizer` as the optimizer.

5. Next, add `TensorBoard` to store losses, as follows:

```
tensorboard = TensorBoard(log_dir="logs/{}".format(time.time()))
tensorboard.set_model(generator)
tensorboard.set_model(discriminator)
```

6. Next, load all images using the `load_data` function, which is defined in the *Preparing the data* section:

```
images, age_list = load_data(wiki_dir=wiki_dir, dataset="wiki")
```

7. Next, convert the age numerical value to the age category, as follows:

```
# Convert age to category
age_cat = age_to_category(age_list)
```

The definition of the `age_to_category` function is as follows:

```
# This method will convert age to respective category
def age_to_category(age_list):
    age_list1 = []

    for age in age_list:
        if 0 < age <= 18:
            age_category = 0
        elif 18 < age <= 29:
            age_category = 1
        elif 29 < age <= 39:
            age_category = 2
        elif 39 < age <= 49:
            age_category = 3
        elif 49 < age <= 59:
```

```
            age_category = 4
        elif age >= 60:
            age_category = 5

        age_list1.append(age_category)
    return age_list1
```

The output of `age_cat` should look as follows:

```
[1, 2, 4, 2, 3, 4, 2, 5, 5, 1, 3, 2, 1, 1, 2, 1, 2, 2, 1, 5, 4 ,
.............]
```

Convert the age categories to one-hot encoded vectors:

```
# Also, convert the age categories to one-hot encoded vectors
final_age_cat = np.reshape(np.array(age_cat), [len(age_cat), 1])
classes = len(set(age_cat))
y = to_categorical(final_age_cat, num_classes=len(set(age_cat)))
```

After we convert the age categories to one-hot encoded vectors, the values of y should be as follows:

```
[[0. 1. 0. 0. 0. 0.]
 [0. 0. 1. 0. 0. 0.]
 [0. 0. 0. 0. 1. 0.]
 ...
 [0. 0. 0. 1. 0. 0.]
 [0. 1. 0. 0. 0. 0.]
 [0. 0. 0. 0. 1. 0.]]
```

The shape of y should be (`total_values`, 5).

8. Next, load all images and create an `ndarray` containing all images:

```
# Read all images and create an ndarray
loaded_images = load_images(wiki_dir, images, (image_shape[0],
image_shape[1]))
```

The definition of the `load_images` function is as follows:

```
def load_images(data_dir, image_paths, image_shape):
    images = None

    for i, image_path in enumerate(image_paths):
        print()
        try:
            # Load image
            loaded_image = image.load_img(os.path.join(data_dir,
```

```
image_path), target_size=image_shape)

            # Convert PIL image to numpy ndarray
            loaded_image = image.img_to_array(loaded_image)

            # Add another dimension (Add batch dimension)
            loaded_image = np.expand_dims(loaded_image, axis=0)

            # Concatenate all images into one tensor
            if images is None:
                images = loaded_image
            else:
                images = np.concatenate([images, loaded_image],
axis=0)
        except Exception as e:
            print("Error:", i, e)

    return images
```

The values inside loaded_images should look like this:

```
[[[[ 97. 122. 178.]
 [ 98. 123. 179.]
 [ 99. 124. 180.]
 ...
 [ 97. 124. 179.]
 [ 96. 123. 178.]
 [ 95. 122. 177.]]
...
[[216. 197. 203.]
 [217. 198. 204.]
 [218. 199. 205.]
 ...
 [ 66. 75. 90.]
 [110. 127. 171.]
 [ 89. 115. 172.]]]
[[[122. 140. 152.]
 [115. 133. 145.]
 [ 95. 113. 123.]
 ...
 [ 41. 73. 23.]
 [ 38. 77. 22.]
 [ 38. 77. 22.]]
[[ 53. 80. 63.]
 [ 47. 74. 57.]
 [ 45. 72. 55.]
 ...
 [ 34. 66...
```

9. Next, create a `for` loop, which should run for the number of times specified by the number of epochs, as follows:

```
for epoch in range(epochs):
    print("Epoch:{}".format(epoch))

    gen_losses = []
    dis_losses = []

    number_of_batches = int(len(loaded_images) / batch_size)
    print("Number of batches:", number_of_batches)
```

10. Next, create another loop inside the epochs loop and make it run for the number of times that is specified by `num_batches`, as follows:

```
for index in range(number_of_batches):
    print("Batch:{}".format(index + 1))
```

Our entire code for the training of the discriminator networks and the adversarial network will be inside this loop.

11. Next, sample a batch of images from the real dataset and a batch of one-hot encoded age vectors:

```
images_batch = loaded_images[index * batch_size:(index + 1)
 * batch_size]
    images_batch = images_batch / 127.5 - 1.0
    images_batch = images_batch.astype(np.float32)

    y_batch = y[index * batch_size:(index + 1) * batch_size]
```

The shape of `image_batch` should be (`batch_size, 64, 64, 3`) and the shape of `y_batch` should be (`batch_size, 6`).

12. Next, sample a batch of noise vectors from a Gaussian distribution, as follows:

```
z_noise = np.random.normal(0, 1, size=(batch_size,
 z_shape))
```

13. Next, generate fake images using the generator network. Keep in mind that we haven't trained the generator network yet:

```
initial_recon_images = generator.predict_on_batch([z_noise,
 y_batch])
```

The generator network takes two inputs, `z_noise` and `y_batch`, which we created in steps 11 and 12.

14. Now, train the discriminator network on real images as well as on fake images:

```
d_loss_real = discriminator.train_on_batch([images_batch,
y_batch], real_labels)
        d_loss_fake =
discriminator.train_on_batch([initial_recon_images, y_batch],
fake_labels)
```

This code should train the discriminator network on one batch of images. In each step, the discriminator will be trained on a batch of samples.

15. Next, train the adversarial network. By freezing the discriminator network, we will train only the generator network:

```
# Again sample a batch of noise vectors from a
Gaussian(normal) distribution
        z_noise2 = np.random.normal(0, 1, size=(batch_size,
z_shape))

        # Samples a batch of random age values
        random_labels = np.random.randint(0, 6,
batch_size).reshape(-1, 1)

        # Convert the random age values to one-hot encoders
        random_labels = to_categorical(random_labels, 6)
        # Train the generator network
        g_loss = adversarial_model.train_on_batch([z_noise2,
sampled_labels], [1] * batch_size)
```

The preceding code will train the generator network on one batch of inputs. The inputs to the adversarial model are z_noise2 and random_labels.

16. Next, calculate and print the losses:

```
d_loss = 0.5 * np.add(d_loss_real, d_loss_fake)
print("d_loss:{}".format(d_loss))
print("g_loss:{}".format(g_loss))
# Add losses to their respective lists
gen_losses.append(g_loss)
dis_losses.append(d_loss)
```

17. Next, write the losses to TensorBoard for visualization:

```
write_log(tensorboard, 'g_loss', np.mean(gen_losses), epoch)
write_log(tensorboard, 'd_loss', np.mean(dis_losses), epoch)
```

18. Sample and save the images after every 10 epochs, as follows:

```
if epoch % 10 == 0:
    images_batch = loaded_images[0:batch_size]
    images_batch = images_batch / 127.5 - 1.0
    images_batch = images_batch.astype(np.float32)

    y_batch = y[0:batch_size]
    z_noise = np.random.normal(0, 1, size=(batch_size,
z_shape))

    gen_images = generator.predict_on_batch([z_noise, y_batch])

    for i, img in enumerate(gen_images[:5]):
        save_rgb_img(img,
path="results/img_{}_{}.png".format(epoch, i))
```

Put the preceding code block inside the epochs loop. After every 10 epochs, it will generate a batch of fake images and save them to the results directory. Here, `save_rgb_img()` is a utility function, defined as follows:

```
def save_rgb_img(img, path):
    """
    Save a rgb image
    """
    fig = plt.figure()
    ax = fig.add_subplot(1, 1, 1)
    ax.imshow(img)
    ax.axis("off")
    ax.set_title("Image")

    plt.savefig(path)
    plt.close()
```

19. Finally, save both models by adding the following lines:

```
# Save weights only
generator.save_weights("generator.h5")
discriminator.save_weights("discriminator.h5")

# Save architecture and weights both
generator.save("generator.h5")
discriminator.save("discriminator.h5")
```

If you have successfully executed the code given in this section, then you have successfully trained both the generator and the discriminator network. After this step, the generator network will start generating blurred face images. In the next section, we will train the encoder model for the initial latent vector approximation.

Initial latent vector approximation

As we have discussed, cGANs don't learn reverse mappings from images to latent vectors. Instead, the encoder learns this reverse mapping and is capable of generating latent vectors that we can use to generate face images at a target age. Let's train the encoder network.

We have already defined the hyperparameters required for the training. Perform the following steps to train the encoder network:

1. Start by building the encoder network. Add the following code to build and compile the network:

```
# Build Encoder
encoder = build_encoder()
encoder.compile(loss=euclidean_distance_loss, optimizer='adam')
```

We haven't defined `euclidean_distance_loss`. Let's define it and add this before we build the encoder network:

```
def euclidean_distance_loss(y_true, y_pred):
    """
    Euclidean distance loss
    """
    return K.sqrt(K.sum(K.square(y_pred - y_true), axis=-1))
```

2. Next, load the generator network, as follows:

```
generator.load_weights("generator.h5")
```

Here, we are loading weights from the previous step, where we successfully trained and saved weights of the generator network.

3. Next, sample a batch of latent vectors, as follows:

```
z_i = np.random.normal(0, 1, size=(1000, z_shape))
```

4. Next, sample a batch of random age numbers and convert the random age numbers to one-hot encoded vectors, as follows:

```
y = np.random.randint(low=0, high=6, size=(1000,), dtype=np.int64)
num_classes = len(set(y))
y = np.reshape(np.array(y), [len(y), 1])
y = to_categorical(y, num_classes=num_classes)
```

You can sample as many samples as you like. In our case, we are sampling 1,000 values.

5. Next, add an epoch loop and a batch steps loop, as shown here:

```
for epoch in range(epochs):
    print("Epoch:", epoch)

    encoder_losses = []

    number_of_batches = int(z_i.shape[0] / batch_size)
    print("Number of batches:", number_of_batches)
    for index in range(number_of_batches):
        print("Batch:", index + 1)
```

6. Now sample a batch of latent vectors and a batch of one-hot encoded vectors from 1,000 samples, as follows:

```
z_batch = z_i[index * batch_size:(index + 1) * batch_size]
y_batch = y[index * batch_size:(index + 1) * batch_size]
```

7. Next, generate fake images using the pre-trained generator network:

```
generated_images = generator.predict_on_batch([z_batch, y_batch])
```

8. Finally, train the encoder network on the generated images by the generator network:

```
encoder_loss = encoder.train_on_batch(generated_images, z_batch)
```

9. Next, after each epoch, write the encoder loss to TensorBoard, as follows:

```
write_log(tensorboard, "encoder_loss", np.mean(encoder_losses), epoch)
```

10. We need to save the trained encoder network. Save the encoder model by adding the following code:

```
encoder.save_weights("encoder.h5")
```

If you have successfully executed the code given in this section, you will have successfully trained the encoder model. Our encoder network is now ready to generate the initial latent vectors. In the next section, we will learn how to perform optimized latent vector approximation.

Latent vector optimization

In the preceding two steps, we successfully trained the generator network, the discriminator network, and the encoder network. In this section, we will improve the encoder and the generator networks. In these steps, we will be using the **face recognition** (**FR**) network, which generates a 128-dimensional embedding of a particular input fed to it, to improve the generator and the encoder network.

Perform the following steps:

1. Start by building and loading the weights for the encoder network and the generator network:

```
encoder = build_encoder()
encoder.load_weights("encoder.h5")

# Load the generator network
generator.load_weights("generator.h5")
```

2. Next, create a network to resize the images from a shape of (64, 64, 3) to a shape of (192, 192, 3), as follows:

```
# Define all functions before you make a call to them
def build_image_resizer():
    input_layer = Input(shape=(64, 64, 3))

    resized_images = Lambda(lambda x: K.resize_images(x,
height_factor=3, width_factor=3,
data_format='channels_last'))(input_layer)

    model = Model(inputs=[input_layer], outputs=[resized_images])
    return model

image_resizer = build_image_resizer()
image_resizer.compile(loss=loss, optimizer='adam')
```

To work with FaceNet, the height and width of our images should be greater than 150 pixels. The preceding network will help us in converting our images to the desired format.

3. Build the face recognition model:

```
# Face recognition model
fr_model = build_fr_model(input_shape=fr_image_shape)
fr_model.compile(loss=loss, optimizer="adam")
```

Refer to `https://github.com/PacktPublishing/Generative-Adversarial-Networks-Projects/Age-cGAN/main.py` for the `build_fr_model()` function.

4. Next, create another adversarial model. In this adversarial model, we will have three networks: the encoder, the generator, and the face recognition model:

```
# Make the face recognition network as non-trainable
fr_model.trainable = False

# Input layers
input_image = Input(shape=(64, 64, 3))
input_label = Input(shape=(6,))

# Use the encoder and the generator network
latent0 = encoder(input_image)
gen_images = generator([latent0, input_label])

# Resize images to the desired shape
resized_images = Lambda(lambda x: K.resize_images(gen_images,
height_factor=3, width_factor=3,
data_format='channels_last'))(gen_images)
embeddings = fr_model(resized_images)

# Create a Keras model and specify the inputs and outputs to the
network
fr_adversarial_model = Model(inputs=[input_image, input_label],
outputs=[embeddings])

# Compile the model
fr_adversarial_model.compile(loss=euclidean_distance_loss,
optimizer=adversarial_optimizer)
```

5. Add an `epoch` loop and a batch steps loop inside the first loop, as follows:

```
for epoch in range(epochs):
    print("Epoch:", epoch)
```

```
number_of_batches = int(len(loaded_images) / batch_size)
print("Number of batches:", number_of_batches)
for index in range(number_of_batches):
    print("Batch:", index + 1)
```

6. Next, sample a batch of images from the list of real images:

```
# Sample and normalize
images_batch = loaded_images[index * batch_size:(index + 1)
* batch_size]
images_batch = images_batch / 255.0
images_batch = images_batch.astype(np.float32)
# Sample a batch of age one-hot encoder vectors
y_batch = y[index * batch_size:(index + 1) * batch_size]
```

7. Next, generate embeddings for the real images using the FR network:

```
images_batch_resized =
image_resizer.predict_on_batch(images_batch)
real_embeddings =
fr_model.predict_on_batch(images_batch_resized)
```

8. Finally, train the adversarial model, which will train the encoder model and the generator model:

```
reconstruction_loss =
fr_adversarial_model.train_on_batch([images_batch, y_batch],
real_embeddings)
```

9. Also, write the reconstruction loss to TensorBoard for further visualization:

```
# Write the reconstruction loss to Tensorboard
write_log(tensorboard, "reconstruction_loss",
reconstruction_loss, index)
```

10. Save the weights for both of the networks:

```
# Save improved weights for both of the networks
generator.save_weights("generator_optimized.h5")
encoder.save_weights("encoder_optimized.h5")
```

Congratulations! We have now successfully trained the Age-cGAN for face aging.

Visualizing the losses

To visualize the losses for the training, start the Tensorboard server, as follows:

```
tensorboard --logdir=logs
```

Now open `localhost:6006` in your browser. The **SCALARS** section
of TensorBoard contains plots for both losses, as shown in the following screenshot:

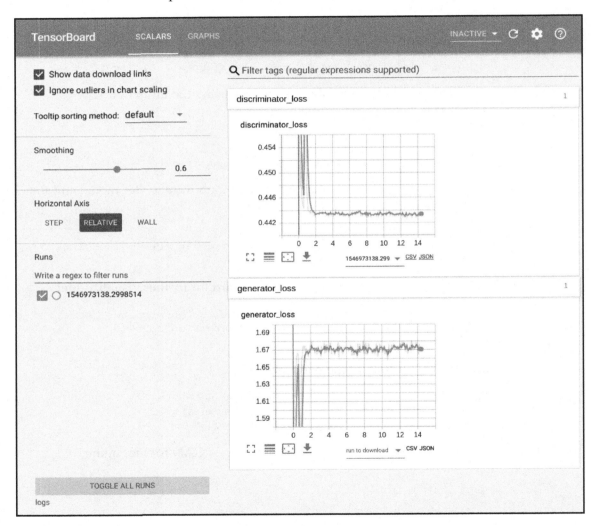

These plots will help you to decide whether to continue or stop the training. If the losses are not decreasing anymore, you can stop the training, as there is no chance of improvement. If the losses keep increasing, you must stop the training. Play with the hyperparameters and select a set of hyperparameters that you think can provide better results. If the losses are decreasing gradually, keep training the model.

Visualizing the graphs

The **GRAPHS** section of TensorBoard contains the graphs for both networks. If the networks are not performing well, these graphs can help you debug the networks. They also show the flow of tensors and different operations inside each graph:

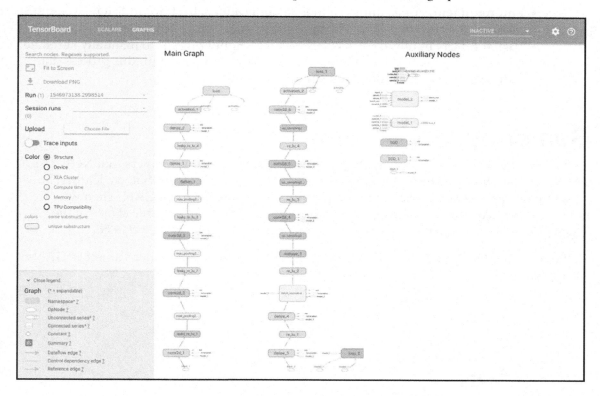

Flow of tensors and different operations inside the graphs

Practical applications of Age-cGAN

Age synthesis and age progression have many industrial and consumer applications:

- **Cross-age face recognition**: This can be incorporated into security applications, such as mobile device unlocking or desktop unlocking. The problem with current face recognition systems is that they need to be updated with time. With Age-cGAN networks, the lifespan of cross-age face recognition systems will be longer.
- **Finding lost children**: This is an interesting application of an Age-cGAN. As the age of a child increases, their facial features change, and it becomes much harder to identify them. An Age-cGAN can simulate a person's face at a specified age.
- **Entertainment**: For example, in mobile applications, to show and share a friend's pictures at a specified age.
- **Visual effects in movies**: It's a tedious and lengthy process to manually simulate a person's face when they are older. Age-cGANs can speed up this process and reduce the costs of creating and simulating faces.

Summary

In this chapter, we were introduced to Age Conditional Generative Adversarial Networks (Age-cGANs). We then studied the architecture of Age-cGANs. After that, we learned how to set up our project and looked at the Keras implementation of Age-cGAN. Then we trained Age-cGAN on a wiki-cropped dataset, and went through all three stages of the Age-cGAN network. Finally, we discussed practical applications of Age-cGANs.

In the next chapter, we will be generating anime characters using another variant of GANs: DCGANs.

4
Generating Anime Characters Using DCGANs

As we know, convolution layers are really good at processing images. They are capable of learning important features, such as edges, shapes, and complex objects, effectively, as shown in neural networks, such as Inception, AlexNet, **Visual Geometry Group (VGG)**, and ResNet. Ian Goodfellow and others proposed a **Generative Adversarial Network (GAN)** with dense layers in their paper titled *Generative Adversarial Nets*, which can be found at the following link: `https://arxiv.org/pdf/1406.2661.pdf`. Complex neural networks, such as **Convolutional Neural Networks (CNNs)**, **Recurrent Neural Networks (RNNs)**, and **Long Short-Term Memory (LSTM)** were not initially tested in GANs. The development of **Deep Convolutional Generative Adversarial Networks (DCGANs)** was an important step toward using CNNs for image generation. A DCGAN uses convolutional layers instead of dense layers. They were proposed by researchers Alec Radford, Luke Metz, Soumith Chintala, and others, in their paper, *Unsupervised Representation Learning with Deep Convolutional Generative Adversarial Networks*, which can be found at the following link: `https://arxiv.org/pdf/1511.06434.pdf`. Since then, DCGANs have been widely used for various image generation tasks. In this chapter, we will use a DCGAN architecture to generate anime characters.

In this chapter, we will be covering the following topics:

- Introducing to DCGANs
- Architectural details of a GAN network
- Setting up the project
- Preparing the dataset for training
- A Keras implementation of a DCGAN for the generation of anime characters
- Training the DCGAN on the anime character dataset
- Evaluating the trained model
- Optimizing the networks by optimizing the hyperparameters
- Practical applications of DCGANs

Introducing to DCGANs

CNNs have been phenomenal in computer vision tasks, be it for classifying images or detecting objects in images. CNNs were so good at understanding images that they inspired researchers to use CNNs in a GAN network. Initially, authors of the official GAN paper introduced **Deep Neural Networks (DNNs)** with dense layers only. Convolutional layers were not used in the original implementation of the GAN network. In the previous GANs, the generator and the discriminator network used dense hidden layers only. Instead, authors suggested that different neural network architectures can be used in a GAN setup.

DCGANs extend the idea of using convolutional layers in the discriminator and the generator network. The setup of a DCGAN is similar to a vanilla GAN. It consists of two networks: a generator and a discriminator. The generator is a DNN with convolutional layers, and the discriminator is a DNN with convolutional layers. Training a DCGAN is similar to training a vanilla GAN network. In the first chapter, we learned that the networks get involved in a non-cooperative game, in which the discriminator network backpropagates its error to the generator network and the generator networks use this error to improve its weights.

We will be exploring the architectures of both networks in the next section.

Architectural details of a DCGAN

As mentioned before, the DCGAN network uses convolutional layers in both networks. To reiterate, a CNN is a network with convolution layers, followed by a normalization or pooling layers, followed by an activation function. In DCGANs, the discriminator network takes an image, downsamples it with the help of convolutional and pooling layers, and uses a dense classification layer to classify the image as real or fake. The generator network takes a random noise vector from latent space, upsamples it using upsampling mechanisms, and finally generates an image. We use Leaky ReLU as the activation function for the hidden layers and dropout between 0.4 and 0.7 to avoid overfitting.

Let's take a look at the configuration for both networks.

Configuring the generator network

Before moving forward, let's have a look at the architecture of the generator network:

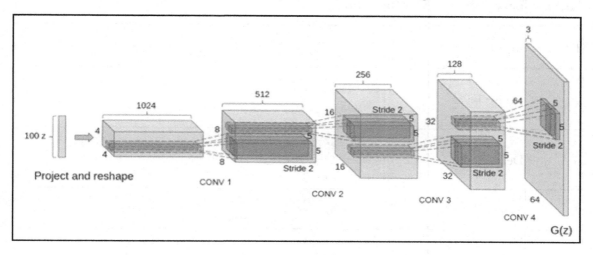

Source: arXiv:1511.06434 [cs.LG]

The preceding diagram contains different layers in the architecture of the generator network and shows how it generates an image of a resolution of 64 x 64 x 3.

The DCGAN's generator network contains 10 layers. It performs strided convolution to increase the spatial resolution of the tensor. In Keras, a combination of upsampling and convolution layers is equal to a strided convolutional layer. Basically, the generator network takes a noise vector sampled from a uniform distribution and keeps transforming it until it generates the final image. In other words, it takes a tensor of shape (`batch_size`, `100`) and outputs a tensor of shape (`batch_size`, `64`, `64`, `3`).

Let's take a look at the different layers in a generator network:

Layer #	Layer name	Configuration
1	Input layer	`input_shape=(batch_size, 100),` `output_shape=(batch_size, 100)`
2	Dense layer	`neurons=2048,input_shape=(batch_size, 100),` `output_shape=(batch_size, 2048),activation='relu'`
3.	Dense layer	`neurons=16384,input_shape=(batch_size, 100),` `output_shape=(batch_size, 2048),` `batch_normalization=Yes,activation='relu'`
4.	Reshape layer	`input_shape=(batch_size=16384),` `output_shape=(batch_size, 8, 8, 256)`
5.	Upsampling layer	`size=(2, 2),input_shape=(batch_size, 8, 8, 256),` `output_shape=(batch_size, 16, 16, 256)`
6.	2D convolution layer	`filters=128,kernel_size=(5, 5),strides=(1, 1),` `padding='same',input_shape=(batch_size, 16, 16, 256),output_shape=(batch_size, 16, 16, 128),activation='relu'`
7.	Upsampling layer	`size=(2, 2),input_shape=(batch_size, 16, 16, 128),` `output_shape=(batch_size, 32, 32, 128)`
8.	2D convolution layer	`filters=64,kernel_size=(5, 5),strides=(1, 1),` `padding='same',activation=ReLU,` `input_shape=(batch_size, 32, 32, 128),` `output_shape=(batch_size, 32, 32, 64),` `activation='relu'`
9.	Upsampling layer	`size=(2, 2),input_shape=(batch_size, 32, 32, 64),` `output_shape=(batch_size, 64, 64, 64)`
10.	2D convolution layer	`filters=3,kernel_size=(5, 5),strides=(1, 1),` `padding='same',activation=ReLU,` `input_shape=(batch_size, 64, 64, 64),` `output_shape=(batch_size, 64, 64, 3),` `activation='tanh'`

Let's have a look at how tensors flow from the first layer to the last layer. The following diagram shows the input and output shapes for the different layers:

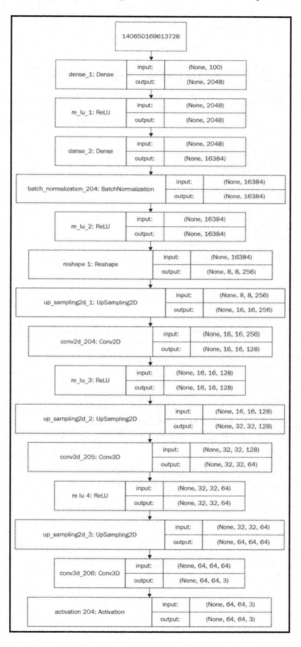

This configuration is valid for Keras APIs with the TensorFlow backend and the `channels_last` format.

Configuring the discriminator network

Before moving forward, let's have a look at the architecture of the discriminator network:

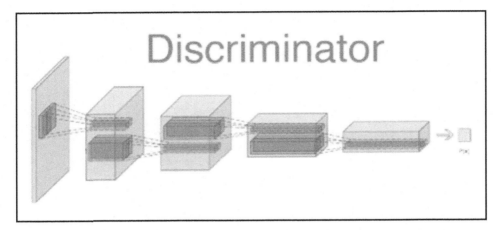

The preceding diagram gives a top-level overview of the architecture of the generator network.

As mentioned, the discriminator network is a CNN that contains 10 layers (you can add more layers to the network according to your requirements). Basically, it takes an image of dimensions of 64 x 64 x 3, downsamples it using 2D convolutional layers, and passes it to the fully connected layers for classification. Its output is a prediction as to whether the given image is a fake image or a real image. This can be either 0 or 1; if the output is 1, the image passed to the discriminator is real and if the output is 0, the image passed is a fake image.

Let's have a look at the layers in the discriminator network:

Layer #	Layer name	Configuration
1.	Input layer	`input_shape=(batch_size, 64, 64, 3), output_shape=(batch_size, 64, 64, 3)`
2.	2D convolutional Layer	`filters=128, kernel_size=(5, 5), strides=(1, 1), padding='valid', input_shape=(batch_size, 64, 64, 3), output_shape=(batch_size, 64, 64, 128), activation='leakyrelu', leaky_relu_alpha=0.2`
3.	MaxPooling2D	`pool_size=(2, 2), input_shape=(batch_size, 64, 64, 128), output_shape=(batch_size, 32, 32, 128)`
4.	2D convolutional layer	`filters=256, kernel_size=(3, 3), strides=(1, 1), padding='valid', input_shape=(batch_size, 32, 32, 128), output_shape=(batch_size, 30, 30, 256), activation='leakyrelu', leaky_relu_alpha=0.2`
5.	MaxPooling2D	`pool_size=(2, 2), input_shape=(batch_size, 30, 30, 256), output_shape=(batch_size, 15, 15, 256)`
6.	2D convolutional layer	`filters=512, kernel_size=(3, 3), strides=(1, 1), padding='valid', input_shape=(batch_size, 15, 15, 256), output_shape=(batch_size, 13, 13, 512), activation='leakyrelu', leaky_relu_alpha=0.2`
7.	MaxPooling2D	`pool_size=(2, 2), input_shape=(batch_size, 13, 13, 512), output_shape=(batch_size, 6, 6, 512)`
8.	Flatten layer	`input_shape=(batch_size, 6, 6, 512), output_shape=(batch_size, 18432)`
9.	Dense layer	`neurons=1024, input_shape=(batch_size, 18432), output_shape=(batch_size, 1024), activation='leakyrelu', 'leakyrelu_alpha'=0.2`
10.	Dense layer	`neurons=1, input_shape=(batch_size, 1024), output_shape=(batch_size, 1), activation='sigmoid'`

Let's have a look at how tensors flow from the first layer to the last layer. The following diagram shows input and output shapes for the different layers:

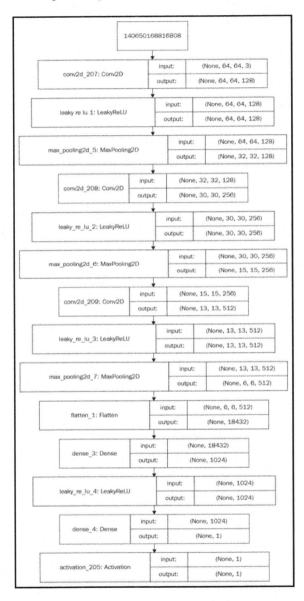

These configurations are valid for Keras APIs with the TensorFlow backend and the `channels_last` format.

Setting up the project

We have already cloned/downloaded the complete code for all the chapters. The downloaded code contains a directory called `Chapter04`, which contains the entire code for this chapter. Execute the following commands to set up the project:

1. Start by navigating to the parent directory, as follows:

    ```
    cd Generative-Adversarial-Networks-Projects
    ```

2. Now, change the directory from the current directory to `Chapter04`:

    ```
    cd Chapter04
    ```

3. Next, create a Python virtual environment for this project:

    ```
    virtualenv venv
    virtualenv venv -p python3 # Create a virtual environment using
                                 python3 interpreter
    virtualenv venv -p python2 # Create a virtual environment using
                                 python2 interpreter
    ```

    We will be using this newly created virtual environment for this project. Each chapter has its own separate virtual environment.

4. Next, activate the virtual environment:

    ```
    source venv/bin/activate
    ```

    After you activate the virtual environment, all further commands will be executed in this virtual environment.

5. Next, install all the requirements given in the `requirements.txt` file by executing the following command:

    ```
    pip install -r requirements.txt
    ```

You can refer to the README.md file for further instructions on how to set up the project. Very often, developers face the problem of mismatching dependencies. Creating a separate virtual environment for each project will take care of this problem.

In this section, we have successfully set up the project and installed the required dependencies. In the next section, we will be working with the dataset, including downloading it and cleaning it.

Downloading and preparing the anime characters dataset

To train a DCGAN network, we need a dataset of anime characters containing cropped faces of the characters. There are multiple ways to collect a dataset. We can either use a publicly available dataset, or we can scrape one, as long as we don't violate the website's scraping policies. In this chapter, we will be scraping images for educational and demonstration purposes only. We have scraped images from pixiv.net using a crawler tool called gallery-dl. This is a command-line tool that can be used to download image collections from websites, such as pixiv.net, exhentai.org, danbooru.donmai.us, and more. It is available at the following link: https://github.com/mikf/gallery-dl.

Downloading the dataset

In this section, we will cover the different steps required to install the dependencies and download the dataset. Before executing the following commands, activate the virtual environment created for this project:

1. Execute the following command to install gallery-dl:

    ```
    pip install --upgrade gallery-dl
    ```

2. Alternatively, you can install the latest development version of gallery-dl using the following command:

    ```
    pip install --upgrade
    https://github.com/mikf/gallery-dl/archive/master.zip
    ```

3. If the preceding commands don't work, follow the instructions given in the official repository:

```
# Official gallery-dl Github repo
https://github.com/mikf/gallery-dl
```

4. Finally, execute the following command to download the images from `danbooru.donmai.us` using `gallery-dl`.:

```
gallery-dl https://danbooru.donmai.us/posts?tags=face
```

 Download images at your own risk. The information given is for educational purposes only and we don't support illegal scraping. We don't have copyright of the images, as the images are hosted by their respective owners. For commercial purposes, please contact the respective owner of the website or the content that you are using.

Exploring the dataset

Before we crop or resize the images, take a look at the downloaded images:

As you see, some images contain other body parts as well, which we don't want in our training images. In the next section, we will crop out only the face part from these images. Also, we will resize all images to a size required for the training.

Cropping and resizing images in the dataset

In this section, we will crop out faces from images. We will be using **python-animeface** to crop the faces from the images. This is an open source GitHub repository that automatically crops faces from images from the command line. It is publicly available at the following link: https://github.com/nya3jp/python-animeface.

Execute the following steps to crop and resize the images:

1. First of all, download python-animeface:

```
pip install animeface
```

2. Next, import the module required for the task:

```
import glob
import os

import animeface
from PIL import Image
```

3. Next, define the parameters:

```
total_num_faces = 0
```

3. Next, iterate over all images to crop and resize them one by one:

```
for index, filename in
enumerate(glob.glob('/path/to/directory/containing/images/*.*')):
```

4. Inside the loop, open the current image and detect a face inside it:

```
try:
    # Open image
    im = Image.open(filename)

    # Detect faces
    faces = animeface.detect(im)
except Exception as e:
    print("Exception:{}".format(e))
    continue
```

5. Next, get coordinates of the face detected in the images:

```
fp = faces[0].face.pos

# Get coordinates of the face detected in the image
coordinates = (fp.x, fp.y, fp.x+fp.width, fp.y+fp.height)
```

6. Now, crop the face out of the image:

```
# Crop image
cropped_image = im.crop(coordinates)
```

7. Next, resize the cropped face image to have a dimension of `(64, 64)`:

```
# Resize image
cropped_image = cropped_image.resize((64, 64), Image.ANTIALIAS)
```

8. Finally, save the cropped and resized image to the desired directory:

```
cropped_image.save("/path/to/directory/to/store/cropped/images/file
name.png"))
```

The complete code wrapped inside a Python function appears as follows:

```
import glob
import os

import animeface
from PIL import Image

total_num_faces = 0

for index, filename in
enumerate(glob.glob('/path/to/directory/containing/images/*.*')):
    # Open image and detect faces
    try:
        im = Image.open(filename)
        faces = animeface.detect(im)
    except Exception as e:
        print("Exception:{}".format(e))
        continue

    # If no faces found in the current image
    if len(faces) == 0:
        print("No faces found in the image")
        continue

    fp = faces[0].face.pos

    # Get coordinates of the face detected in the image
    coordinates = (fp.x, fp.y, fp.x+fp.width, fp.y+fp.height)

    # Crop image
    cropped_image = im.crop(coordinates)
```

```
    # Resize image
    cropped_image = cropped_image.resize((64, 64), Image.ANTIALIAS)

    # Show cropped and resized image
    # cropped_image.show()

    # Save it in the output directory
cropped_image.save("/path/to/directory/to/store/cropped/images/filename.png
"))

    print("Cropped image saved successfully")
    total_num_faces += 1
    print("Number of faces detected till now:{}".format(total_num_faces))

    print("Total number of faces:{}".format(total_num_faces))
```

The preceding script will load all of the images from the folder containing downloaded images, detect faces using the `python-animeface` library, and **crop out** the face part from the initial image. Then, the cropped images will be resized to a size of 64 x 64. If you want to change the dimensions of the images, change the architecture of the generator and the discriminator accordingly. We are now ready to work on our network.

Implementing a DCGAN using Keras

In this section, we will write an implementation of a DCGAN in the Keras framework. Keras is a meta-framework that uses TensorFlow or Teano as a backend. It provides high-level APIs for working with neural networks. It also has pre-built neural network layers, optimizers, regularizers, initializers, and data-preprocessing layers for easy prototyping compared to low-level frameworks, such as TensorFlow. Let's start by writing the implementation of the generator network.

Generator

As mentioned in the *Architecture of DCGAN* section, the generator network consists of some 2D convolutional layers, upsampling layers, a reshape layer, and a batch normalization layer. In Keras, every operation can be specified as a layer. Even activation functions are layers in Keras and can be added to a model just like a normal dense layer.

Perform the following steps to create a generator network:

1. Let's start by creating a `Sequential` Keras model:

   ```
   gen_model = Sequential()
   ```

2. Next, add a dense layer that has 2,048 nodes, followed by an activation layer, `tanh`:

   ```
   gen_model.add(Dense(units=2048))
   gen_model.add(Activation('tanh'))
   ```

3. Next, add the second layer, which is also a dense layer that has 16,384 neurons. This is followed by a `batch normalization` layer with `default hyperparameters` and `tanh` as the **activation function**:

   ```
   gen_model.add(Dense(256*8*8))
   gen_model.add(BatchNormalization())
   gen_model.add(Activation('tanh'))
   ```

   The output of the second dense layer is a tensor of a size of (**16384,**). Here, (**256, 8, 8**) is the number of neurons in the dense layer.

4. Next, add a reshape layer to the network to reshape the tensor from the last layer to a tensor of a shape of (`batch_size, 8, 8, 256`):

   ```
   # Reshape layer
   gen_model.add(Reshape((8, 8, 256), input_shape=(256*8*8,)))
   ```

5. Next, add a 2D upsampling layer to alter the shape from (8, 8, 256) to (16, 16, 256). The upsampling size is (2, 2), which increases the size of the tensor to double its original size. Here, we have 256 tensors of a dimension of 16 x 16:

   ```
   gen_model.add(UpSampling2D(size=(2, 2)))
   ```

6. Next, add a 2D convolutional layer. This applies 2D convolutions on the tensor using a specified number of filters. Here, we are using 64 filters and a kernel of a shape of (`5, 5`):

   ```
   gen_model.add(Conv2D(128, (5, 5), padding='same'))
   gen_model.add(Activation('tanh'))
   ```

7. Next, add a 2D upsampling layer to change the shape of the tensor from (`batch_size, 16, 16, 64`) to (`batch_size, 32, 32, 64`):

   ```
   gen_model.add(UpSampling2D(size=(2, 2)))
   ```

A 2D upsampling layer repeats the rows and columns of the tensor by a size of [0] and a size of [1], respectively.

8. Next, add a second 2D convolutional layer with 64 filters and a **kernel size** of (5, 5) followed by `tanh` as the activation function:

```
gen_model.add(Conv2D(64, (5, 5), padding='same'))
gen_model.add(Activation('tanh'))
```

9. Next, add a 2D upsampling layer to change the shape from (batch_size, 32, 32, 64) to (batch_size, 64, 64, 64):

```
gen_model.add(UpSampling2D(size=(2, 2)))
```

10. Finally, add the third 2D convolutional layer with three **filters** and a **kernel size** of (5, 5) followed by `tanh` as the activation function:

```
gen_model.add(Conv2D(3, (5, 5), padding='same'))
gen_model.add(Activation('tanh'))
```

The generator network will output a tensor of a shape of (batch_size, 64, 64, 3). One image tensor from this batch of tensors is similar to an image of a dimension of 64 x 64 with three channels: **Red, Green, and Blue (RGB)**.

The complete code for the generator network wrapped in a Python method looks as follows:

```
def get_generator():
    gen_model = Sequential()

    gen_model.add(Dense(input_dim=100, output_dim=2048))
    gen_model.add(LeakyReLU(alpha=0.2))

    gen_model.add(Dense(256 * 8 * 8))
    gen_model.add(BatchNormalization())
    gen_model.add(LeakyReLU(alpha=0.2))

    gen_model.add(Reshape((8, 8, 256), input_shape=(256 * 8 * 8,)))
    gen_model.add(UpSampling2D(size=(2, 2)))

    gen_model.add(Conv2D(128, (5, 5), padding='same'))
    gen_model.add(LeakyReLU(alpha=0.2))

    gen_model.add(UpSampling2D(size=(2, 2)))

    gen_model.add(Conv2D(64, (5, 5), padding='same'))
    gen_model.add(LeakyReLU(alpha=0.2))
```

```
gen_model.add(UpSampling2D(size=(2, 2)))

gen_model.add(Conv2D(3, (5, 5), padding='same'))
gen_model.add(LeakyReLU(alpha=0.2))
return gen_model
```

Now we have created the generator network, let's work on creating the discriminator network.

Discriminator

As mentioned in the *Architecture of DCGAN* section, the discriminator network has three 2D convolutional layers, each followed by an activation function followed by two max pooling layers. The tail of the network contains two fully-connected (dense) layers that work as a classification layer. Before anything else, let's have a look at the different layers in the discriminator network:

- All convolutional layers have LeakyReLU as the activation function with an alpha value of 0.2
- The convolutional layers have 128, 256, and 512 filters, respectively. Their kernel sizes are (5, 5), (3, 3), and (3, 3), respectively.
- After the convolutional layers, we have a flatten layer, which flattens the input to a one-dimensional tensor.
- Following this, the network has two dense layers with 1,024 neurons and one neuron, respectively.
- The first dense layer has LeakyReLU as the activation function, while the second layer has sigmoid as the activation function. Sigmoid activation is used for binary classification. We are training the discriminator network to classify between real or fake images.

Perform the following steps to create a discriminator network:

1. Let's start by creating a Sequential Keras model:

   ```
   dis_model = Sequential()
   ```

2. Add a 2D convolutional layer that takes an input image of a shape of (64, 64, 3). The hyperparameters for this layer are the following. Also, add LeakyReLU with an alpha value of 0.2 as the activation function:
   - **Filters:** 128
   - **Kernel Size:** (5, 5)

- **Padding:** Same:

```
dis_model.add(Conv2D(filters=128, kernel_size=5, padding='same',
                input_shape=(64, 64, 3)))
dis_model.add(LeakyReLU(alpha=0.2))
```

3. Next, add a 2D max pooling layer with a pool size of (2, 2). Max pooling is used to downsample an image representation and it is applied by using a max-filter over non-overlapping sub-regions of the representation:

```
dis_model.add(MaxPooling2D(pool_size=(2, 2)))
```

The shape of the output tensor from the first layer will be (batch_size, 32, 32, 128).

4. Next, add another 2D convolutional layer with the following configurations:
   - **Filters**: 256
   - **Kernel size**: (3, 3)
   - **Activation function**: LeakyReLU with alpha 0.2
   - **Pool size in 2D max pooling**: (2, 2):

```
dis_model.add(Conv2D(filters=256, kernel_size=3))
dis_model.add(LeakyReLU(alpha=0.2))
dis_model.add(MaxPooling2D(pool_size=(2, 2)))
```

The shape of the output tensor from this layer will be (batch_size, 30, 30, 256).

5. Next, add the third 2D convolutional layer with the following configurations:
   - **Filters**: 512
   - **Kernel size**: (3, 3)
   - **Activation function**: LeakyReLU with alpha 0.2
   - **Pool size in 2D Max Pooling**: (2, 2):

```
dis_model.add(Conv2D(512, (3, 3)))
dis_model.add(LeakyReLU(alpha=0.2))
dis_model.add(MaxPooling2D(pool_size=(2, 2)))
```

The shape of the output tensor from this layer will be (batch_size, 13, 13, 512).

6. Next, add a flatten layer. This flattens the input without affecting the batch size. It produces a two-dimensional tensor:

```
dis_model.add(Flatten())
```

The output shape of the tensor from the flattened layer will be `(batch_size, 18432,)`.

7. Next, add a dense layer with `1024` neurons and `LeakyReLU` with `alpha` 0.2 as the activation function:

```
dis_model.add(Dense(1024))
dis_model.add(LeakyReLU(alpha=0.2))
```

8. Finally, add a dense layer with one neuron for binary classification. The sigmoid function is the best for binary classification, as it gives the probability of the classes:

```
dis_model.add(Dense(1))
dis_model.add(Activation('tanh'))
```

The network will generate an output tensor of a shape of `(batch_size, 1)`. The output tensor contains the probability of the classes.

The complete code for the discriminator network wrapped inside a Python method looks as follows:

```
def get_discriminator():
    dis_model = Sequential()
    dis_model.add(
        Conv2D(128, (5, 5),
               padding='same',
               input_shape=(64, 64, 3))
    )
    dis_model.add(LeakyReLU(alpha=0.2))
    dis_model.add(MaxPooling2D(pool_size=(2, 2)))

    dis_model.add(Conv2D(256, (3, 3)))
    dis_model.add(LeakyReLU(alpha=0.2))
    dis_model.add(MaxPooling2D(pool_size=(2, 2)))

    dis_model.add(Conv2D(512, (3, 3)))
    dis_model.add(LeakyReLU(alpha=0.2))
    dis_model.add(MaxPooling2D(pool_size=(2, 2)))

    dis_model.add(Flatten())
    dis_model.add(Dense(1024))
```

```
dis_model.add(LeakyReLU(alpha=0.2))

dis_model.add(Dense(1))
dis_model.add(Activation('sigmoid'))

return dis_model
```

In this section, we have successfully implemented the discriminator and generator networks. In the next section, we will train the model on the dataset that we prepared in the *Downloading and preparing the anime characters dataset* section.

Training the DCGAN

Again, training a DCGAN is similar to training a Vanilla GAN network. It is a four-step process:

1. Load the dataset.
2. Build and compile the networks.
3. Train the discriminator network.
4. Train the generator network.

We will work on these steps one by one in this section.

Let's start by defining the variables and the hyperparameters:

```
dataset_dir = "/Path/to/dataset/directory/*.*"
batch_size = 128
z_shape = 100
epochs = 10000
dis_learning_rate = 0.0005
gen_learning_rate = 0.0005
dis_momentum = 0.9
gen_momentum = 0.9
dis_nesterov = True
gen_nesterov = True
```

Here, we have specified different hyperparameters for the training. We will now see how to load the dataset for the training.

Loading the samples

To train the DCGAN network, we need to load the dataset in memory and we need to define a mechanism to load batches of memory. Perform the following steps to load the dataset:

1. Start by loading all images that you cropped, resized, and saved in the `cropped` folder. Specify the path of the directory correctly, so that the `glob.glob` method can create a list of all files in it. To read an image, use the `imread` method from the `scipy.misc` module. The following code shows the different steps to load all images inside the directory:

    ```
    # Loading images
    all_images = []
    for index, filename in
    enumerate(glob.glob('/Path/to/cropped/images/directory/*.*')):
        image = imread(filename, flatten=False, mode='RGB')
        all_images.append(image)
    ```

2. Next, create a `ndarray` of all the images. The shape of the final `ndarray` will be `(total_num_images, 64, 64, 3)`. Also, normalize all the images:

    ```
    # Convert to Numpy ndarray
    X = np.array(all_images)
    X = (X - 127.5) / 127.5
    ```

Now we have loaded the dataset, next we will see how to build and compile the networks.

Building and compiling the networks

In this section, we will build and compile our networks required for the training:

1. Start by defining the optimizers required for the training, as shown here:

    ```
    # Define optimizers
    dis_optimizer = SGD(lr=dis_learning_rate, momentum=dis_momentum,
    nesterov=dis_nesterov)
    gen_optimizer = SGD(lr=gen_learning_rate, momentum=gen_momentum,
    nesterov=gen_nesterov)
    ```

2. Next, create an instance of the generator model, and compile the generator model (compiling will initialize the weights parameters, the optimizer algorithm, the loss function, and other essential steps required to use the network):

```
gen_model = build_generator()
gen_model.compile(loss='binary_crossentropy',
optimizer=gen_optimizer)
```

Use `binary_crossentropy` as the `loss` function for the generator networks and `gen_optimizer` as the optimizer.

3. Next, create an instance of the discriminator model, and compile it, as shown here:

```
dis_model = build_discriminator()
dis_model.compile(loss='binary_crossentropy',
optimizer=dis_optimizer)
```

Similarly, use `binary_crossentropy` as the loss function for the discriminator network and `dis_optimizer` as the optimizer.

4. Next, create an adversarial model. An adversarial contains both networks in a single model. The architecture of the adversarial model will be as follows:
   - *input -> generator->discriminator->output*

The code to create and compile an adversarial model is as follows:

```
adversarial_model = Sequential()
adversarial_model.add(gen_model)
dis_model.trainable = False
adversarial_model.add(dis_model)
```

When we train this network, we don't want to train the discriminator network, so make it non-trainable before we add it to the adversarial model.

Compile the adversarial model, as follows:

```
adversarial_model.compile(loss='binary_crossentropy',
optimizer=gen_optimizer)
```

Use `binary_crossentropy` as the loss function and `gen_optimizer` as the optimizer for the adversarial model.

Before starting the training, add TensorBoard to visualize the losses, as follows:

```
tensorboard = TensorBoard(log_dir="logs/{}".format(time.time()),
write_images=True, write_grads=True, write_graph=True)
tensorboard.set_model(gen_model)
tensorboard.set_model(dis_model)
```

We will train the network for a specified number of iterations, so create a loop that should run for a specified number of epochs. Inside each epoch, we will train our networks on a mini-batch of a size of 128. Calculate the number of batches that need to be processed:

```
for epoch in range(epcohs):
    print("Epoch is", epoch)
    number_of_batches = int(X.shape[0] / batch_size)
    print("Number of batches", number_of_batches)
    for index in range(number_of_batches):
```

We will now take a closer look at the training process. The following points explain the different steps involved in the training of DCGAN:

- Initially, both of the networks are naive and have random weights.
- The standard process to train a DCGAN network is to first train the discriminator on the batch of samples.
- To do this, we need fake samples as well as real samples. We already have the real samples, so we now need to generate the fake samples.
- To generate fake samples, create a latent vector of a shape of (100,) over a uniform distribution. Feed this latent vector to the untrained generator network. The generator network will generate fake samples that we use to train our discriminator network.
- Concatenate the real images and the fake images to create a new set of sample images. We also need to create an array of labels: label 1 for real images and label 0 for fake images.

Training the discriminator network

Perform the following steps to train the discriminator network:

1. Start by sampling a batch of noise vectors from a normal distribution, as follows:

    ```
    z_noise = np.random.normal(0, 1, size=(batch_size, z_shape))
    ```

    To sample the values, use the `normal()` method from the `np.random` module in the Numpy library.

2. Next, sample a batch of real images from the set of all images:

    ```
    image_batch = X[index * batch_size:(index + 1) * batch_size]
    ```

3. Next, generate a batch of fake images using the generator network:

    ```
    generated_images = gen_model.predict_on_batch(z_noise)
    ```

4. Next, create real labels and fake labels:

    ```
    y_real = np.ones(batch_size) - np.random.random_sample(batch_size)
    * 0.2
    y_fake = np.random.random_sample(batch_size) * 0.2
    ```

5. Next, train the discriminator network on real images and real labels:

    ```
    dis_loss_real = dis_model.train_on_batch(image_batch, y_real)
    ```

6. Similarly, train it on fake images and fake labels:

    ```
    dis_loss_fake = dis_model.train_on_batch(generated_images, y_fake)
    ```

7. Next, calculate the average loss and print it to the console:

    ```
    d_loss = (dis_loss_real+dis_loss_fake)/2
    print("d_loss:", d_loss)
    ```

Up until now, we have been training the discriminator network. In the next section, let's train the generator network.

Training the generator network

To train the generator network, we have to train the adversarial model. When we train the adversarial model, it trains the generator network only but freezes the discriminator network. We won't train the discriminator network, as we have already trained it. Perform the following steps to train the adversarial model:

1. Start by creating a batch of noise vectors again. Sample these noise vectors from a Gaussian/Normal distribution:

```
z_noise = np.random.normal(0, 1, size=(batch_size, z_shape))
```

2. Next, train the adversarial model on this batch of noise vectors, as follows:

```
g_loss = adversarial_model.train_on_batch(z_noise, [1] *
batch_size)
```

We train the adversarial model on the batch of noise vectors and real labels. Here, *real labels* is a vector with all values equal to 1. We are also training the generator to fool the discriminator network. To do this, we provide it with a vector that has all the values equal to 1. In this step, the generator will receive feedback from the generator network and improve itself accordingly.

3. Finally, print the generator loss to the console to keep track of the losses:

```
print("g_loss:", g_loss)
```

There is a passive method to evaluate the training process. After every 10 epochs, generate fake images and manually check the quality of the images:

```
if epoch % 10 == 0:
    z_noise = np.random.normal(0, 1, size=(batch_size, z_shape))
    gen_images1 = gen_model.predict_on_batch(z_noise)

    for img in gen_images1[:2]:
        save_rgb_img(img, "results/one_{}.png".format(epoch))
```

These images will help you to decide whether to continue the training or to stop it early. Stop the training if quality of the generated high-resolution images is good. Or continue the training until your model becomes good.

We have successfully trained a DCGAN network on the ANIME character dataset. Now we can use the model to generate images of anime characters.

Generating images

To generate images, we need a noise vector, sampled from latent space. Numpy has a method called `uniform()` that generates a vector from a uniform distribution. Let's see how to generate images in the following steps:

1. Create a noise vector of a dimension of `(batch_size, 100)` by adding the following line of code:

```
z_noise = np.random.normal(0, 1, size=(batch_size, z_shape))
```

2. Then, use the generator model's `predict_on_batch` method to generate an image. Feed it with the noise vector created in the previous step:

```
gen_images = gen_model.predict_on_batch(z_noise)
```

3. Now that we have generated the image, save it by adding the following line of code. Create a directory called `results` to store the generated images:

```
imsave('results/image_{}.jpg'.format(epoch),gen_images[0])
```

You can now open these generated images to measure the quality of the generated model. This is a passive method to estimate the performance of the model.

Saving the model

Saving a model in Keras requires just one line of code. To save the generator model, add the following line:

```
# Specify the path for the generator model
gen_model.save("directory/for/the/generator/model.h5")
```

Similarly, save the discriminator model by adding the following line:

```
# Specify the path for the discriminator model
dis_model.save("directory/for/the/discriminator/model.h5")
```

Visualizing generated images

After training the network for 100 epochs, the generator will start generating plausible images. Let's have a look at the generated images.

After 100 epochs, the images appear as follows:

After 200 epochs, the images appear as follows:

To generate really good images, train the network for 10,000 epochs.

Visualizing losses

To visualize the losses for the training, start the TensorBoard server, as follows:

```
tensorboard --logdir=logs
```

Now, open `localhost:6006` in your browser. The **SCALARS** section of Tensorboard contains plots for both losses:

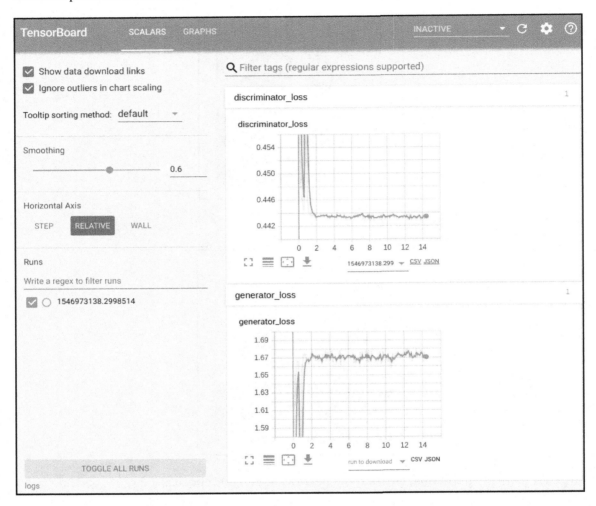

These plots will help you to decide whether to continue or stop the training. If the losses are not decreasing anymore, you can stop the training, as there is no chance of improvement. If the losses keep increasing, you must stop the training. Play with the hyperparameters and select a set of hyperparameters that you think can provide better results. If the losses are decreasing gradually, keep training the model.

Visualizing graphs

The **GRAPHS** section of Tensorboard contains the graphs for both networks. If the networks are not performing well, these graphs can help you debug the networks. They also show the flow of tensors and different operations inside each graph:

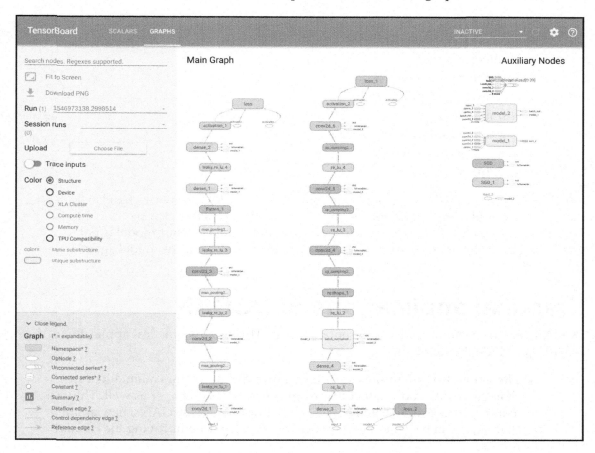

Tuning the hyperparameters

The hyperparameters are the properties of a model, which are fixed during the training of the model. Different parameters can have different accuracy. Let's take a look at some of the common hyperparameters used:

- Learning rate
- Batch size
- Number of epochs
- Generator optimizer
- Discriminator optimizer
- Number of layers
- Number of units in a dense layer
- Activation function
- Loss function

In the *Implementing a DCGAN using Keras* section, the learning rates were fixed: 0.0005 for the generator model and 0.0005 for the discriminator model. The batch size was 128. Tweaking these values might lead us to create a better model. If your model is not generating plausible images, try changing these values and run your model again.

Practical applications of DCGAN

DCGANs can be customized for different use cases. The various practical applications of DCGANs include the following:

- **The generation of anime characters**: Currently, animators manually draw characters with computer software and sometimes on paper as well. This is a manual process that usually takes a lot of time. With DCGANs, new anime characters can be generated in much less time, hence improving the creative process.
- **The augmentation of datasets**: If you want to train a supervised machine learning model, to train a good model, you would require a large dataset. DCGANs can help by augmenting the existing dataset, therefore increasing the size of the dataset required for supervised model training.

- **The generation of MNIST characters**: The MNIST dataset contains 60,000 images of handwritten digits. To train a complex supervised learning model, the MNIST dataset is not sufficient. DCGAN, once trained, will generate new digits that can be added to the original dataset.

- **Human face generation**: DCGANs use convolution neural networks and are pretty good at generating realistic-looking images.

- **Feature extractors**: Once trained, a discriminator can be used to extract features from an intermediate layer. These extracted features can be useful in tasks such as style transfer and face recognition. Style transfer involves generating internal representations of images, which are used to calculate style and content losses. Refer to the following paper to learn more about style transfer: `https://arxiv.org/pdf/1508.06576.pdf`.

Summary

In this chapter, we have introduced deep convolutional generative adversarial networks. We started with a basic introduction to DCGANs and then explored the architecture of the DCGAN network in depth. After that, we set up the project and installed the necessary dependencies. Then, we looked at the different steps required to download and prepare the dataset. We then prepared a Keras implementation of the network and trained it on our dataset. Once it was trained, we used it to generate new anime characters. We also explored different applications of DCGAN for real-world use cases.

In the next chapter, we will work on SRGANs for high-resolution image generation.

5
Using SRGANs to Generate Photo-Realistic Images

Super-Resolution Generative Adversarial Network, or **SRGAN**, is a **Generative Adversarial Network (GAN)** that can generate super-resolution images from low-resolution images, with finer details and higher quality. CNNs were earlier used to produce high-resolution images that train quicker and achieve high-level accuracy. However, in some cases, they are incapable of recovering finer details and often generate blurry images. In this chapter, we will implement an SRGAN network in the Keras framework that will be capable of generating high-resolution images. SRGANs were introduced in the paper titled, *Photo-Realistic Single Image Super-Resolution Using a Generative Adversarial Network*, by Christian Ledig, Lucas Theis, Ferenc Huszar, Jose Caballero, Andrew Cunningham, and others, which is available at the following link: `https://arxiv.org/pdf/1609.04802.pdf`.

Moving forward in this chapter, we will be covering the following topics:

- Introducing SRGANs
- Setting up the project
- Downloading the CelebA dataset
- The Keras implementation of SRGANs
- Training the SRGANs and network optimization
- Practical applications of SRGANs

Introducing SRGANs

Like any other GAN, SRGANs contain a generator network and a discriminator network. Both networks are deep. The functionality of both of these networks is specified as follows:

- **The generator**: The generator network takes a low-resolution image of a dimension of 64x64x3, and, after a series of convolution and upsampling layers, generates a super-resolution image of a shape of 256x256x3
- **The discriminator**: The discriminator network takes a high-resolution image and tries to identify whether the given image is real (from the real data samples) or fake (generated by the generator)

The architecture of SRGANs

In SRGANs, both of the networks are deep convolution neural networks. They contain convolution layers and upsampling layers. Each convolution layer is followed by a batch normalization operation and an activation layer. We will explore the networks in detail in the following sections. The architecture of an SRGAN is shown in the following diagram:

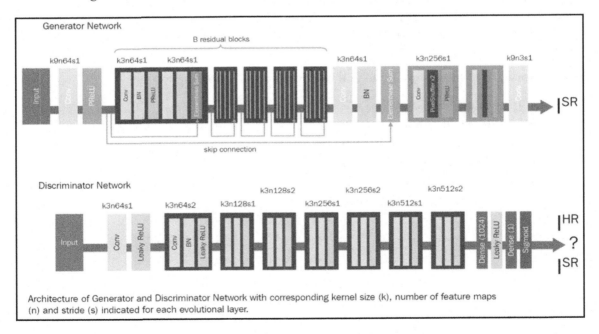

Architecture of Generator and Discriminator Network with corresponding kernel size (k), number of feature maps (n) and stride (s) indicated for each evolutional layer.

Let's have a look at the architecture of the networks in detail in the following sections.

The architecture of the generator network

As mentioned in the previous section, the generator network is a deep convolution neural network. The generator network contains the following blocks:

- The pre-residual block
- The residual block
- The post-residual block
- The upsampling block
- The final convolution layer

Let's explore these blocks one by one:

- **The pre-residual block**: The pre-residual block contains a single 2D convolution layer and relu as the activation function. The configuration of the block is as follows:

Layer name	Hyperparameters	Input shape	Output shape
2D convolution layer	`Filters=64, kernel_size=3, strides=1, padding='same', activation='relu'`	(64, 64, 3)	(64, 64, 64)

- **The residual block**: The residual block contains two 2D convolution layers. Both layers are followed by a batch normalization layer with a value of momentum equal to 0.8. The configuration of each residual block is as follows:

Layer name	Hyperparameters	Input shape	Output shape
2D convolution layer	`Filters=64, kernel_size=3, strides=1, padding='same', activation='relu'`	(64, 64, 64)	(64, 64, 64)
Batch normalization layer	`Momentum=0.8`	(64, 64, 64)	(64, 64, 64)
2D convolution layer	`Filters=64, kernel_size=3, strides=1, padding='same'`	(64, 64, 64)	(64, 64, 64)

| Batch normalization layer | Momentum=0.8 | (64, 64, 64) | (64, 64, 64) |
| Addition layer | None | (64, 64, 64) | (64, 64, 64) |

The addition layer calculates the sum of the input tensor to the block and the output of the last batch normalization layer. The generator network contains 16 residual blocks with the preceding configuration.

- **The post-residual block**: The post-residual block also contains a single 2D convolution layer and `relu` as the activation function. The convolution layer is followed by a batch normalization layer with the value of momentum equal to 0.8. The configuration of the post-residual block is as follows:

Layer name	Hyperparameters	Input Shape	Output Shape
2D convolution layer	Filters=64, kernel_size=3, strides=1, padding='same'	(64, 64, 64)	(64, 64, 64)
Batch normalization layer	Momentum=0.8	(64, 64, 64)	(64, 64, 64)

- **The upsampling block**: The upsampling block contains one upsampling layer and one 2D convolution layer and uses relu as the activation function. There are two upsampling blocks in the generator network. The configuration of the first upsampling block is as follows:

Layer name	Hyperparameters	Input shape	Output shape
2D upsampling layer	Size=(2, 2)	(64, 64, 64)	(128, 128, 64)
2D convolution layer	Filters=256, kernel_size=3, strides=1, padding='same', activation='relu'	(128, 128, 256)	(128, 128, 256)

The configuration of the second upsampling block is as follows:

Layer name	Hyperparameters	Input shape	Output shape
2D upsampling layer	Size=(2, 2)	(128, 128, 256)	(256, 256, 256)
2D convolution layer	Filters=256, kernel_size=3, strides=1, padding='same', activation='relu'	(256, 256, 256)	(256, 256, 256)

- **The last convolution layer**: The last layer is a 2D convolution layer that uses tanh as the activation function. It generates an image of a shape of (256, 256, 3). The configuration of the last layer is as follows:

Layer name	Hyperparameters	Input shape	Output shape
2D convolution layer	Filters=3, kernel_size=9, strides=1, padding='same', activation='tanh'	(256, 256, 256)	(256, 256, 3)

 These hyperparameters are best-suited for the Keras framework. If you are using any other framework, modify them accordingly.

The architecture of the discriminator network

The discriminator network is also a deep convolutional network. It contains eight convolution blocks followed by two dense (fully connected) layers. Each convolution block is followed by a batch normalization layer. There are two dense layers at the end of the network, which work as a classification block. The last layer predicts the probability of an image belonging to the real dataset or to the fake dataset. The detailed configuration of the discriminator network is shown in the following table:

Layer name	Hyperparameters	Input shape	Output shape
Input layer	None	(256, 256, 3)	(256, 256, 3)
2D convolution layer	filters=64, kernel_size=3, strides=1, padding='same', activation='leakyrelu'	(256, 256, 3)	(256, 256, 64)
2D convolution layer	filters=64, kernel_size=3, strides=2, padding='same', activation='leakyrelu'	(256, 256, 64)	(128, 128, 64)

Batch normalization layer	momentum=0.8	(128, 128, 64)	(128, 128, 64)
2D convolution layer	filters=128, kernel_size=3, strides=1, padding='same', activation='leakyrelu'	(128, 128, 64)	(128, 128, 128)
Batch normalization layer	momentum=0.8	(128, 128, 128)	(128, 128, 128)
2D convolution layer	filters=128, kernel_size=3, strides=2, padding='same', activation='leakyrelu'	(128, 128, 128)	(64, 64, 128)
Batch normalization layer	momentum=0.8	(64, 64, 128)	(64, 64, 128)
2D convolution layer	filters=256, kernel_size=3, strides=1, padding='same', activation='leakyrelu'	(64, 64, 128)	(64, 64, 256)
Batch normalization layer	momentum=0.8	(64, 64, 256)	(64, 64, 256)
2D convolution layer	filters=256, kernel_size=3, strides=2, padding='same', activation='leakyrelu'	(64, 64, 256)	(32, 32, 256)

We now have a clear understanding of the architecture of both networks. In the next section, let's have a look at the objective function required to train SRGANs.

The training objective function

To train SRGANs, there is an objective function or loss function, which we need to minimize to train the model. The objective function for SRGANs is called the **perceptual loss** function, which is a weighted sum of the two loss functions, as follows:

- Content loss
- Adversarial loss

Let's explore the content loss and the adversarial loss in detail in the following sections.

Content loss

There are two types of content loss, as follows:

- Pixel-wise MSE loss
- VGG loss

Let's discuss these losses in detail.

Pixel-wise MSE loss

The content loss is the mean squared error calculated between each pixel value from the real image and each pixel value from the generated image. The pixel-wide MSE loss calculates how different the generated images are from the real images. The formula for calculating the pixel-wide MSE loss is as follows:

$$l_{MSE}^{SR} = \frac{1}{r^2 WH} \sum_{x=1}^{rW} \sum_{y=1}^{rH} (I_{x,y}^{HR} - G_{\theta_G}(I^{LR})x, y)^2$$

Here, $G_{\theta_G}(I^{LR})$ represents a high-resolution image generated by the generated network. I^{HR} represents a high-resolution image sampled from the real dataset.

VGG loss

The VGG loss is another content loss function, which is applied over generated images and real images. VGG19 is a very popular deep neural network that is mostly used for image classification. VGG19 was introduced by Simonyan and Zisserman in their paper titled *Very Deep Convolutional Networks for Large-Scale Image Recognition*, which is available at https://arxiv.org/pdf/1409.1556.pdf. The intermediate layers of a pre-trained VGG19 network work as feature extractors and can be used to extract feature maps of the generated images and the real images. The VGG loss is based on these extracted feature maps. It is calculated as the Euclidean distance between the feature maps of the generated image and the real image. The formula for the VGG loss is as follows:

$$l_{VGG/i,j}^{SR} = \frac{1}{W_{i,j}H_{i,j}} \sum_{x=1}^{W_{i,j}} \sum_{y=1}^{H_{i,j}} (\Phi_{i,j}(I^{HR})x, y - \Phi_{i,j}(G_{\theta_G}(I^{LR}))x, y)^2$$

Here, $\emptyset_{i,j}$ represents the feature map generated by the VGG19 network. $\emptyset_{i,j}(I^{HR})$ represents the extracted feature maps of the real image and $\emptyset_{i,j}(G_{\theta_G}(I^{LR}))$ represents the extracted feature maps of the high-resolution generated image. The whole equation represents the Euclidean distance between the feature maps of the generated image and the real image.

Either of the preceding content losses can be used to train SRGANs. For our implementation, we will use the VGG loss.

Adversarial loss

The adversarial loss is calculated on the probabilities returned by the discriminator network. In the adversarial model, the discriminator network is fed with generated images, which are generated by the generated network. The adversarial loss can be represented by an equation, as follows:

$$l_{Gen}^{SR} = \sum_{n=1}^{N} -logD_{\theta_D}(G_{\theta_G}(I^{LR}))$$

Here, $G_{\theta_G}(I^{LR})$ is the generated image and $D_{\theta_D}(G_{\theta_G}(I^{LR}))$ represents the probability that the generated image is a real image.

The perceptual loss function is a weighted sum of the content loss and the adversarial loss, which is represented as the following equation:

$$l^{SR} = 1.0 * l_X^{SR} + 0.001 * l_{Gen}^{SR}$$

Here, the total perceptual loss is represented by l^{SR}. l_X^{SR} is the content loss, which can be either a pixel-wise MSE loss or VGG loss.

By minimizing the perceptual loss value, the generator network tries to fool the discriminator. As the value of the perceptual loss decreases, the generator network starts generating more realistic images.

Let's now start working on the project.

Setting up the project

If you haven't already cloned the repository with the complete code for all the chapters, clone the repository now. The downloaded code has a directory called `Chapter05`, which contains the entire code for this chapter. Execute the following commands to set up the project:

1. Start by navigating to the parent directory, as follows:

   ```
   cd Generative-Adversarial-Networks-Projects
   ```

2. Now change the directory from the current directory to `Chapter05`:

   ```
   cd Chapter05
   ```

3. Next, create a Python virtual environment for this project:

   ```
   virtualenv venv
   virtualenv venv -p python3 # Create a virtual environment using
             python3 interpreter
   virtualenv venv -p python2 # Create a virtual environment using
             python2 interpreter
   ```

   We will be using this newly created virtual environment for this project. Each chapter has its own separate virtual environment.

4. Next, activate the newly created virtual environment:

   ```
   source venv/bin/activate
   ```

   After you activate the virtual environment, all further commands will be executed in this virtual environment.

5. Next, install all the libraries given in the `requirements.txt` file by executing the following command:

   ```
   pip install -r requirements.txt
   ```

You can refer to the `README.md` file for further instructions on how to set up the project. Very often, developers face the problem of mismatching dependencies. Creating a separate virtual environment for each project will take care of this problem.

In this section, we have successfully set up the project and installed the required dependencies. In the next section, let's work on the dataset. We will explore various steps to download and format the dataset.

Downloading the CelebA dataset

For this chapter, we will use the large-scale **CelebFaces Attributes (CelebA)** dataset, which is available at `http://mmlab.ie.cuhk.edu.hk/projects/CelebA.html`. The dataset contains 202, 599 face images of celebrities.

 The dataset is available for non-commercial research purposes only and can't be used for commercial purposes. If you intend to use the dataset for commercial purposes, seek permissions from the owners of the images.

We will use the `CelebA` dataset to train our SRGAN network. Perform the following steps to download and extract the dataset:

1. Download the dataset from the following link:

   ```
   https://www.dropbox.com/sh/8oqt9vytwxb3s4r/AAB06FXaQRUNtjW9ntaoPGvC
   a?dl=0
   ```

2. Extract images from the downloaded `img_align_celeba.zip` by executing the following command:

   ```
   unzip img_align_celeba.zip
   ```

We have now downloaded and extracted the dataset. We can now start working on the Keras implementation of SRGAN.

The Keras implementation of SRGAN

As we discussed, SRGAN has three neural networks, a generator, a discriminator, and a pre-trained VGG19 network on the Imagenet dataset. In this section, we will write the implementation for all the networks. Let's start by implementing the generator network.

Before starting to write the implementations, create a Python file called `main.py` and import the essential modules, as follows:

```
import glob
import os

import numpy as np
import tensorflow as tf
from keras import Input
from keras.applications import VGG19
from keras.callbacks import TensorBoard
```

```
from keras.layers import BatchNormalization, Activation, LeakyReLU, Add,
Dense, PReLU, Flatten
from keras.layers.convolutional import Conv2D, UpSampling2D
from keras.models import Model
from keras.optimizers import Adam
from keras_preprocessing.image import img_to_array, load_img
from scipy.misc import imsave
```

The generator network

We have already explored the architecture of the generator network in *The architecture of the generator network* section. Let's start by writing the layers for the generator network in the Keras framework and then create a Keras model, using the functional API of the Keras framework.

Perform the following steps to implement the generator network in Keras:

1. Start by defining the hyperparameters required for the generator network:

   ```
   residual_blocks = 16
   momentum = 0.8
   input_shape = (64, 64, 3)
   ```

2. Next, create an input layer to feed input to the network, as follows:

   ```
   input_layer = Input(shape=input_shape)
   ```

   The input layer takes an input image of a shape of (64, 64, 3) and passes it to the next layer in the network.

3. Next, add the pre-residual block (2D convolution layer), as follows:
   Configuration:
   - **Filters**: 64
   - **Kernel size**: 9
   - **Strides**: 1
   - **Padding**: same
   - **Activation**: relu:

   ```
   gen1 = Conv2D(filters=64, kernel_size=9, strides=1, padding='same',
   activation='relu')(input_layer)
   ```

4. Next, write a method with the entire code for the residual block, as shown here:

```python
def residual_block(x):
    """
    Residual block
    """
    filters = [64, 64]
    kernel_size = 3
    strides = 1
    padding = "same"
    momentum = 0.8
    activation = "relu"

    res = Conv2D(filters=filters[0], kernel_size=kernel_size,
                strides=strides, padding=padding)(x)
    res = Activation(activation=activation)(res)
    res = BatchNormalization(momentum=momentum)(res)

    res = Conv2D(filters=filters[1], kernel_size=kernel_size,
                strides=strides, padding=padding)(res)
    res = BatchNormalization(momentum=momentum)(res)

    # Add res and x
    res = Add()([res, x])
    return res
```

5. Now, add 16 residual blocks using the `residual_block` function, defined in the last step:

```python
res = residual_block(gen1)
for i in range(residual_blocks - 1):
    res = residual_block(res)
```

The output of the pre-residual block goes to the first residual block. The output of the first residual block goes to the second residual block, and so on, up to the 16th residual block.

6. Next, add the post-residual block (a 2D convolution layer followed by a batch normalization layer), as follows:
Configuration:
- **Filters**: 64
- **Kernel size**: 3
- **Strides**: 1

- **Padding**: same
- **Batchnormalization**: Yes (momentum=0.8):

```
gen2 = Conv2D(filters=64, kernel_size=3, strides=1,
padding='same')(res)
gen2 = BatchNormalization(momentum=momentum)(gen2)
```

7. Now, add an `Add` layer to take the sum of the output from the pre-residual block, which is `gen1`, and the output from the post-residual block, which is `gen2`. This layer generates another tensor of similar shape. Refer to the section, *The architecture of the generator network,* for more details:

```
gen3 = Add()([gen2, gen1])
```

8. Next, add an upsampling block, as follows:
   Configuration:
   - **Upsampling size**: 2
   - **Filers**: 256
   - **Kernel size**: 3
   - **Strides**: 1
   - **Padding**: same
   - **Activation**: PReLU:

```
gen4 = UpSampling2D(size=2)(gen3)
gen4 = Conv2D(filters=256, kernel_size=3, strides=1,
padding='same')(gen4)
gen4 = Activation('relu')(gen4)
```

9. Next, add another upsampling block, as follows:
   Configuration:
   - **Upsampling size**: 2
   - **Filers**: 256
   - **Kernel size**: 3
   - **Strides**: 1
   - **Padding**: same
   - **Activation**: PReLU:

```
gen5 = UpSampling2D(size=2)(gen4)
gen5 = Conv2D(filters=256, kernel_size=3, strides=1,
padding='same')(gen5)
gen5 = Activation('relu')(gen5)
```

10. Finally, add the output convolution layer:
    Configuration:
    - **Filters**: 3 (equal to number of channels)
    - **Kernel size**: 9
    - **Strides**: 1
    - **Padding**: same
    - **Activation**: tanh:

```
gen6 = Conv2D(filters=3, kernel_size=9, strides=1,
padding='same')(gen5)
output = Activation('tanh')(gen6)
```

Once you have defined all the layers in the network, you can create a Keras model. We have defined a Keras sequential graph using Keras's functional API. Let's create a Keras model by specifying the input and output for the network.

11. Now, create a Keras model and specify the inputs and the outputs for the model, as follows:

```
model = Model(inputs=[input_layer], outputs=[output],
name='generator')
```

We have successfully created a Keras model for the generator network. Now wrap the entire code for the generator network inside a Python function, as follows:

```
def build_generator():
    """
    Create a generator network using the hyperparameter values defined
below
    :return:
    """
    residual_blocks = 16
    momentum = 0.8
    input_shape = (64, 64, 3)

    # Input Layer of the generator network
    input_layer = Input(shape=input_shape)

    # Add the pre-residual block
    gen1 = Conv2D(filters=64, kernel_size=9, strides=1, padding='same',
                  activation='relu')(input_layer)

    # Add 16 residual blocks
    res = residual_block(gen1)
    for i in range(residual_blocks - 1):
```

```
    res = residual_block(res)

    # Add the post-residual block
    gen2 = Conv2D(filters=64, kernel_size=3, strides=1,
padding='same')(res)
    gen2 = BatchNormalization(momentum=momentum)(gen2)

    # Take the sum of the output from the pre-residual block(gen1) and
        the post-residual block(gen2)
    gen3 = Add()([gen2, gen1])

    # Add an upsampling block
    gen4 = UpSampling2D(size=2)(gen3)
    gen4 = Conv2D(filters=256, kernel_size=3, strides=1,
padding='same')(gen4)
    gen4 = Activation('relu')(gen4)

    # Add another upsampling block
    gen5 = UpSampling2D(size=2)(gen4)
    gen5 = Conv2D(filters=256, kernel_size=3, strides=1,
                  padding='same')(gen5)
    gen5 = Activation('relu')(gen5)

    # Output convolution layer
    gen6 = Conv2D(filters=3, kernel_size=9, strides=1,
padding='same')(gen5)
    output = Activation('tanh')(gen6)

    # Keras model
    model = Model(inputs=[input_layer], outputs=[output],
                  name='generator')
    return model
```

We have successfully created a Keras model for the generator network. In the next section, we will create a Keras model for the discriminator network.

The discriminator network

We have already explored the architecture of the discriminator network in *The architecture of the discriminator network* section. Let's start by writing the layers for the discriminator network in the Keras framework and then create a Keras model, using the functional API of the Keras framework.

Perform the following steps to implement the discriminator network in Keras:

1. Start by defining the hyperparameters required for the discriminator network:

```
leakyrelu_alpha = 0.2
momentum = 0.8
input_shape = (256, 256, 3)
```

2. Next, create an input layer to feed input to the network, as follows:

```
input_layer = Input(shape=input_shape)
```

3. Next, add a convolution block, as follows:
Configuration:
   - **Filters**: 64
   - **Kernel size**: 3
   - **Strides**: 1
   - **Padding**: same
   - **Activation**: LeakyReLU with alpha equal to 0.2:

```
dis1 = Conv2D(filters=64, kernel_size=3, strides=1,
padding='same')(input_layer)
dis1 = LeakyReLU(alpha=leakyrelu_alpha)(dis1)
```

4. Next, add another seven convolution blocks, as follows:
Configuration:
   - **Filters**: 64, 128, 128, 256, 256, 512, 512
   - **Kernel size**: 3, 3, 3, 3, 3, 3, 3
   - **Strides**: 2, 1, 2, 1, 2, 1, 2
   - **Padding**: same for each convolution layer
   - **Activation**: LealyReLU with alpha equal to 0.2 for each convolution layer:

```
# Add the 2nd convolution block
dis2 = Conv2D(filters=64, kernel_size=3, strides=2,
padding='same')(dis1)
dis2 = LeakyReLU(alpha=leakyrelu_alpha)(dis2)
dis2 = BatchNormalization(momentum=momentum)(dis2)

# Add the third convolution block
dis3 = Conv2D(filters=128, kernel_size=3, strides=1,
padding='same')(dis2)
dis3 = LeakyReLU(alpha=leakyrelu_alpha)(dis3)
dis3 = BatchNormalization(momentum=momentum)(dis3)
```

```
# Add the fourth convolution block
dis4 = Conv2D(filters=128, kernel_size=3, strides=2,
padding='same')(dis3)
dis4 = LeakyReLU(alpha=leakyrelu_alpha)(dis4)
dis4 = BatchNormalization(momentum=0.8)(dis4)

# Add the fifth convolution block
dis5 = Conv2D(256, kernel_size=3, strides=1, padding='same')(dis4)
dis5 = LeakyReLU(alpha=leakyrelu_alpha)(dis5)
dis5 = BatchNormalization(momentum=momentum)(dis5)

# Add the sixth convolution block
dis6 = Conv2D(filters=256, kernel_size=3, strides=2,
padding='same')(dis5)
dis6 = LeakyReLU(alpha=leakyrelu_alpha)(dis6)
dis6 = BatchNormalization(momentum=momentum)(dis6)

# Add the seventh convolution block
dis7 = Conv2D(filters=512, kernel_size=3, strides=1,
padding='same')(dis6)
dis7 = LeakyReLU(alpha=leakyrelu_alpha)(dis7)
dis7 = BatchNormalization(momentum=momentum)(dis7)

# Add the eight convolution block
dis8 = Conv2D(filters=512, kernel_size=3, strides=2,
padding='same')(dis7)
dis8 = LeakyReLU(alpha=leakyrelu_alpha)(dis8)
dis8 = BatchNormalization(momentum=momentum)(dis8)
```

5. Next, add a dense layer with 1,024 nodes, as follows:
Configuration:

- **Nodes**: 1024
- **Activation**: LeakyReLU with alpha equal to 0.2:

```
dis9 = Dense(units=1024)(dis8)
dis9 = LeakyReLU(alpha=0.2)(dis9)
```

6. Then, add a dense layer to return the probabilities, as follows:

```
output = Dense(units=1, activation='sigmoid')(dis9)
```

7. Finally, create a Keras model and specify the inputs and the outputs for the network:

```
model = Model(inputs=[input_layer], outputs=[output],
              name='discriminator')
```

Wrap the entire code for the discriminator network inside a function, as follows:

```python
def build_discriminator():
    """
    Create a discriminator network using the hyperparameter values defined
below
    :return:
    """
    leakyrelu_alpha = 0.2
    momentum = 0.8
    input_shape = (256, 256, 3)

    input_layer = Input(shape=input_shape)

    # Add the first convolution block
    dis1 = Conv2D(filters=64, kernel_size=3, strides=1,
padding='same')(input_layer)
    dis1 = LeakyReLU(alpha=leakyrelu_alpha)(dis1)

    # Add the 2nd convolution block
    dis2 = Conv2D(filters=64, kernel_size=3, strides=2,
padding='same')(dis1)
    dis2 = LeakyReLU(alpha=leakyrelu_alpha)(dis2)
    dis2 = BatchNormalization(momentum=momentum)(dis2)

    # Add the third convolution block
    dis3 = Conv2D(filters=128, kernel_size=3, strides=1,
padding='same')(dis2)
    dis3 = LeakyReLU(alpha=leakyrelu_alpha)(dis3)
    dis3 = BatchNormalization(momentum=momentum)(dis3)

    # Add the fourth convolution block
    dis4 = Conv2D(filters=128, kernel_size=3, strides=2,
padding='same')(dis3)
    dis4 = LeakyReLU(alpha=leakyrelu_alpha)(dis4)
    dis4 = BatchNormalization(momentum=0.8)(dis4)

    # Add the fifth convolution block
    dis5 = Conv2D(256, kernel_size=3, strides=1, padding='same')(dis4)
    dis5 = LeakyReLU(alpha=leakyrelu_alpha)(dis5)
    dis5 = BatchNormalization(momentum=momentum)(dis5)

    # Add the sixth convolution block
    dis6 = Conv2D(filters=256, kernel_size=3, strides=2,
padding='same')(dis5)
    dis6 = LeakyReLU(alpha=leakyrelu_alpha)(dis6)
    dis6 = BatchNormalization(momentum=momentum)(dis6)
```

```
    # Add the seventh convolution block
    dis7 = Conv2D(filters=512, kernel_size=3, strides=1,
padding='same')(dis6)
    dis7 = LeakyReLU(alpha=leakyrelu_alpha)(dis7)
    dis7 = BatchNormalization(momentum=momentum)(dis7)

    # Add the eight convolution block
    dis8 = Conv2D(filters=512, kernel_size=3, strides=2,
padding='same')(dis7)
    dis8 = LeakyReLU(alpha=leakyrelu_alpha)(dis8)
    dis8 = BatchNormalization(momentum=momentum)(dis8)

    # Add a dense layer
    dis9 = Dense(units=1024)(dis8)
    dis9 = LeakyReLU(alpha=0.2)(dis9)

    # Last dense layer - for classification
    output = Dense(units=1, activation='sigmoid')(dis9)

    model = Model(inputs=[input_layer], outputs=[output],
name='discriminator')
    return model
```

In this section, we have successfully created a Keras model for the discriminator network. In the next section, we will build the VGG19 network, as shown in the *Introducing SRGAN* section.

VGG19 network

We will use the pre-trained VGG19 network. The purpose of the VGG19 network is to extract feature maps of the generated and the real images. In this section, we will build and compile the VGG19 network with pre-trained weights in Keras:

1. Start by specifying the input shape:

```
input_shape = (256, 256, 3)
```

2. Next, load a pre-trained VGG19 and specify the outputs for the model:

```
vgg = VGG19(weights="imagenet")
vgg.outputs = [vgg.layers[9].output]
```

3. Next, create a symbolic `input_tensor`, which will be our symbolic input to the VGG19 network, as follows:

```
input_layer = Input(shape=input_shape)
```

4. Next, use the VGG19 network to extract the features:

```
features = vgg(input_layer)
```

5. Finally, create a Keras `model` and specify the `inputs` and `outputs` for the network:

```
model = Model(inputs=[input_layer], outputs=[features])
```

Finally, wrap the entire code for the VGG19 model inside a function, as follows:

```
def build_vgg():
    """
    Build the VGG network to extract image features
    """
    input_shape = (256, 256, 3)

    # Load a pre-trained VGG19 model trained on 'Imagenet' dataset
    vgg = VGG19(weights="imagenet")
    vgg.outputs = [vgg.layers[9].output]

    input_layer = Input(shape=input_shape)

    # Extract features
    features = vgg(input_layer)

    # Create a Keras model
    model = Model(inputs=[input_layer], outputs=[features])
    return model
```

The adversarial network

The adversarial network is a combined network that uses the generator, the discriminator, and VGG19. In this section, we will create an adversarial network.

Perform the following steps to create an adversarial network:

1. Start by creating an input layer for the network:

```
input_low_resolution = Input(shape=(64, 64, 3))
```

The adversarial network will receive an image of a shape of (64, 64, 3), which is why we have created an input layer.

2. Next, generate fake high-resolution images using the generator network, as follows:

```
fake_hr_images = generator(input_low_resolution)
```

3. Next, extract the features of the fake images using the VGG19 network, as follows:

```
fake_features = vgg(fake_hr_images)
```

4. Next, make the discriminator network non-trainable in the adversarial network:

```
discriminator.trainable = False
```

We are making the discriminator network non-trainable because we don't want to train the discriminator network while we train the generator network.

5. Next, pass the fake images to the discriminator network:

```
output = discriminator(fake_hr_images)
```

6. Finally, create a Keras model, which will be our adversarial model:

```
model = Model(inputs=[input_low_resolution], outputs=[output,
              fake_features])
```

7. Wrap the entire code for the adversarial model inside a Python function:

```
def build_adversarial_model(generator, discriminator, vgg):

    input_low_resolution = Input(shape=(64, 64, 3))

    fake_hr_images = generator(input_low_resolution)
    fake_features = vgg(fake_hr_images)

    discriminator.trainable = False

    output = discriminator(fake_hr_images)

    model = Model(inputs=[input_low_resolution],
                  outputs=[output, fake_features])

    for layer in model.layers:
        print(layer.name, layer.trainable)

    print(model.summary())
    return model
```

We have now successfully implemented the networks in Keras. Next, we will train the network on the dataset that we downloaded in the *Data preparation* section.

Training the SRGAN

Training the SRGAN network is a two-step process. In the first step, we train the discriminator network. In the second step, we train the adversarial network, which eventually trains the generator network. Let's start training the network.

Perform the following steps to train the SRGAN network:

1. Start by defining the hyperparameters required for the training:

```
# Define hyperparameters
data_dir = "Paht/to/the/dataset/img_align_celeba/*.*"
epochs = 20000
batch_size = 1

# Shape of low-resolution and high-resolution images
low_resolution_shape = (64, 64, 3)
high_resolution_shape = (256, 256, 3)
```

2. Next, define the training optimizer. For all networks, we will use Adam optimizer with the learning rate equal to 0.0002 and `beta_1` equal to `0.5`:

```
# Common optimizer for all networks
common_optimizer = Adam(0.0002, 0.5)
```

Building and compiling the networks

In this section, we will go through the different steps required to build and compile the networks:

1. Build and compile the VGG19 network:

```
vgg = build_vgg()
vgg.trainable = False
vgg.compile(loss='mse', optimizer=common_optimizer, metrics=
            ['accuracy'])
```

To compile VGG19, use `mse` as the loss, `accuracy` as the metrics, and `common_optimizer` as the optimizer. Before compiling the network, disable the training, as we don't want to train the VGG19 network.

2. Next, build and compile the `discriminator` network, as follows:

```
discriminator = build_discriminator()
discriminator.compile(loss='mse', optimizer=common_optimizer,
                      metrics=['accuracy'])
```

To compile the discriminator network, use `mse` as the loss, `accuracy` as the metrics, and `common_optimizer` as the optimizer.

3. Next, build the generator network:

```
generator = build_generator()
```

4. Next, create an adversarial model. Start by creating two input layers:

```
input_high_resolution = Input(shape=high_resolution_shape)
input_low_resolution = Input(shape=low_resolution_shape)
```

5. Next, use the generator network to symbolically generate high-resolution images from the low-resolution images:

```
generated_high_resolution_images = generator(input_low_resolution)
```

Use VGG19 to extract feature maps for the generated images:

```
features = vgg(generated_high_resolution_images)
```

Make the discriminator network non-trainable, because we don't want to train the discriminator model during the training of the adversarial model:

```
discriminator.trainable = False
```

6. Next, use the discriminator network to get the probabilities of the generated high-resolution fake images:

```
probs = discriminator(generated_high_resolution_images)
```

Here, `probs` represents the probability of the generated images belonging to a real dataset.

7. Finally, create and compile the adversarial network:

```
adversarial_model = Model([input_low_resolution,
input_high_resolution], [probs, features])
adversarial_model.compile(loss=['binary_crossentropy', 'mse'],
            loss_weights=[1e-3, 1], optimizer=common_optimizer)
```

To compile the adversarial model, use `binary_crossentropy` and `mse` as the loss functions, `common_optimizer` as the optimizer, and `[0.001, 1]` as the loss weights.

8. Add `Tensorboard` to visualize the training losses and to visualize the network graphs:

```
tensorboard = TensorBoard(log_dir="logs/".format(time.time()))
tensorboard.set_model(generator)
tensorboard.set_model(discriminator)
```

9. Create a loop that should run for the specified number of epochs:

```
for epoch in range(epochs):
    print("Epoch:{}".format(epoch))
```

After this step, all of the code will be inside this for loop.

10. Next, sample a batch of high-resolution and low-resolution images, as follows:

```
high_resolution_images, low_resolution_images =
    sample_images(data_dir=data_dir,
batch_size=batch_size,low_resolution_shape=low_resolution_shape,
    high_resolution_shape=high_resolution_shape)
```

The code for the `sample_images` function is as follows. It is quite descriptive and can be understood by going through it. It contains different steps to load and resize the images to generate high-resolution as well as low-resolution images:

```
def sample_images(data_dir, batch_size, high_resolution_shape,
low_resolution_shape):
    # Make a list of all images inside the data directory
    all_images = glob.glob(data_dir)

    # Choose a random batch of images
    images_batch = np.random.choice(all_images, size=batch_size)

    low_resolution_images = []
    high_resolution_images = []

    for img in images_batch:
        # Get an ndarray of the current image
        img1 = imread(img, mode='RGB')
        img1 = img1.astype(np.float32)

        # Resize the image
        img1_high_resolution = imresize(img1,
```

```
high_resolution_shape)
        img1_low_resolution = imresize(img1, low_resolution_shape)

        # Do a random flip
        if np.random.random() < 0.5:
            img1_high_resolution = np.fliplr(img1_high_resolution)
            img1_low_resolution = np.fliplr(img1_low_resolution)

        high_resolution_images.append(img1_high_resolution)
        low_resolution_images.append(img1_low_resolution)

    return np.array(high_resolution_images),
            np.array(low_resolution_images)
```

11. Next, normalize the images to convert the pixel values to a range between `[-1, 1]`, as follows:

```
high_resolution_images = high_resolution_images / 127.5 - 1.
low_resolution_images = low_resolution_images / 127.5 - 1.
```

It is very important to convert the pixel values to a range of between -1 to 1. Our generator network has `tanh` at the end of the network. The `tanh` activation function squashes values to the same range. While calculating the loss, it is necessary to have all values in the same range.

Training the discriminator network

The steps given in this section show how to train the discriminator network. This is a continuation of the last series of steps:

1. Generate fake high-resolution images using the `generator` network:

```
generated_high_resolution_images =
        generator.predict(low_resolution_images)
```

2. Create a batch of real labels and fake labels:

```
real_labels = np.ones((batch_size, 16, 16, 1))
fake_labels = np.zeros((batch_size, 16, 16, 1))
```

3. Train the discriminator network on real images and real labels:

```
d_loss_real = discriminator.train_on_batch(high_resolution_images,
    real_labels)
```

4. Train the discriminator on generated images and fake labels:

```
d_loss_fake =
discriminator.train_on_batch(generated_high_resolution_images,
fake_labels)
```

5. Finally, calculate the total discriminator loss:

```
d_loss = 0.5 * np.add(d_loss_real, d_loss_fake)
```

We have now added the code to train the discriminator network. Next, add the code to train the adversarial model, which trains the generator network.

Training the generator network

The steps given in this section show how to train the generator network. This is a continuation of the last series of steps:

1. Again, sample a batch of high-resolution and low-resolution images and normalize them:

```
        high_resolution_images, low_resolution_images =
    sample_images(data_dir=data_dir,
    batch_size=batch_size,low_resolution_shape=low_resolution_shape,
    high_resolution_shape=high_resolution_shape)
        # Normalize images
        high_resolution_images = high_resolution_images / 127.5 - 1.
        low_resolution_images = low_resolution_images / 127.5 - 1.
```

2. Use the VGG19 network to extract feature maps (internal representations) of real high-resolution images:

```
image_features = vgg.predict(high_resolution_images)
```

3. Finally, train the adversarial model and provide it with appropriate inputs, as follows:

```
    g_loss =
adversarial_model.train_on_batch([low_resolution_images,
high_resolution_images],
                    [real_labels, image_features])
```

4. After the completion of each epoch, write the losses to TensorBoard to visualize them:

```
write_log(tensorboard, 'g_loss', g_loss[0], epoch)
write_log(tensorboard, 'd_loss', d_loss[0], epoch)
```

5. After every 100 epochs, generate high-resolution fake images using the generator network and save them to visualize them:

```
if epoch % 100 == 0:
    high_resolution_images, low_resolution_images =
sample_images(data_dir=data_dir,
batch_size=batch_size,low_resolution_shape=low_resolution_shape,
high_resolution_shape=high_resolution_shape)
    # Normalize images
    high_resolution_images = high_resolution_images / 127.5 -
1.
    low_resolution_images = low_resolution_images / 127.5 - 1.
    # Generate fake high-resolution images
    generated_images =
generator.predict_on_batch(low_resolution_images)
    # Save
    for index, img in enumerate(generated_images):
        save_images(low_resolution_images[index],
high_resolution_images[index], img,
                    path="results/img_{}_{}".format(epoch,
index))
```

These images will help you to decide whether to continue the training or to stop it early. Stop the training if the quality of the generated high-resolution images is good. Alternatively, continue the training until your model becomes good.

We have now successfully trained an SRGAN network on the `CelebA` dataset. After the training is complete, generating high-resolution images is very easy. Take a low-resolution image with a dimension of 64 x 64x3 and pass it to the `generator.predict()` function, which will generate a high-resolution image.

Saving the models

Saving a model in Keras requires just one line of code. To save the `generator` model, add the following line:

```
# Specify the path for the generator model
gen_model.save("directory/for/the/generator/model.h5")
```

Similarly, save the `discriminator` model by adding the following line:

```
# Specify the path for the discriminator model
dis_model.save("directory/for/the/discriminator/model.h5")
```

Visualizing generated images

After a large number of epochs, the generator will start generating good images. Let's have a look at the generated images:

- After 1,000 epochs, the images appear as follows:

- After 5,000 epochs, the images appear as follows:

- After 10,000 epochs, the images appear as follows:

- After 15,000 epochs, the images appear as follows:

- After 20,000 epochs, the images appear as follows:

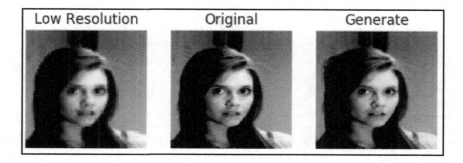

To generate really good images, train the network for 30,000-50,000 epochs.

Visualizing losses

To visualize the losses for the training, start the `tensorboard` server, as follows:

```
tensorboard --logdir=logs
```

Now, open `localhost:6006` in your browser. The **SCALARS** section of TensorBoard contains plots for both losses:

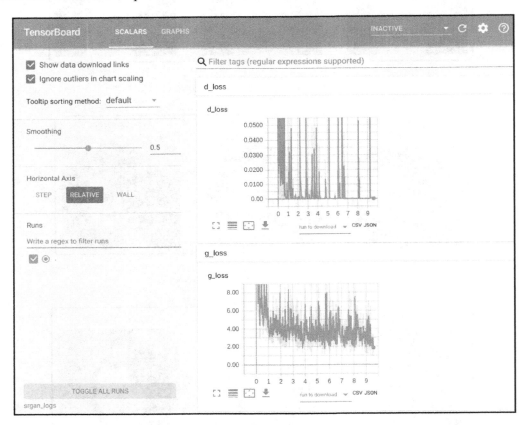

These plots will help you to decide whether to continue or stop the training. If the losses are not decreasing anymore, you can stop the training, as there is no chance of improvement. If the losses keep increasing, you must stop the training. Play with the hyperparameters and select a set of hyperparameters that you think might provide better results. If the losses are decreasing gradually, keep training the model.

Visualizing graphs

The **GRAPHS** section of TensorBoard contains the graphs for both networks. If the networks are not performing well, these graphs can help you to debug the networks. They also show the flow of tensors and different operations inside each graph:

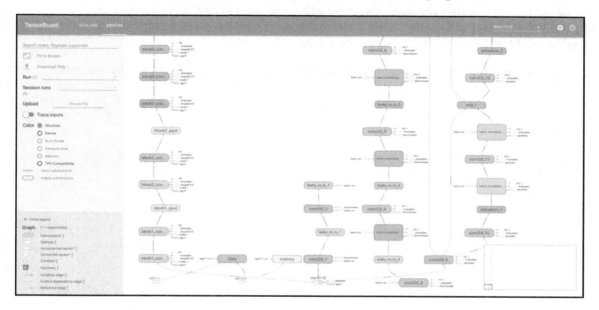

Practical applications of SRGANs

Now, let's look at the practical applications of SRGANs:

- Recovery of old photographs
- Industry applications, such as automatically increasing the resolution of logos, banners, and pamphlets
- Automatically increasing the resolution of social media images for users
- Automatically enhancing pictures on cameras while capturing them
- Increasing the resolution of medical images

Summary

In this chapter, we began by introducing SRGANs. Then, we looked at the architecture of the generator and discriminator networks. Later, we carried out the required setup for the project. Then, we gathered and explored the dataset. After that, we implemented the project in Keras before training the SRGAN, evaluating the trained SRGAN network, and optimizing the trained model using hyperparameter optimization techniques. Finally, we took a brief look at some different applications of SRGANs.

In the next chapter, we will be going through StackGAN and its different applications.

6
StackGAN - Text to Photo-Realistic Image Synthesis

Text to image synthesis is one of the use cases for **Generative Adversarial Networks (GANs)** that has many industrial applications, just like the GANs described in previous chapters. Synthesizing images from text descriptions is very hard, as it is very difficult to build a model that can generate images that reflect the meaning of the text. One network that tries to solve this problem is StackGAN. In this chapter, we will implement a StackGAN in the Keras framework, using TensorFlow as the backend.

In this chapter, we will cover the following topics:

- Introduction to StackGAN
- The architecture of StackGAN
- Data gathering and preparation
- A Keras implementation of StackGAN
- Training a StackGAN
- Evaluating the model
- Practical applications of a pix2pix network

Introduction to StackGAN

A StackGAN is named as such because it has two GANs that are stacked together to form a network that is capable of generating high-resolution images. It has two stages, Stage-I and Stage-II. The Stage-I network generates low-resolution images with basic colors and rough sketches, conditioned on a text embedding, while the Stage-II network takes the image generated by the Stage-I network and generates a high-resolution image that is conditioned on a text embedding. Basically, the second network corrects defects and adds compelling details, yielding a more realistic high-resolution image.

We can compare a StackGAN network to the work of a painter. As a painter starts working, they draw primitive shapes such as lines, circles, and rectangles. Then, they try to fill in the colors. As the painting progresses, more and more detail is added. In a StackGAN, Stage-I is about drawing primitive shapes, while Stage-II is about correcting defects in the image generated by the Stage-I network. Stage-II also adds more detail to make the image look more photo-realistic. The generator networks in both stages are **Conditional Generative Adversarial Networks (CGANs)**. The first GAN is conditioned on the text descriptions, while the second network is conditioned on the text descriptions and the images generated by the first GAN as well.

Architecture of StackGAN

StackGAN is a two-stage network. Each stage has two generators and two discriminators. StackGAN is made up of many networks, which are as follows:

- **Stack-I GAN**: text encoder, Conditioning Augmentation network, generator network, discriminator network, embedding compressor network
- **Stack-II GAN**: text encoder, Conditioning Augmentation network, generator network, discriminator network, embedding compressor network

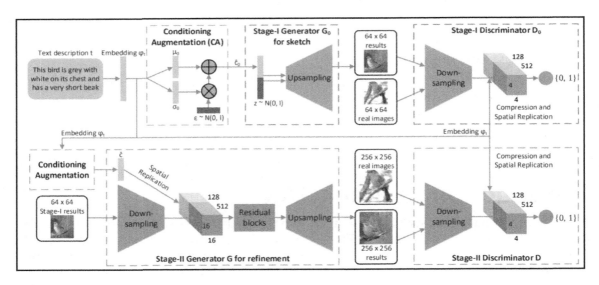

Source: arXiv:1612.03242 [cs.CV]

The preceding image is self-explanatory. It represents both stages of the StackGAN network. As you can see, the first stage is generating images with dimensions of `64x64`. Then the second stage takes these low-resolution images and generates high-resolution images with dimensions of `256x256`. In the next few sections, we will explore the different components in the StackGAN network. Before doing this, however, let's get familiar with the notations that are used in this chapter:

Notation	Description
t	This is a text description of the true data distribution.
z	This is a randomly sampled noise vector from a Gaussian distribution .
φ_t	This is a text embedding of the given text description generated by a pre-trained encoder.
$\hat{c}_0$	This text conditioning variable is a Gaussian conditioning variable sampled from a distribution . It captures the different meanings of .
$N(\mu(\varphi_t), \sum(\varphi_t))$	This is a conditioning Gaussian distribution.
N(0,I)	This is a normal distribution.
$\sum(\varphi_t)$	This is a diagonal covariance matrix.
pdata	This is the true data distribution.
Pz	This is the Gaussian distribution.
D1	This is the Stage-I discriminator.
G1	This is the Stage-I generator.
D2	This is the Stage-II discriminator.
G2	This is the Stage-II generator.
N2	These are the dimensions of the random noise variable.
$\hat{c}$	These are the Gaussian latent variables for the Stack-II GAN.

The text encoder network

The sole purpose of the text encoder network is to convert a text description (t) to a text embedding (φ_t). In this chapter, we won't train the text encoder network. We will be working with pre-trained text embeddings. Follow the steps given in the *Data preparation* section to download the pre-trained text embeddings. If you want to train your own text encoder, refer to the paper *Learning Deep Representations of Fine-Grained Visual Descriptions*, which is available at `https://arxiv.org/pdf/1605.05395.pdf`. The text encoder network encodes a sentence to a 1,024-dimensional text embedding. The text encoder network is common to both of the stages.

The conditioning augmentation block

A **conditioning augmentation (CA)** network samples random latent variables $\hat{c}$ from a distribution, which is represented as $N(\mu(\varphi_t), \sum(\varphi_t))$. We will learn more about this distribution in later sections. There are many advantages to adding a CA block, as follows:

- It adds randomness to the network.
- It makes the generator network robust by capturing various objects with various poses and appearances.
- It produces more image-text pairs. With a higher number of image-text pairs, we can train a robust network that can handle perturbations.

Getting the conditioning augmentation variable

After we get the text embeddings (φ_t) from the text encoder, these are fed to a fully connected layer to generate values such as the mean equal to μ_0 and the standard deviation equal to σ_0. These are then used to create a diagonal covariance matrix by placing σ_0 in a diagonal of the matrix ($\Sigma(\varphi_t)$). Finally, we create a Gaussian distribution using μ_0 and Σ_0, which can be represented as follows:

$$N(\mu_0(\varphi_t), \Sigma_0(\varphi_t))$$

Then, we sample $\hat{c}_0$ from the Gaussian distribution that we just created. The formula to compute $\hat{c}_0$ is as follows:

$$\hat{c}_0 = \mu_0 + \sigma_0 \odot N(0, I)$$

The preceding equation is pretty self-explanatory. To sample $\hat{c}_0$, we first take the element-wise multiplication of σ_0 and then add the output to μ_0. We will cover how to calculate the CA variable $\hat{c}_0$ in more detail in the *Keras implementation of StackGAN* section.

Stage-I

The main components of the StackGAN network are the generator network and the discriminator network. In this section, we will explore both networks in detail.

The generator network

The Stage-I generator network is a deep convolutional neural network with several upsampling layers. The generator network is a CGAN, which is conditioned on $\hat{c}_0$ and the random variable z. The generator network takes the Gaussian conditioning variable $\hat{c}_0$ and random noise variable z and generates an image of dimensions `64x64x3`. The generated low-resolution image might have primitive shapes and basic colors but it will have various defects. Here, z is the random noise variable sampled from a Gaussian distribution p_z with dimension N_z. Images generated by the generator network can be represented as $s_0 = G_0(z, \hat{c}_0)$. Let's have a look at the architecture of the generator network, as shown in the following screenshots:

```
Layer (type)                    Output Shape          Param #     Connected to
=====================================================================================
input_1 (InputLayer)            (None, 1024)          0

dense_1 (Dense)                 (None, 256)           262400      input_1[0][0]

leaky_re_lu_1 (LeakyReLU)       (None, 256)           0           dense_1[0][0]

lambda_1 (Lambda)               (None, 128)           0           leaky_re_lu_1[0][0]

input_2 (InputLayer)            (None, 100)           0

concatenate_1 (Concatenate)     (None, 228)           0           lambda_1[0][0]
                                                                  input_2[0][0]

dense_2 (Dense)                 (None, 16384)         3735552     concatenate_1[0][0]

re_lu_1 (ReLU)                  (None, 16384)         0           dense_2[0][0]

reshape_1 (Reshape)             (None, 4, 4, 1024)    0           re_lu_1[0][0]

up_sampling2d_1 (UpSampling2D)  (None, 8, 8, 1024)    0           reshape_1[0][0]

conv2d_1 (Conv2D)               (None, 8, 8, 512)     4718592     up_sampling2d_1[0][0]

batch_normalization_1 (BatchNor (None, 8, 8, 512)     2048        conv2d_1[0][0]

re_lu_2 (ReLU)                  (None, 8, 8, 512)     0           batch_normalization_1[0][0]

up_sampling2d_2 (UpSampling2D)  (None, 16, 16, 512)   0           re_lu_2[0][0]
```

```
-------------------------------------------------------------------------------------------
conv2d_2 (Conv2D)                  (None, 16, 16, 256)  1179648   up_sampling2d_2[0][0]
-------------------------------------------------------------------------------------------
batch_normalization_2 (BatchNor    (None, 16, 16, 256)  1024      conv2d_2[0][0]
-------------------------------------------------------------------------------------------
re_lu_3 (ReLU)                     (None, 16, 16, 256)  0         batch_normalization_2[0][0]
-------------------------------------------------------------------------------------------
up_sampling2d_3 (UpSampling2D)     (None, 32, 32, 256)  0         re_lu_3[0][0]
-------------------------------------------------------------------------------------------
conv2d_3 (Conv2D)                  (None, 32, 32, 128)  294912    up_sampling2d_3[0][0]
-------------------------------------------------------------------------------------------
batch_normalization_3 (BatchNor    (None, 32, 32, 128)  512       conv2d_3[0][0]
-------------------------------------------------------------------------------------------
re_lu_4 (ReLU)                     (None, 32, 32, 128)  0         batch_normalization_3[0][0]
-------------------------------------------------------------------------------------------
up_sampling2d_4 (UpSampling2D)     (None, 64, 64, 128)  0         re_lu_4[0][0]
-------------------------------------------------------------------------------------------
conv2d_4 (Conv2D)                  (None, 64, 64, 64)   73728     up_sampling2d_4[0][0]
-------------------------------------------------------------------------------------------
batch_normalization_4 (BatchNor    (None, 64, 64, 64)   256       conv2d_4[0][0]
-------------------------------------------------------------------------------------------
re_lu_5 (ReLU)                     (None, 64, 64, 64)   0         batch_normalization_4[0][0]
-------------------------------------------------------------------------------------------
conv2d_5 (Conv2D)                  (None, 64, 64, 3)    1728      re_lu_5[0][0]
-------------------------------------------------------------------------------------------
activation_1 (Activation)          (None, 64, 64, 3)    0         conv2d_5[0][0]
===========================================================================================
Total params: 10,270,400
Trainable params: 10,268,480
Non-trainable params: 1,920
-------------------------------------------------------------------------------------------
```

The architecture of the generator network in Stage-I

As you saw, the generator network contains several convolutional layers, where each convolutional layer is either followed by a batch normalization layer or an activation layer. The sole purpose of it is to generate images with the dimensions of 64x64x3. Now we have a basic idea of the generator network, let's explore the discriminator network.

The discriminator network

Similar to the generator network, the discriminator network is a deep convolutional neural network, containing a series of downsampling convolutional layers. The downsampling layers generate feature maps from images, whether they are real images from the real data distribution P_{data} or images generated by the generator network. Then, we concatenate the feature maps to the text embedding. We use compression and spatial replication to convert a text embedding to the format required for concatenation. The spatial compression and replication include a fully connected layer, which is used to compress the text embedding to an N_d dimensional output, which is then converted to an $M_d \times M_d \times N_d$ dimensional tensor by replicating it spatially. The feature maps and compressed and spatially replicated text embedding are then concatenated along the channel dimension. Finally, we have a fully connected layer with one node, which is used for binary classification. Let's have a look at the architecture of the discriminator network, as shown in the following screenshots:

```
Layer (type)                    Output Shape         Param #    Connected to
==================================================================================
input_3 (InputLayer)            (None, 64, 64, 3)    0

conv2d_6 (Conv2D)               (None, 32, 32, 64)   3072       input_3[0][0]

leaky_re_lu_2 (LeakyReLU)       (None, 32, 32, 64)   0          conv2d_6[0][0]

conv2d_7 (Conv2D)               (None, 16, 16, 128)  131072     leaky_re_lu_2[0][0]

batch_normalization_5 (BatchNor (None, 16, 16, 128)  512        conv2d_7[0][0]

leaky_re_lu_3 (LeakyReLU)       (None, 16, 16, 128)  0          batch_normalization_5[0][0]

conv2d_8 (Conv2D)               (None, 8, 8, 256)    524288     leaky_re_lu_3[0][0]

batch_normalization_6 (BatchNor (None, 8, 8, 256)    1024       conv2d_8[0][0]

leaky_re_lu_4 (LeakyReLU)       (None, 8, 8, 256)    0          batch_normalization_6[0][0]

conv2d_9 (Conv2D)               (None, 4, 4, 512)    2097152    leaky_re_lu_4[0][0]

batch_normalization_7 (BatchNor (None, 4, 4, 512)    2048       conv2d_9[0][0]

leaky_re_lu_5 (LeakyReLU)       (None, 4, 4, 512)    0          batch_normalization_7[0][0]

input_4 (InputLayer)            (None, 4, 4, 128)    0

concatenate_2 (Concatenate)     (None, 4, 4, 640)    0          leaky_re_lu_5[0][0]
                                                                input_4[0][0]
==================================================================================
```

```
conv2d_10 (Conv2D)              (None, 4, 4, 512)      328192      concatenate_2[0][0]
--------------------------------------------------------------------------------------
batch_normalization_8 (BatchNor (None, 4, 4, 512)      2048        conv2d_10[0][0]
--------------------------------------------------------------------------------------
leaky_re_lu_6 (LeakyReLU)       (None, 4, 4, 512)      0           batch_normalization_8[0][0]
--------------------------------------------------------------------------------------
flatten_1 (Flatten)             (None, 8192)           0           leaky_re_lu_6[0][0]
--------------------------------------------------------------------------------------
dense_3 (Dense)                 (None, 1)              8193        flatten_1[0][0]
--------------------------------------------------------------------------------------
activation_2 (Activation)       (None, 1)              0           dense_3[0][0]
======================================================================================
Total params: 3,097,601
Trainable params: 3,094,785
Non-trainable params: 2,816
```

The architecture of the Stage-I discriminator network

As you saw, the generator network contains several convolutional layers. The sole purpose of the discriminator network is to discriminate between images from the real data distribution and images generated by the generator network. Now, we will have a look at the losses used in Stage-I of StackGAN.

Losses for Stage-I of StackGAN

There are two losses used in Stage-I of StackGAN as follows:

- Generator loss
- Discriminator loss

The discriminator loss $\mathcal{L}_D$ can be represented as follows:

$$\mathcal{L}_{D_0} = \mathbb{E}_{(I_0,t) \sim p_{data}}[\log D_0(I_0, \varphi_t)] + \\ \mathbb{E}_{z \sim p_z, t \sim p_{data}}[\log(1 - D_0(G_0(z, \hat{c}_0), \varphi_t))],$$

The preceding equation is pretty self-explanatory. It represents the loss function for the discriminator network, in which both networks are conditioned on the text embeddings.

The generator loss $\mathcal{L}_G$ can be represented as follows:

$$\mathcal{L}_{G_0} = \mathbb{E}_{z \sim p_z, t \sim p_{data}}[\log(1 - D_0(G_0(z, \hat{c}_0), \varphi_t))] +$$
$$\lambda D_{KL}(\mathcal{N}(\mu_0(\varphi_t), \Sigma_0(\varphi_t)) \, || \, \mathcal{N}(0, I)),$$

The preceding equation is pretty self-explanatory too. It represents the loss function for the generator network, in which both networks are conditioned on the text embeddings. Also, it includes a KL-divergence term to the loss function.

Stack-II

The main components of the Stage-II StackGAN are a generator network and a discriminator network. The generator network is an encoder-decoder type of network. The random noise z is not used during this stage, on the assumption that the randomness has already been preserved by s_0, where s_0 is the image generated by the generator network of Stage-I.

We start by using the pre-trained text encoder to generate Gaussian conditioning variables $\hat{c}$. This generates the same text embedding φ_t. The Stage-I and Stage-II Conditioning Augmentations have different fully connected layers for generating different means and standard deviations. This means that the Stage-II GAN learns to capture useful information in the text embedding that is omitted by the Stage-I GAN.

The problems with the images generated by the Stack-I GAN are that they can lack vivid object parts, they may contain shape distortions, and that they may omit important details that are very important for the generation of photo-realistic images. A Stack-II GAN is built upon the output of the Stack-I GAN. The Stack-II GAN is conditioned on the low-resolution image generated by the Stack-I GAN and the text description. It produces high-resolution images by correcting defects.

The generator network

The generator network is again a deep convolutional neural network. The Stage-I result, which is the low-resolution image, is passed through several downsampling layers to generate image features. Then, the image features and the text conditioning variables are concatenated along the channel dimensions. After that, the concatenated tensor is fed into some residual blocks that learn multimodal representations across image and text features. Finally, the output of the last operation is fed into a set of upsampling layers, which generate a high-resolution image with dimensions of 256x256x3. Let's have a look at the architecture of the generator network, as shown in the following images:

```
Layer (type)                     Output Shape          Param #      Connected to
==================================================================================
input_2 (InputLayer)             (None, 64, 64, 3)     0

zero_padding2d_1 (ZeroPadding2D  (None, 66, 66, 3)     0            input_2[0][0]

conv2d_1 (Conv2D)                (None, 64, 64, 128)   3456         zero_padding2d_1[0][0]

re_lu_1 (ReLU)                   (None, 64, 64, 128)   0            conv2d_1[0][0]

zero_padding2d_2 (ZeroPadding2D  (None, 66, 66, 128)   0            re_lu_1[0][0]

conv2d_2 (Conv2D)                (None, 32, 32, 256)   524288       zero_padding2d_2[0][0]

batch_normalization_1 (BatchNor  (None, 32, 32, 256)   1024         conv2d_2[0][0]

re_lu_2 (ReLU)                   (None, 32, 32, 256)   0            batch_normalization_1[0][0]

input_1 (InputLayer)             (None, 1024)          0

zero_padding2d_3 (ZeroPadding2D  (None, 34, 34, 256)   0            re_lu_2[0][0]

dense_1 (Dense)                  (None, 256)           262400       input_1[0][0]

conv2d_3 (Conv2D)                (None, 16, 16, 512)   2097152      zero_padding2d_3[0][0]

leaky_re_lu_1 (LeakyReLU)        (None, 256)           0            dense_1[0][0]

batch_normalization_2 (BatchNor  (None, 16, 16, 512)   2048         conv2d_3[0][0]
```

lambda_1 (Lambda)	(None, 128)	0	leaky_re_lu_1[0][0]
re_lu_3 (ReLU)	(None, 16, 16, 512)	0	batch_normalization_2[0][0]
lambda_2 (Lambda)	(None, 16, 16, 640)	0	lambda_1[0][0] re_lu_3[0][0]
zero_padding2d_4 (ZeroPadding2D	(None, 18, 18, 640)	0	lambda_2[0][0]
conv2d_4 (Conv2D)	(None, 16, 16, 512)	2949120	zero_padding2d_4[0][0]
batch_normalization_3 (BatchNor	(None, 16, 16, 512)	2048	conv2d_4[0][0]
re_lu_4 (ReLU)	(None, 16, 16, 512)	0	batch_normalization_3[0][0]
conv2d_5 (Conv2D)	(None, 16, 16, 512)	2359808	re_lu_4[0][0]
batch_normalization_4 (BatchNor	(None, 16, 16, 512)	2048	conv2d_5[0][0]
re_lu_5 (ReLU)	(None, 16, 16, 512)	0	batch_normalization_4[0][0]
conv2d_6 (Conv2D)	(None, 16, 16, 512)	2359808	re_lu_5[0][0]
batch_normalization_5 (BatchNor	(None, 16, 16, 512)	2048	conv2d_6[0][0]
add_1 (Add)	(None, 16, 16, 512)	0	batch_normalization_5[0][0] re_lu_4[0][0]
re_lu_6 (ReLU)	(None, 16, 16, 512)	0	add_1[0][0]

conv2d_7 (Conv2D)	(None, 16, 16, 512)	2359808	re_lu_6[0][0]
batch_normalization_6 (BatchNor	(None, 16, 16, 512)	2048	conv2d_7[0][0]
re_lu_7 (ReLU)	(None, 16, 16, 512)	0	batch_normalization_6[0][0]
conv2d_8 (Conv2D)	(None, 16, 16, 512)	2359808	re_lu_7[0][0]
batch_normalization_7 (BatchNor	(None, 16, 16, 512)	2048	conv2d_8[0][0]
add_2 (Add)	(None, 16, 16, 512)	0	batch_normalization_7[0][0] re_lu_6[0][0]
re_lu_8 (ReLU)	(None, 16, 16, 512)	0	add_2[0][0]
conv2d_9 (Conv2D)	(None, 16, 16, 512)	2359808	re_lu_8[0][0]
batch_normalization_8 (BatchNor	(None, 16, 16, 512)	2048	conv2d_9[0][0]
re_lu_9 (ReLU)	(None, 16, 16, 512)	0	batch_normalization_8[0][0]
conv2d_10 (Conv2D)	(None, 16, 16, 512)	2359808	re_lu_9[0][0]
batch_normalization_9 (BatchNor	(None, 16, 16, 512)	2048	conv2d_10[0][0]
add_3 (Add)	(None, 16, 16, 512)	0	batch_normalization_9[0][0] re_lu_8[0][0]
re_lu_10 (ReLU)	(None, 16, 16, 512)	0	add_3[0][0]

```
--------------------------------------------------------------------------------------------
conv2d_11 (Conv2D)                 (None, 16, 16, 512)   2359808    re_lu_10[0][0]
--------------------------------------------------------------------------------------------
batch_normalization_10 (BatchNo    (None, 16, 16, 512)   2048       conv2d_11[0][0]
--------------------------------------------------------------------------------------------
re_lu_11 (ReLU)                    (None, 16, 16, 512)   0          batch_normalization_10[0][0]
--------------------------------------------------------------------------------------------
conv2d_12 (Conv2D)                 (None, 16, 16, 512)   2359808    re_lu_11[0][0]
--------------------------------------------------------------------------------------------
batch_normalization_11 (BatchNo    (None, 16, 16, 512)   2048       conv2d_12[0][0]
--------------------------------------------------------------------------------------------
add_4 (Add)                        (None, 16, 16, 512)   0          batch_normalization_11[0][0]
                                                                    re_lu_10[0][0]
--------------------------------------------------------------------------------------------
re_lu_12 (ReLU)                    (None, 16, 16, 512)   0          add_4[0][0]
--------------------------------------------------------------------------------------------
up_sampling2d_1 (UpSampling2D)     (None, 32, 32, 512)   0          re_lu_12[0][0]
--------------------------------------------------------------------------------------------
conv2d_13 (Conv2D)                 (None, 32, 32, 512)   2359296    up_sampling2d_1[0][0]
--------------------------------------------------------------------------------------------
batch_normalization_12 (BatchNo    (None, 32, 32, 512)   2048       conv2d_13[0][0]
--------------------------------------------------------------------------------------------
re_lu_13 (ReLU)                    (None, 32, 32, 512)   0          batch_normalization_12[0][0]
--------------------------------------------------------------------------------------------
up_sampling2d_2 (UpSampling2D)     (None, 64, 64, 512)   0          re_lu_13[0][0]
--------------------------------------------------------------------------------------------
conv2d_14 (Conv2D)                 (None, 64, 64, 256)   1179648    up_sampling2d_2[0][0]
--------------------------------------------------------------------------------------------
batch_normalization_13 (BatchNo    (None, 64, 64, 256)   1024       conv2d_14[0][0]
--------------------------------------------------------------------------------------------
re_lu_14 (ReLU)                    (None, 64, 64, 256)   0          batch_normalization_13[0][0]
--------------------------------------------------------------------------------------------
```

```
up_sampling2d_3 (UpSampling2D)    (None, 128, 128, 256 0        re_lu_14[0][0]

conv2d_15 (Conv2D)                (None, 128, 128, 128 294912   up_sampling2d_3[0][0]

batch_normalization_14 (BatchNo   (None, 128, 128, 128 512      conv2d_15[0][0]

re_lu_15 (ReLU)                   (None, 128, 128, 128 0        batch_normalization_14[0][0]

up_sampling2d_4 (UpSampling2D)    (None, 256, 256, 128 0        re_lu_15[0][0]

conv2d_16 (Conv2D)                (None, 256, 256, 64) 73728    up_sampling2d_4[0][0]

batch_normalization_15 (BatchNo   (None, 256, 256, 64) 256      conv2d_16[0][0]

re_lu_16 (ReLU)                   (None, 256, 256, 64) 0        batch_normalization_15[0][0]

conv2d_17 (Conv2D)                (None, 256, 256, 3)  1728     re_lu_16[0][0]

activation_1 (Activation)         (None, 256, 256, 3)  0        conv2d_17[0][0]
=================================================================================
Total params: 28,649,536
Trainable params: 28,636,864
Non-trainable params: 12,672
```

The architecture of the Stage-II generator

The sole purpose of this generator network is to generate high-resolution images from low-resolution images. Low-resolution images are first generated by the generator network of Stage-I and then fed to the generator network of Stage-II, which generates high-resolution images.

The discriminator network

Similar to the generator network, the discriminator network is a deep convolutional neural network and contains extra downsampling layers as the image is of a larger size than the discriminator network in Stage-I. The discriminator is a matching-aware discriminator (more information about which can be found at the following link: `https://arxiv.org/pdf/1605.05396.pdf`), which allows us to achieve better alignment between the image and the conditioning text. During training, the discriminator takes real images and their corresponding text descriptions as positive sample pairs, whereas negative sample pairs consist of two groups. The first group is real images with mismatched text embeddings, while the second is synthetic images with their corresponding text embeddings. Let's have a look at the architecture of the discriminator network, as shown in the following images:

Layer (type)	Output Shape	Param #	Connected to
input_3 (InputLayer)	(None, 256, 256, 3)	0	
conv2d_18 (Conv2D)	(None, 128, 128, 64)	3072	input_3[0][0]
leaky_re_lu_2 (LeakyReLU)	(None, 128, 128, 64)	0	conv2d_18[0][0]
conv2d_19 (Conv2D)	(None, 64, 64, 128)	131072	leaky_re_lu_2[0][0]
batch_normalization_16 (BatchNo	(None, 64, 64, 128)	512	conv2d_19[0][0]
leaky_re_lu_3 (LeakyReLU)	(None, 64, 64, 128)	0	batch_normalization_16[0][0]
conv2d_20 (Conv2D)	(None, 32, 32, 256)	524288	leaky_re_lu_3[0][0]
batch_normalization_17 (BatchNo	(None, 32, 32, 256)	1024	conv2d_20[0][0]
leaky_re_lu_4 (LeakyReLU)	(None, 32, 32, 256)	0	batch_normalization_17[0][0]
conv2d_21 (Conv2D)	(None, 16, 16, 512)	2097152	leaky_re_lu_4[0][0]
batch_normalization_18 (BatchNo	(None, 16, 16, 512)	2048	conv2d_21[0][0]
leaky_re_lu_5 (LeakyReLU)	(None, 16, 16, 512)	0	batch_normalization_18[0][0]
conv2d_22 (Conv2D)	(None, 8, 8, 1024)	8388608	leaky_re_lu_5[0][0]
batch_normalization_19 (BatchNo	(None, 8, 8, 1024)	4096	conv2d_22[0][0]

```
leaky_re_lu_6 (LeakyReLU)        (None, 8, 8, 1024)    0          batch_normalization_19[0][0]
_____
conv2d_23 (Conv2D)               (None, 4, 4, 2048)    33554432   leaky_re_lu_6[0][0]
_____
batch_normalization_20 (BatchNo  (None, 4, 4, 2048)    8192       conv2d_23[0][0]
_____
leaky_re_lu_7 (LeakyReLU)        (None, 4, 4, 2048)    0          batch_normalization_20[0][0]
_____
conv2d_24 (Conv2D)               (None, 4, 4, 1024)    2097152    leaky_re_lu_7[0][0]
_____
batch_normalization_21 (BatchNo  (None, 4, 4, 1024)    4096       conv2d_24[0][0]
_____
leaky_re_lu_8 (LeakyReLU)        (None, 4, 4, 1024)    0          batch_normalization_21[0][0]
_____
conv2d_25 (Conv2D)               (None, 4, 4, 512)     524288     leaky_re_lu_8[0][0]
_____
batch_normalization_22 (BatchNo  (None, 4, 4, 512)     2048       conv2d_25[0][0]
_____
conv2d_26 (Conv2D)               (None, 4, 4, 128)     65536      batch_normalization_22[0][0]
_____
batch_normalization_23 (BatchNo  (None, 4, 4, 128)     512        conv2d_26[0][0]
_____
leaky_re_lu_9 (LeakyReLU)        (None, 4, 4, 128)     0          batch_normalization_23[0][0]
_____
conv2d_27 (Conv2D)               (None, 4, 4, 128)     147456     leaky_re_lu_9[0][0]
_____
batch_normalization_24 (BatchNo  (None, 4, 4, 128)     512        conv2d_27[0][0]
_____
leaky_re_lu_10 (LeakyReLU)       (None, 4, 4, 128)     0          batch_normalization_24[0][0]
_____
```

```
conv2d_28 (Conv2D)               (None, 4, 4, 512)    589824    leaky_re_lu_10[0][0]

batch_normalization_25 (BatchNo  (None, 4, 4, 512)    2048      conv2d_28[0][0]

add_5 (Add)                      (None, 4, 4, 512)    0         batch_normalization_22[0][0]
                                                                batch_normalization_25[0][0]

leaky_re_lu_11 (LeakyReLU)       (None, 4, 4, 512)    0         add_5[0][0]

input_4 (InputLayer)             (None, 4, 4, 128)    0

concatenate_1 (Concatenate)      (None, 4, 4, 640)    0         leaky_re_lu_11[0][0]
                                                                input_4[0][0]

conv2d_29 (Conv2D)               (None, 4, 4, 512)    328192    concatenate_1[0][0]

batch_normalization_26 (BatchNo  (None, 4, 4, 512)    2048      conv2d_29[0][0]

leaky_re_lu_12 (LeakyReLU)       (None, 4, 4, 512)    0         batch_normalization_26[0][0]

flatten_1 (Flatten)              (None, 8192)         0         leaky_re_lu_12[0][0]

dense_2 (Dense)                  (None, 1)            8193      flatten_1[0][0]

activation_2 (Activation)        (None, 1)            0         dense_2[0][0]
=================================================================================
Total params: 48,486,401
Trainable params: 48,472,833
Non-trainable params: 13,568
```

The architecture of the Stage-II discriminator network.

More information about the architecture of the discriminator network can be found in the *Keras implementation of StackGAN* section.

Losses for Stage-II of StackGAN

Similar to any other GAN, the generator G and the discriminator D in the Stack-II GAN can also be trained by maximizing the loss for the discriminator and minimizing the loss for the generator network.

The generator loss $\mathcal{L}_G$ can be represented as follows:

$$\mathcal{L}_D = \mathbb{E}_{(I,t)\sim p_{data}}[\log D(I, \varphi_t)] + \\ \mathbb{E}_{s_0\sim p_{G_0}, t\sim p_{data}}[\log(1 - D(G(s_0, \hat{c}), \varphi_t))],$$

The preceding equation is pretty self-explanatory. It represents the loss function for the discriminator network, in which both networks are conditioned on the text embeddings. One major difference is that the generator network has s_0 and $\hat{c}$ as inputs, where s_0 is the image generated by the Stage-I and $\hat{c}$ is the CA variable.

The discriminator loss $\mathcal{L}_D$ can be represented as follows:

$$\mathcal{L}_G = \mathbb{E}_{s_0\sim p_{G_0}, t\sim p_{data}}[\log(1 - D(G(s_0, \hat{c}), \varphi_t))] + \\ \lambda D_{KL}(\mathcal{N}(\mu(\varphi_t), \Sigma(\varphi_t)) \,\|\, \mathcal{N}(0, I)),$$

The preceding equation is also pretty self-explanatory. It represents the loss function for the generator network, in which both networks are conditioned on the text embeddings. It also includes a **Kullback-Leibler (KL)** divergence term to the loss function.

Setting up the project

If you haven't already cloned the repository with the complete code for all chapters, clone the repository now. The downloaded code has a directory called `Chapter06`, which contains the entire code for this chapter. Execute the following commands to set up the project:

1. Start by navigating to the parent directory as follows:

```
cd Generative-Adversarial-Networks-Projects
```

2. Now, change the directory from the current directory to `Chapter06`:

```
cd Chapter06
```

3. Next, create a Python virtual environment for this project:

```
virtualenv venv
virtualenv venv -p python3 # Create a virtual environment using
          python3 interpreter
virtualenv venv -p python2 # Create a virtual environment using
          python2 interpreter
```

We will be using this newly created virtual environment for this project. Each chapter has its own separate virtual environment.

4. Activate the newly created virtual environment:

```
source venv/bin/activate
```

After you activate the virtual environment, all further commands will be executed in it.

5. Install all libraries given in the requirements.txt file by executing the following command:

```
pip install -r requirements.txt
```

You can refer to the README.md file for further instructions on how to set up the project. Very often, developers face the problem of mismatching dependencies. Creating a separate virtual environment for each project will take care of this problem.

In this section, we have successfully set up the project and installed the required dependencies. In the next section, we'll work on the dataset.

Data preparation

In this section, we will be working with the CUB dataset, which is an image dataset of different bird species and can found at the following link: http://www.vision.caltech.edu/visipedia/CUB-200-2011.html. The CUB dataset contains 11,788 high-resolution images. We will also need the char-CNN-RNN text embeddings, which can be found at the following link: https://drive.google.com/open?id=0B3y_msrWZaXLT1BZdVdycDY5TEE. These are pretrained text embeddings. Follow the instructions given in the next few sections to download and extract the dataset.

Downloading the dataset

The CUB dataset can be downloaded manually from `http://www.vision.caltech.edu/visipedia/CUB-200-2011.html`. Alternatively, we can execute the following command to download the dataset:

```
wget
http://www.vision.caltech.edu/visipedia-data/CUB-200-2011/CUB_200_2011.tgz
```

After downloading the dataset, we can extract it and put it in the `data/birds/` directory.

Download the char-CNN-RNN embeddings from this link: `https://drive.google.com/open?id=0B3y_msrWZaXLT1BZdVdycDY5TEE`.

Extracting the dataset

The CUB dataset is a compressed file and needs to be extracted. Extract the CUB dataset using the following command:

```
tar -xvzf CUB_200_2011.tgz
```

Extract the char-CNN-RNN embedding using the following command:

```
unzip birds.zip
```

Finally, put `CUB_200_2011` inside the `data/birds` directory. Our dataset is now ready to use.

Exploring the dataset

The CUB dataset contains a total of 11,788 images of 200 different species of birds. The images in the CUB dataset include the following:

These four images show a black-footed albatross, a parakeet auklet, a bobolink, and a Brandt's cormorant.

It is very important to understand the dataset before designing the network. Make sure you go through the images in the CUB dataset carefully.

A Keras implementation of StackGAN

The Keras implementation of StackGAN is divided into two parts: Stage-I and Stage-II. We will implement these stages in the following sections.

Stage-I

A Stage-I StackGAN contains both a generator network and a discriminator network. It also has a text encoder network and a Conditional Augmentation network (CA network), which are explained in detail in the following section. The generator network gets the text conditioning variable ($\hat{c}_0$), along with a noise vector (x). After a set of upsampling layers, it produces a low-resolution image with dimensions of 64x64x3. The discriminator network takes this low-resolution image and tries to identify whether the image is real or fake. The generator network is a network with a set of downsampling layers, followed by a concatenation and then a classification layer. We will explore the architecture of StackGAN in detail in the following sections.

The networks used in the Stage-I StackGAN network are as follows:

- A text encoder network
- A conditioning augmentation network
- A generator network
- A discriminator network

Before starting to write the implementations, however, create a Python file, `main.py`, and import the essential modules as follows:

```
import os
import pickle
import random
import time

import PIL
import numpy as np
import pandas as pd
import tensorflow as tf
from PIL import Image
from keras import Input, Model
from keras import backend as K
from keras.callbacks import TensorBoard
from keras.layers import Dense, LeakyReLU, BatchNormalization, ReLU,
Reshape, UpSampling2D, Conv2D, Activation, \
    concatenate, Flatten, Lambda, Concatenate
from keras.optimizers import Adam
from keras_preprocessing.image import ImageDataGenerator
from matplotlib import pyplot as plt
```

Text encoder network

The sole purpose of the text encoder network is to convert a text description (t) to a text embedding (ϕ_t). This network encodes a sentence to a 1,024-dimensional text embedding. We have already downloaded the pretrained char-CNN-RNN text embeddings. We will use these to train our network.

Conditional augmentation network

The purpose of the CA network is to convert a text embedding vector (ϕ_t) to a conditioning latent variable ($\hat{c}_0$). In the CA network, the text embedding vector is passed through a fully connected layer with nonlinearity, which produces the mean $\mu(\phi_t)$ and the diagonal covariance matrix $\sum(\phi_t)$.

The following code shows how to create a CA network:

1. Start by creating a fully connected layer with 256 nodes and `LeakyReLU` as the activation function:

   ```
   input_layer = Input(shape=(1024,))
   x = Dense(256)(input_layer)
   mean_logsigma = LeakyReLU(alpha=0.2)(x)
   ```

   The input shape is (`batch_size`, `1024`), and the output shape is (`batch_size`, `256`).

2. Next, split `mean_logsigma` into `mean` and `log_sigma` tensors:

   ```
   mean = x[:, :128]
   log_sigma = x[:, 128:]
   ```

   This operation creates two tensors of dimensions (`batch_size`, `128`) and (`batch_size`, `128`).

3. Next, calculate the text conditioning variable using the following code. Refer to the *Conditional Augmentation (CA) block* section inside the *Architecture of StackGAN* subsection for more information on how to generate text conditioning variables:

   ```
   stddev = K.exp(log_sigma)
   epsilon = K.random_normal(shape=K.constant((mean.shape[1], ),
   dtype='int32'))
   c = stddev * epsilon + mean
   ```

This produces a tensor with a dimension of (`batch_size`, `128`), which is our text conditioning variable. The complete code for the CA network is as follows:

```
def generate_c(x):
    mean = x[:, :128]
    log_sigma = x[:, 128:]

    stddev = K.exp(log_sigma)
    epsilon = K.random_normal(shape=K.constant((mean.shape[1], ),
```

```
        dtype='int32'))
    c = stddev * epsilon + mean

    return c
```

The entire code for the conditioning block looks as follows:

```
def build_ca_model():
    input_layer = Input(shape=(1024,))
    x = Dense(256)(input_layer)
    mean_logsigma = LeakyReLU(alpha=0.2)(x)

    c = Lambda(generate_c)(mean_logsigma)
    return Model(inputs=[input_layer], outputs=[c])
```

In the preceding code, the build_ca_model() method creates a Keras model with one fully connected layer and LeakyReLU as the activation function.

The generator network

The generator network is a **Conditional Generative Adversarial Network (CGAN)**. The generator network we are going to create is conditioned on the text-conditioning variable. It takes a random noise vector sampled from a latent space and generates an image with a shape of 64x64x3.

Let's start by writing the code for the generator network:

1. Start by creating an input layer to feed the input (the noise variable) to the network:

```
input_layer2 = Input(shape=(100, ))
```

2. Next, concatenate the text-conditioning variable with the noise variable along dimension 1:

```
gen_input = Concatenate(axis=1)([c, input_layer2])
```

Here, c is the text-conditioning variable. In the previous step, we have written code to generate text-conditioning variables and gen_input will be our input to the generator network.

3. Next, create a `dense layer` with `128*8*4*4` `(16,384)` nodes, and a `ReLU` activation layer as follows:

```
x = Dense(128 * 8 * 4 * 4, use_bias=False)(gen_input)
x = ReLU()(x)
```

4. After that, reshape the output from the last layer to a tensor with a dimension of `(batch_size, 4, 4, 128*8)`:

```
x = Reshape((4, 4, 128 * 8), input_shape=(128 * 8 * 4 * 4,))(x)
```

This operation reshapes a two-dimensional tensor to a four-dimensional tensor.

5. Next, create a 2D upsampling convolutional block. This block contains an upsampling layer, a convolutional layer, and a batch normalization layer. After batch normalization, use `ReLU` as the activation function for this block:

```
x = UpSampling2D(size=(2, 2))(x)
x = Conv2D(512, kernel_size=3, padding="same", strides=1,
use_bias=False)(x)
x = BatchNormalization()(x)
x = ReLU()(x)
```

6. After that, create three more 2D upsampling convolutional blocks, as follows:

```
x = UpSampling2D(size=(2, 2))(x)
x = Conv2D(256, kernel_size=3, padding="same", strides=1,
use_bias=False)(x)
x = BatchNormalization()(x)
x = ReLU()(x)


x = UpSampling2D(size=(2, 2))(x)
x = Conv2D(128, kernel_size=3, padding="same", strides=1,
use_bias=False)(x)
x = BatchNormalization()(x)
x = ReLU()(x)


x = UpSampling2D(size=(2, 2))(x)
x = Conv2D(64, kernel_size=3, padding="same", strides=1,
use_bias=False)(x)
x = BatchNormalization()(x)
x = ReLU()(x)
```

7. Finally, create a convolutional layer, which will generate a low-resolution image:

```
x = Conv2D(3, kernel_size=3, padding="same", strides=1,
use_bias=False)(x)
x = Activation(activation='tanh')(x)
```

8. Now, create a Keras model by specifying the inputs and outputs for the network as follows:

```
stage1_gen = Model(inputs=[input_layer, input_layer2], outputs=[x,
mean_logsigma])
```

Here, *x* will be the output of the model and its shape will be (batch_size, 64, 64, 3).

The entire code for the generator network looks as follows:

```
def build_stage1_generator():
    """
    Builds a generator model
    """

    input_layer = Input(shape=(1024,))
    x = Dense(256)(input_layer)
    mean_logsigma = LeakyReLU(alpha=0.2)(x)

    c = Lambda(generate_c)(mean_logsigma)

    input_layer2 = Input(shape=(100,))

    gen_input = Concatenate(axis=1)([c, input_layer2])

    x = Dense(128 * 8 * 4 * 4, use_bias=False)(gen_input)
    x = ReLU()(x)

    x = Reshape((4, 4, 128 * 8), input_shape=(128 * 8 * 4 * 4,))(x)

    x = UpSampling2D(size=(2, 2))(x)
    x = Conv2D(512, kernel_size=3, padding="same", strides=1,
use_bias=False)(x)
    x = BatchNormalization()(x)
    x = ReLU()(x)

    x = UpSampling2D(size=(2, 2))(x)
    x = Conv2D(256, kernel_size=3, padding="same", strides=1,
use_bias=False)(x)
    x = BatchNormalization()(x)
    x = ReLU()(x)

    x = UpSampling2D(size=(2, 2))(x)
    x = Conv2D(128, kernel_size=3, padding="same", strides=1,
use_bias=False)(x)
    x = BatchNormalization()(x)
    x = ReLU()(x)
```

```
    x = UpSampling2D(size=(2, 2))(x)
    x = Conv2D(64, kernel_size=3, padding="same", strides=1,
use_bias=False)(x)
    x = BatchNormalization()(x)
    x = ReLU()(x)

    x = Conv2D(3, kernel_size=3, padding="same", strides=1,
use_bias=False)(x)
    x = Activation(activation='tanh')(x)

    stage1_gen = Model(inputs=[input_layer, input_layer2], outputs=[x,
mean_logsigma])
    return stage1_gen
```

This model has both the CA network and the generator network inside a single network. It takes two inputs and returns two outputs. The inputs are the text embedding and the noise variable, while the outputs are the generated images and `mean_logsigma`.

We have now successfully implemented the generator network. Let's move on to the discriminator network.

The discriminator network

The discriminator network is a classifier network; it contains a set of downsampling layers and classifies whether a given image is real or fake.

Let's start by writing the code for the network:

1. Start by creating an input layer to feed input to the network:

   ```
   input_layer = Input(shape=(64, 64, 3))
   ```

2. Next, add a 2D convolutional layer with the following parameters:
   - **Filters** = 64
   - **Kernel size** = (4, 4)
   - **Strides** = 2
   - **Padding** = 'same'
   - **Use bias** = False

- **Activation** = LeakyReLU with alpha=0.2

```
stage1_dis = Conv2D(64, (4, 4),
                    padding='same', strides=2,
                    input_shape=(64, 64, 3),
use_bias=False)(input_layer)
stage1_dis = LeakyReLU(alpha=0.2)(stage1_dis)
```

3. After that, add two convolutional layers, each followed by a batch normalization layer and a LeakyReLU activation function, with the following parameters:
    - **Filters:** 128
    - **Kernel size:** (4, 4)
    - **Strides** = 2
    - **Padding** = 'same'
    - **Use bias** = False
    - **Activation** = LeakyReLU with alpha=0.2

```
x = Conv2D(128, (4, 4), padding='same', strides=2,
use_bias=False)(x)
x = BatchNormalization()(x)
x = LeakyReLU(alpha=0.2)(x)
```

4. Next, add one more 2D convolutional layer, followed by a batch normalization layer and a LeakyReLU activation function, with the following parameters:
    - **Filters:** 256
    - **Kernel size:** (4, 4)
    - **Strides** = 2
    - **Padding** = 'same'
    - **Use bias** = False
    - **Activation** = LeakyReLU with alpha=0.2

```
x = Conv2D(256, (4, 4), padding='same', strides=2,
use_bias=False)(x)
x = BatchNormalization()(x)
x = LeakyReLU(alpha=0.2)(x)
```

5. After that, add one more 2D convolutional layer, followed by a batch normalization layer and LeakyReLU activation function, with the following parameters:
    - **Filters:** 512
    - **Kernel size:** (4, 4)

- **Strides** = 2
- **Padding** = `'same'`
- **Use bias** = `False`
- **Activation** = `LeakyReLU` with `alpha=0.2`

```
x = Conv2D(512, (4, 4), padding='same', strides=2,
use_bias=False)(x)
x = BatchNormalization()(x)
x = LeakyReLU(alpha=0.2)(x)
```

6. Then, create another input layer to receive the spatial replicated and compressed text embedding:

```
input_layer2 = Input(shape=(4, 4, 128))
```

7. Add a concatenate layer to concatenate x and the `input_layer2`:

```
merged_input = concatenate([x, input_layer2])
```

8. After that, add another 2D convolution layer, followed by a batch normalization layer and `LeakyReLU` as the activation function, with the following parameters:

- **Filters** = `512`
- **Kernel size** = `1`
- **Strides** = `1`
- **Padding** = `'same'`
- **Batch normalization** = Yes
- **Activation** = `LeakyReLU` with `alpha 0.2`

```
x2 = Conv2D(64 * 8, kernel_size=1,
                     padding="same", strides=1)(merged_input)
x2 = BatchNormalization()(x2)
x2 = LeakyReLU(alpha=0.2)(x2)
```

9. Now, flatten the tensor and add a dense classifier layer:

```
# Flatten the tensor
x2 = Flatten()(x2)

# Classifier layer
x2 = Dense(1)(x2)
x2 = Activation('sigmoid')(x2)
```

10. Finally, create the Keras model:

```
stage1_dis = Model(inputs=[input_layer, input_layer2],
outputs=[x2])
```

The model outputs the probability of the input image either belonging to the real class or the fake class. The entire code for the discriminator network is as follows:

```
def build_stage1_discriminator():
    input_layer = Input(shape=(64, 64, 3))

    x = Conv2D(64, (4, 4),
                        padding='same', strides=2,
                        input_shape=(64, 64, 3),
use_bias=False)(input_layer)
    x = LeakyReLU(alpha=0.2)(x)

    x = Conv2D(128, (4, 4), padding='same', strides=2, use_bias=False)(x)
    x = BatchNormalization()(x)
    x = LeakyReLU(alpha=0.2)(x)

    x = Conv2D(256, (4, 4), padding='same', strides=2, use_bias=False)(x)
    x = BatchNormalization()(x)
    x = LeakyReLU(alpha=0.2)(x)

    x = Conv2D(512, (4, 4), padding='same', strides=2, use_bias=False)(x)
    x = BatchNormalization()(x)
    x = LeakyReLU(alpha=0.2)(x)

    input_layer2 = Input(shape=(4, 4, 128))

    merged_input = concatenate([x, input_layer2])

    x2 = Conv2D(64 * 8, kernel_size=1,
                        padding="same", strides=1)(merged_input)
    x2 = BatchNormalization()(x2)
    x2 = LeakyReLU(alpha=0.2)(x2)
    x2 = Flatten()(x2)
    x2 = Dense(1)(x2)
    x2 = Activation('sigmoid')(x2)

    stage1_dis = Model(inputs=[input_layer, input_layer2], outputs=[x2])
    return stage1_dis
```

This model has two inputs and one output. The inputs are the low-resolution images and compressed text embedding, while the output is the probability. Now that we've successfully written the implementation of the discriminator network, let's create the adversarial network.

The adversarial model

To create an adversarial model, take both the generator and discriminator networks and create a new Keras model.

1. Start by creating three input layers to feed inputs to the network:

```
def build_adversarial_model(gen_model, dis_model):
    input_layer = Input(shape=(1024,))
    input_layer2 = Input(shape=(100,))
    input_layer3 = Input(shape=(4, 4, 128))
```

2. Then, use the generator network to generate low-resolution images:

```
# Get output of the generator model
x, mean_logsigma = gen_model([input_layer, input_layer2])

# Make discriminator trainable false
dis_model.trainable = False
```

3. Next, use the discriminator network to get the probabilities:

```
# Get output of the discriminator models
valid = dis_model([x, input_layer3])
```

4. Finally, create the adversarial model, taking three inputs and returning two outputs.

```
model = Model(inputs=[input_layer, input_layer2, input_layer3],
outputs=[valid, mean_logsigma])
    return model
```

Now, our adversarial model is ready. This adversarial model is an end-to-end trainable model. In this section, we've looked at the networks involved in Stage-I of the StackGAN model. In the next section, we'll work on the implementations of the networks involved in Stage-II of StackGAN.

Stage-II

The Stage-II StackGAN is slightly different from the Stage-I StackGAN. The inputs to the generator models are the conditioning variable ($\hat{c}_0$) and the low-resolution images generated by the generator network in Stage-I.

It has five components:

- The text encoder
- The conditioning augmentation network
- Downsampling blocks
- Residual blocks
- Upsampling blocks

The text encoder and the CA network are similar to those used previously in the Stage-I section. We will now go through the three components of the generator network, which are downsampling blocks, residual blocks, and upsampling blocks.

Generator network

The generator network is built up of three different modules. We will write the code for each module one by one. Let's start with the downsampling blocks.

Downsampling blocks

This block takes a low-resolution image of the dimensions `64x64x3` from the generator of Stage-I and downsamples it to generate a tensor with a shape of `16x16x512`. The image goes through a series of 2D convolution blocks.

In this section, we will write the implementation for the downsampling blocks.

1. Start by creating with the first downsampling block. This block contains a 2D convolution layer with `ReLU` as the activation function. Before applying the 2D convolution, pad the input with zeros on all sides. The configurations for the different layers in this block are the following:
    - **Padding size:** `(1, 1)`
    - **Filters:** `128`
    - **Kernel size:** `(3, 3)`
    - **Strides:** `1`

- **Activation:** ReLU

```
x = ZeroPadding2D(padding=(1, 1))(input_lr_images)
x = Conv2D(128, kernel_size=(3, 3), strides=1, use_bias=False)(x)
x = ReLU()(x)
```

2. Next, add a second convolution block with the following configurations:
   - **Padding size:** (1, 1)
   - **Filters:** 256
   - **Kernel size:** (4, 4)
   - **Strides:** 2
   - **Batch normalization:** Yes
   - **Activation:** ReLU

```
x = ZeroPadding2D(padding=(1, 1))(x)
x = Conv2D(256, kernel_size=(4, 4), strides=2, use_bias=False)(x)
x = BatchNormalization()(x)
x = ReLU()(x)
```

3. After that, add another convolution block with the following configurations:
   - **Padding size:** (1, 1)
   - **Filters:** 512
   - **Kernel size:** (4, 4)
   - **Strides:** 2
   - **Batch normalization:** Yes
   - **Activation:** ReLU

```
x = ZeroPadding2D(padding=(1, 1))(x)
x = Conv2D(512, kernel_size=(4, 4), strides=2, use_bias=False)(x)
x = BatchNormalization()(x)
x = ReLU()(x)
```

The downsampling block generates a tensor with a shape of 16x16x512. After that, we have a series of residual blocks. Before feeding this tensor to the residual block, we need to concatenate it to the text-conditioning variable. The code to do this is as follows:

```
# This block will extend the text conditioning variable and concatenate it
to the encoded images tensor.
def joint_block(inputs):
    c = inputs[0]
    x = inputs[1]

    c = K.expand_dims(c, axis=1)
```

```
    c = K.expand_dims(c, axis=1)
    c = K.tile(c, [1, 16, 16, 1])
    return K.concatenate([c, x], axis=3)
# This is the lambda layer which we will add to the generator network
c_code = Lambda(joint_block)([c, x])
```

Here, the shape of c is (batch_size, 228) and the shape of x is (batch_size, 16, 16, 512). The shape of the c_code will be (batch_size, 640).

The residual blocks

The residual blocks contain two 2D convolutional layers, each followed by a batch normalization layer and an activation function.

1. Let's define the residual blocks. This code describes the residual blocks completely:

```
def residual_block(input):
    """
    Residual block in the generator network
    :return:
    """
    x = Conv2D(128 * 4, kernel_size=(3, 3), padding='same',
strides=1)(input)
    x = BatchNormalization()(x)
    x = ReLU()(x)

    x = Conv2D(128 * 4, kernel_size=(3, 3), strides=1,
padding='same')(x)
    x = BatchNormalization()(x)

    x = add([x, input])
    x = ReLU()(x)

    return x
```

The initial input is added to the output of the second 2D convolutional layer. The resultant tensor will be the output of the block.

2. Next, add a 2D convolutional block with the following hyperparameters:
   - **Padding size:** (1, 1)
   - **Filters:** 512
   - **Kernel size:** (3, 3)

- **Strides:** 1
- **Batch normalization:** Yes
- **Activation:** ReLU

```
x = ZeroPadding2D(padding=(1, 1))(c_code)
x = Conv2D(512, kernel_size=(3, 3), strides=1, use_bias=False)(x)
x = BatchNormalization()(x)
x = ReLU()(x)
```

3. After that, add four residual blocks sequentially:

```
x = residual_block(x)
x = residual_block(x)
x = residual_block(x)
x = residual_block(x)
```

The upsampling blocks will receive this output tensor from the residual blocks. Let's write the code for the upsampling blocks.

Upsampling Blocks

Upsampling blocks contain layers that increase the spatial resolution of images and generate a high-resolution image of dimensions 256x256x3.

Let's write the code for the upsampling blocks:

1. Firstly, add an upsampling block that contains a 2D upsampling layer, a 2D convolutional layer, a batch normalization, and an activation function. The different parameters that are used in the block are the following:
   - **Upsampling size:** (2, 2)
   - **Filters:** 512
   - **Kernel size:** 3
   - **Padding:** "same"
   - **Strides:** 1
   - **Batch normalization:** Yes
   - **Activation:** ReLU

```
x = UpSampling2D(size=(2, 2))(x)
x = Conv2D(512, kernel_size=3, padding="same", strides=1,
use_bias=False)(x)
x = BatchNormalization()(x)
x = ReLU()(x)
```

2. Next, add three more upsampling blocks. The hyperparameters used in the block can easily be inferred from the code given as follows:

```
x = UpSampling2D(size=(2, 2))(x)
x = Conv2D(256, kernel_size=3, padding="same", strides=1,
use_bias=False)(x)
x = BatchNormalization()(x)
x = ReLU()(x)

x = UpSampling2D(size=(2, 2))(x)
x = Conv2D(128, kernel_size=3, padding="same", strides=1,
use_bias=False)(x)
x = BatchNormalization()(x)
x = ReLU()(x)

x = UpSampling2D(size=(2, 2))(x)
x = Conv2D(64, kernel_size=3, padding="same", strides=1,
use_bias=False)(x)
x = BatchNormalization()(x)
x = ReLU()(x)
```

3. Add the final convolutional layer. This layer is the last layer and it is responsible for generating high-resolution images.

```
x = Conv2D(3, kernel_size=3, padding="same", strides=1,
use_bias=False)(x)
x = Activation('tanh')(x)
```

Finally, create the generator model using the preceding parts:

```
model = Model(inputs=[input_layer, input_lr_images], outputs=[x,
mean_logsigma])
```

We now have the generator model ready and we use the model to generate high-resolution images. The following is the complete code for the generator network for the purposes of clarity:

```
def build_stage2_generator():
    """
    Create a generator network for Stage-II StackGAN
    """

    # 1. CA Augementation Network
    input_layer = Input(shape=(1024,))
    input_lr_images = Input(shape=(64, 64, 3))

    ca = Dense(256)(input_layer)
    mean_logsigma = LeakyReLU(alpha=0.2)(ca)
```

```
    c = Lambda(generate_c)(mean_logsigma)

    # 2. Image Encoder
    x = ZeroPadding2D(padding=(1, 1))(input_lr_images)
    x = Conv2D(128, kernel_size=(3, 3), strides=1, use_bias=False)(x)
    x = ReLU()(x)

    x = ZeroPadding2D(padding=(1, 1))(x)
    x = Conv2D(256, kernel_size=(4, 4), strides=2, use_bias=False)(x)
    x = BatchNormalization()(x)
    x = ReLU()(x)

    x = ZeroPadding2D(padding=(1, 1))(x)
    x = Conv2D(512, kernel_size=(4, 4), strides=2, use_bias=False)(x)
    x = BatchNormalization()(x)
    x = ReLU()(x)

    # Concatenation block
    c_code = Lambda(joint_block)([c, x])
    # 3. Residual Blocks
    x = ZeroPadding2D(padding=(1, 1))(c_code)
    x = Conv2D(512, kernel_size=(3, 3), strides=1, use_bias=False)(x)
    x = BatchNormalization()(x)
    x = ReLU()(x)

    x = residual_block(x)
    x = residual_block(x)
    x = residual_block(x)
    x = residual_block(x)

    # 4. Upsampling blocks
    x = UpSampling2D(size=(2, 2))(x)
    x = Conv2D(512, kernel_size=3, padding="same", strides=1,
use_bias=False)(x)
    x = BatchNormalization()(x)
    x = ReLU()(x)

    x = UpSampling2D(size=(2, 2))(x)
    x = Conv2D(256, kernel_size=3, padding="same", strides=1,
use_bias=False)(x)
    x = BatchNormalization()(x)
    x = ReLU()(x)

    x = UpSampling2D(size=(2, 2))(x)
    x = Conv2D(128, kernel_size=3, padding="same", strides=1,
use_bias=False)(x)
    x = BatchNormalization()(x)
    x = ReLU()(x)
```

```
    x = UpSampling2D(size=(2, 2))(x)
    x = Conv2D(64, kernel_size=3, padding="same", strides=1,
use_bias=False)(x)
    x = BatchNormalization()(x)
    x = ReLU()(x)

    x = Conv2D(3, kernel_size=3, padding="same", strides=1,
use_bias=False)(x)
    x = Activation('tanh')(x)

    model = Model(inputs=[input_layer, input_lr_images], outputs=[x,
mean_logsigma])
    return model
```

The discriminator network

The discriminator network for the Stage-II StackGAN is a series of downsampling layers, then a concatenation block, followed by a classifier. Let's write the code for each block.

Start by creating an input layer as follows:

```
input_layer = Input(shape=(256, 256, 3))
```

Downsampling blocks

The downsampling blocks have several layers that downsample the images.

Start by adding different layers in the downsampling blocks. The code in this section is pretty explanatory and can be understood easily:

```
x = Conv2D(64, (4, 4), padding='same', strides=2, input_shape=(256, 256,
3), use_bias=False)(input_layer)
x = LeakyReLU(alpha=0.2)(x)

x = Conv2D(128, (4, 4), padding='same', strides=2, use_bias=False)(x)
x = BatchNormalization()(x)
x = LeakyReLU(alpha=0.2)(x)

x = Conv2D(256, (4, 4), padding='same', strides=2, use_bias=False)(x)
x = BatchNormalization()(x)
x = LeakyReLU(alpha=0.2)(x)

x = Conv2D(512, (4, 4), padding='same', strides=2, use_bias=False)(x)
x = BatchNormalization()(x)
x = LeakyReLU(alpha=0.2)(x)
```

```
x = Conv2D(1024, (4, 4), padding='same', strides=2, use_bias=False)(x)
x = BatchNormalization()(x)
x = LeakyReLU(alpha=0.2)(x)

x = Conv2D(2048, (4, 4), padding='same', strides=2, use_bias=False)(x)
x = BatchNormalization()(x)
x = LeakyReLU(alpha=0.2)(x)

x = Conv2D(1024, (1, 1), padding='same', strides=1, use_bias=False)(x)
x = BatchNormalization()(x)
x = LeakyReLU(alpha=0.2)(x)

x = Conv2D(512, (1, 1), padding='same', strides=1, use_bias=False)(x)
x = BatchNormalization()(x)

x2 = Conv2D(128, (1, 1), padding='same', strides=1, use_bias=False)(x)
x2 = BatchNormalization()(x2)
x2 = LeakyReLU(alpha=0.2)(x2)

x2 = Conv2D(128, (3, 3), padding='same', strides=1, use_bias=False)(x2)
x2 = BatchNormalization()(x2)
x2 = LeakyReLU(alpha=0.2)(x2)

x2 = Conv2D(512, (3, 3), padding='same', strides=1, use_bias=False)(x2)
x2 = BatchNormalization()(x2)
```

After that, we have two outputs, which are x and x2. Add these two tensors to create a tensor of the same shape. We also need to apply the LeakyReLU activation function:

```
added_x = add([x, x2])
added_x = LeakyReLU(alpha=0.2)(added_x)
```

The concatenation block

Create another input layer for spatially replicated and compressed embeddings:

```
input_layer2 = Input(shape=(4, 4, 128))
```

Concatenate the output of the downsampling blocks to the spatially compressed embeddings:

```
input_layer2 = Input(shape=(4, 4, 128))

merged_input = concatenate([added_x, input_layer2])
```

The fully connected classifier

This merged input is then fed to a block with one convolutional layer and a dense layer for classification purposes:

```
x3 = Conv2D(64 * 8, kernel_size=1, padding="same", strides=1)(merged_input)
x3 = BatchNormalization()(x3)
x3 = LeakyReLU(alpha=0.2)(x3)
x3 = Flatten()(x3)
x3 = Dense(1)(x3)
x3 = Activation('sigmoid')(x3)
```

x3 is the output of this discriminator network. This outputs a probability of whether the passed image is real or fake.

Finally, create a model:

```
stage2_dis = Model(inputs=[input_layer, input_layer2], outputs=[x3])
```

As you can see, this model takes two inputs and returns one output.

The complete code for the discriminator network is as follows:

```
def build_stage2_discriminator():
    input_layer = Input(shape=(256, 256, 3))

    x = Conv2D(64, (4, 4), padding='same', strides=2, input_shape=(256,
256, 3), use_bias=False)(input_layer)
    x = LeakyReLU(alpha=0.2)(x)

    x = Conv2D(128, (4, 4), padding='same', strides=2, use_bias=False)(x)
    x = BatchNormalization()(x)
    x = LeakyReLU(alpha=0.2)(x)

    x = Conv2D(256, (4, 4), padding='same', strides=2, use_bias=False)(x)
    x = BatchNormalization()(x)
    x = LeakyReLU(alpha=0.2)(x)

    x = Conv2D(512, (4, 4), padding='same', strides=2, use_bias=False)(x)
    x = BatchNormalization()(x)
    x = LeakyReLU(alpha=0.2)(x)

    x = Conv2D(1024, (4, 4), padding='same', strides=2, use_bias=False)(x)
    x = BatchNormalization()(x)
    x = LeakyReLU(alpha=0.2)(x)

    x = Conv2D(2048, (4, 4), padding='same', strides=2, use_bias=False)(x)
    x = BatchNormalization()(x)
```

```
    x = LeakyReLU(alpha=0.2)(x)

    x = Conv2D(1024, (1, 1), padding='same', strides=1, use_bias=False)(x)
    x = BatchNormalization()(x)
    x = LeakyReLU(alpha=0.2)(x)

    x = Conv2D(512, (1, 1), padding='same', strides=1, use_bias=False)(x)
    x = BatchNormalization()(x)

    x2 = Conv2D(128, (1, 1), padding='same', strides=1, use_bias=False)(x)
    x2 = BatchNormalization()(x2)
    x2 = LeakyReLU(alpha=0.2)(x2)

    x2 = Conv2D(128, (3, 3), padding='same', strides=1, use_bias=False)(x2)
    x2 = BatchNormalization()(x2)
    x2 = LeakyReLU(alpha=0.2)(x2)

    x2 = Conv2D(512, (3, 3), padding='same', strides=1, use_bias=False)(x2)
    x2 = BatchNormalization()(x2)
    added_x = add([x, x2])
    added_x = LeakyReLU(alpha=0.2)(added_x)

    input_layer2 = Input(shape=(4, 4, 128))
    # Concatenation block
    merged_input = concatenate([added_x, input_layer2])

    x3 = Conv2D(64 * 8, kernel_size=1, padding="same",
strides=1)(merged_input)
    x3 = BatchNormalization()(x3)
    x3 = LeakyReLU(alpha=0.2)(x3)
    x3 = Flatten()(x3)
    x3 = Dense(1)(x3)
    x3 = Activation('sigmoid')(x3)

    stage2_dis = Model(inputs=[input_layer, input_layer2], outputs=[x3])
    return stage2_dis
```

We have now successfully created models for both StackGANs: Stage-I and Stage-II. Let's move on to training the model.

Training a StackGAN

In this section, we will learn how to train both the StackGANs. In the first subsection, we will train the Stage-I StackGAN. In the second subsection, we will train the Stage-II StackGAN.

Training the Stage-I StackGAN

Before starting the training, we need to specify the essential hyperparameters. Hyperparameters are values that don't change during the training. Let's do this first:

```
data_dir = "Specify your dataset directory here/Data/birds"
train_dir = data_dir + "/train"
test_dir = data_dir + "/test"
image_size = 64
batch_size = 64
z_dim = 100
stage1_generator_lr = 0.0002
stage1_discriminator_lr = 0.0002
stage1_lr_decay_step = 600
epochs = 1000
condition_dim = 128

embeddings_file_path_train = train_dir + "/char-CNN-RNN-embeddings.pickle"
embeddings_file_path_test = test_dir + "/char-CNN-RNN-embeddings.pickle"

filenames_file_path_train = train_dir + "/filenames.pickle"
filenames_file_path_test = test_dir + "/filenames.pickle"

class_info_file_path_train = train_dir + "/class_info.pickle"
class_info_file_path_test = test_dir + "/class_info.pickle"

cub_dataset_dir = data_dir + "/CUB_200_2011"
```

We then need to load the dataset.

Loading the dataset

Loading the dataset is a process that takes several steps. Let's explore each step one by one.

1. The first step is to load the class IDs, which are stored in a pickle file. The following code will load the class IDs and return a list of all of them:

```
def load_class_ids(class_info_file_path):
    """
    Load class ids from class_info.pickle file
    """
    with open(class_info_file_path, 'rb') as f:
        class_ids = pickle.load(f, encoding='latin1')
        return class_ids
```

2. Next, load the filenames, which are also stored in a pickle file. This can be done as follows:

```
def load_filenames(filenames_file_path):
    """
    Load filenames.pickle file and return a list of all file names
    """
    with open(filenames_file_path, 'rb') as f:
        filenames = pickle.load(f, encoding='latin1')
    return filenames
```

3. After that, we need to load the text embeddings, which are in a pickle file as well. Load the files and retrieve the text embeddings as follows:

```
def load_embeddings(embeddings_file_path):
    """
    Load embeddings
    """
    with open(embeddings_file_path, 'rb') as f:
        embeddings = pickle.load(f, encoding='latin1')
        embeddings = np.array(embeddings)
        print('embeddings: ', embeddings.shape)
    return embeddings
```

4. Next, get the bounding boxes, which are used to extract objects from the raw images. The following self-explanatory code shows how to retrieve the bounding boxes:

```
def load_bounding_boxes(dataset_dir):
    """
    Load bounding boxes and return a dictionary of file names and
corresponding bounding boxes
    """
    # Paths
    bounding_boxes_path = os.path.join(dataset_dir,
'bounding_boxes.txt')
    file_paths_path = os.path.join(dataset_dir, 'images.txt')

    # Read bounding_boxes.txt and images.txt file
    df_bounding_boxes = pd.read_csv(bounding_boxes_path,
                                    delim_whitespace=True,
header=None).astype(int)
    df_file_names = pd.read_csv(file_paths_path,
delim_whitespace=True, header=None)

    # Create a list of file names
    file_names = df_file_names[1].tolist()
```

```
        # Create a dictionary of file_names and bounding boxes
        filename_boundingbox_dict = {img_file[:-4]: [] for img_file in
file_names[:2]}

        # Assign a bounding box to the corresponding image
        for i in range(0, len(file_names)):
            # Get the bounding box
            bounding_box = df_bounding_boxes.iloc[i][1:].tolist()
            key = file_names[i][:-4]
            filename_boundingbox_dict[key] = bounding_box

        return filename_boundingbox_dict
```

5. Next, write a method to load and crop an image. The following code loads the image and crops it around the provided bounding box. It also resizes the image to a specified size:

```
def get_img(img_path, bbox, image_size):
    """
    Load and resize image
    """
    img = Image.open(img_path).convert('RGB')
    width, height = img.size
    if bbox is not None:
        R = int(np.maximum(bbox[2], bbox[3]) * 0.75)
        center_x = int((2 * bbox[0] + bbox[2]) / 2)
        center_y = int((2 * bbox[1] + bbox[3]) / 2)
        y1 = np.maximum(0, center_y - R)
        y2 = np.minimum(height, center_y + R)
        x1 = np.maximum(0, center_x - R)
        x2 = np.minimum(width, center_x + R)
        img = img.crop([x1, y1, x2, y2])
    img = img.resize(image_size, PIL.Image.BILINEAR)
    return img
```

6. Finally, combine all of the preceding methods to get the dataset, which we need for our training. This code returns all the images, their labels, and the corresponding embeddings. We need these for the training:

```
def load_dataset(filenames_file_path, class_info_file_path,
cub_dataset_dir, embeddings_file_path, image_size):
    filenames = load_filenames(filenames_file_path)
    class_ids = load_class_ids(class_info_file_path)
    bounding_boxes = load_bounding_boxes(cub_dataset_dir)
    all_embeddings = load_embeddings(embeddings_file_path)

    X, y, embeddings = [], [], []
```

```
        # TODO: Change filenames indexing
        for index, filename in enumerate(filenames[:500]):
            # print(class_ids[index], filenames[index])
            bounding_box = bounding_boxes[filename]

            try:
                # Load images
                img_name = '{}/images/{}.jpg'.format(cub_dataset_dir,
filename)

                img = get_img(img_name, bounding_box, image_size)

                all_embeddings1 = all_embeddings[index, :, :]

                embedding_ix = random.randint(0,
all_embeddings1.shape[0] - 1)
                embedding = all_embeddings1[embedding_ix, :]

                X.append(np.array(img))
                y.append(class_ids[index])
                embeddings.append(embedding)
            except Exception as e:
                print(e)

    X = np.array(X)
    y = np.array(y)
    embeddings = np.array(embeddings)

    return X, y, embeddings
```

7. Finally, load the dataset and make it available for the training:

```
X_train, y_train, embeddings_train =
load_dataset(filenames_file_path=filenames_file_path_train,
class_info_file_path=class_info_file_path_train,
cub_dataset_dir=cub_dataset_dir,
embeddings_file_path=embeddings_file_path_train,
                                            image_size=(64,
64))

X_test, y_test, embeddings_test =
load_dataset(filenames_file_path=filenames_file_path_test,
class_info_file_path=class_info_file_path_test,
cub_dataset_dir=cub_dataset_dir,
embeddings_file_path=embeddings_file_path_test,
                                    image_size=(64, 64))
```

Now that we have successfully loaded the dataset for training, let's create some models.

Creating models

Let's create models using the methods in the previous *Stage-I StackGAN* section under *A Keras Implementation of StackGAN*. We will use four models: a generator model, a discriminator model, a compressor model that compresses the text embedding, and an adversarial model containing both the generator and discriminator:

1. Start by defining the optimizers required for the training:

```
dis_optimizer = Adam(lr=stage1_discriminator_lr, beta_1=0.5,
beta_2=0.999)
gen_optimizer = Adam(lr=stage1_generator_lr, beta_1=0.5,
beta_2=0.999)
```

2. Then build and compile different networks as follows:

```
ca_model = build_ca_model()
ca_model.compile(loss="binary_crossentropy", optimizer="adam")

stage1_dis = build_stage1_discriminator()
stage1_dis.compile(loss='binary_crossentropy',
optimizer=dis_optimizer)

stage1_gen = build_stage1_generator()
stage1_gen.compile(loss="mse", optimizer=gen_optimizer)

embedding_compressor_model = build_embedding_compressor_model()
embedding_compressor_model.compile(loss="binary_crossentropy",
optimizer="adam")

adversarial_model = build_adversarial_model(gen_model=stage1_gen,
dis_model=stage1_dis)
adversarial_model.compile(loss=['binary_crossentropy', KL_loss],
loss_weights=[1, 2.0],
                          optimizer=gen_optimizer, metrics=None)
```

Here, `KL_loss` is a custom loss function, which is defined as follows:

```
def KL_loss(y_true, y_pred):
    mean = y_pred[:, :128]
    logsigma = y_pred[:, :128]
    loss = -logsigma + .5 * (-1 + K.exp(2. * logsigma) + K.square(mean))
    loss = K.mean(loss)
    return loss
```

We now have the dataset and the models ready, so we can start training the model.

Also, add TensorBoard to store losses for visualization, as follows:

```
tensorboard = TensorBoard(log_dir="logs/".format(time.time()))
tensorboard.set_model(stage1_gen)
tensorboard.set_model(stage1_dis)
tensorboard.set_model(ca_model)
tensorboard.set_model(embedding_compressor_model)
```

Training the model

Training a model takes several steps:

1. Create two tensors with the real and fake labels. These will be required during the training of the generator and the discriminator. Use label smoothing, which is covered in `Chapter 1`, *Introduction to Generative Adversarial Networks*:

   ```
   real_labels = np.ones((batch_size, 1), dtype=float) * 0.9
   fake_labels = np.zeros((batch_size, 1), dtype=float) * 0.1
   ```

2. Next, create a for loop, which should run for the number of times specified by the number of epochs, as follows:

   ```
   for epoch in range(epochs):
       print("========================================")
       print("Epoch is:", epoch)
       print("Number of batches", int(X_train.shape[0] / batch_size))

       gen_losses = []
       dis_losses = []
   ```

3. After that, calculate a number of batches and write a for loop that will run for a specified number of batches:

   ```
   number_of_batches = int(X_train.shape[0] / batch_size)
   for index in range(number_of_batches):
       print("Batch:{}".format(index+1))
   ```

4. Sample a batch of data (a mini-batch) for the current iteration. Create a noise vector, select a batch of images and a batch of embeddings, and normalize the images:

   ```
   # Create a batch of noise vectors
   z_noise = np.random.normal(0, 1, size=(batch_size, z_dim))
   image_batch = X_train[index * batch_size:(index + 1) *
   ```

```
batch_size]
        embedding_batch = embeddings_train[index *
batch_size:(index + 1) * batch_size]

        # Normalize images
        image_batch = (image_batch - 127.5) / 127.5
```

5. Next, generate fake images using the generator model by passing the embedding_batch **and** z_noise:

```
        fake_images, _ = stage1_gen.predict([embedding_batch,
z_noise], verbose=3)
```

This will generate a batch of fake images conditioned on a batch of embeddings and a batch of noise vectors.

6. Use the compressor model to compress the embedding. Spatially replicate it to convert it to a tensor with a shape of (batch_size, 4, 4, 128):

```
        compressed_embedding =
embedding_compressor_model.predict_on_batch(embedding_batch)
        compressed_embedding = np.reshape(compressed_embedding,
(-1, 1, 1, condition_dim))
        compressed_embedding = np.tile(compressed_embedding, (1, 4,
4, 1))
```

7. Next, train the discriminator model on the fake images generated by the generator, the real images from the real dataset, and the wrong images:

```
        dis_loss_real = stage1_dis.train_on_batch([image_batch,
compressed_embedding],
                                        np.reshape(real_labels,
(batch_size, 1)))
        dis_loss_fake = stage1_dis.train_on_batch([fake_images,
compressed_embedding],
                                        np.reshape(fake_labels,
(batch_size, 1)))
        dis_loss_wrong =
stage1_dis.train_on_batch([image_batch[:(batch_size - 1)],
compressed_embedding[1:]],
np.reshape(fake_labels[1:], (batch_size-1, 1)))
```

We have now successfully trained the discriminator on three sets of data: real images, fake images, and wrong images. Let's now train the adversarial model:

8. Next, train the adversarial model. Provide it with three inputs and the corresponding truth values. This operation will calculate gradients and update the weights of one batch of data.

```
g_loss = adversarial_model.train_on_batch([embedding_batch,
z_noise, compressed_embedding],[K.ones((batch_size, 1)) * 0.9,
K.ones((batch_size, 256)) * 0.9])
```

9. Next, calculate the losses and store them for evaluation purposes. It is a good idea to keep printing the different losses to keep track of the training:

```
d_loss = 0.5 * np.add(dis_loss_real, 0.5 * np.add(dis_loss_wrong,
dis_loss_fake))

    print("d_loss:{}".format(d_loss))
    print("g_loss:{}".format(g_loss))

    dis_losses.append(d_loss)
    gen_losses.append(g_loss)
```

10. After the completion of each epoch, store any losses to TensorBoard:

```
    write_log(tensorboard, 'discriminator_loss',
np.mean(dis_losses), epoch)
    write_log(tensorboard, 'generator_loss',
np.mean(gen_losses[0]), epoch)
```

11. After each epoch, to evaluate the progress, generate images and save them in the results directory.

```
    z_noise2 = np.random.normal(0, 1, size=(batch_size, z_dim))
    embedding_batch = embeddings_test[0:batch_size]
    fake_images, _ = stage1_gen.predict_on_batch([embedding_batch,
z_noise2])

    # Save images
    for i, img in enumerate(fake_images[:10]):
        save_rgb_img(img, "results/gen_{}_{}.png".format(epoch, i))
```

Here, `save_rgb_img()` is a utility function and defined as follows:

```
def save_rgb_img(img, path):
    """
    Save a rgb image
    """
    fig = plt.figure()
    ax = fig.add_subplot(1, 1, 1)
    ax.imshow(img)
    ax.axis("off")
    ax.set_title("Image")

    plt.savefig(path)
    plt.close()
```

12. Save the weights for each model in Stage-I of the StackGAN.

```
stage1_gen.save_weights("stage1_gen.h5")
stage1_dis.save_weights("stage1_dis.h5")
```

Congratulations, we have successfully trained Stage-I of the StackGAN. We now have a trained generator network that can generate images with dimensions of `64x64x3`. These images will have basic colors and primitive shapes. In the next section, we will train the Stage-II StackGAN.

Training the Stage-II StackGAN

Undertake the following steps to train the Stage-II StackGAN.

Start by specifying the hyperparameters for the training of the Stage-II StackGAN:

```
# Specify hyperparamters
data_dir = "Path to the dataset/Data/birds"
train_dir = data_dir + "/train"
test_dir = data_dir + "/test"
hr_image_size = (256, 256)
lr_image_size = (64, 64)
batch_size = 8
z_dim = 100
stage1_generator_lr = 0.0002
stage1_discriminator_lr = 0.0002
stage1_lr_decay_step = 600
epochs = 10
condition_dim = 128

embeddings_file_path_train = train_dir + "/char-CNN-RNN-embeddings.pickle"
```

```
embeddings_file_path_test = test_dir + "/char-CNN-RNN-embeddings.pickle"

filenames_file_path_train = train_dir + "/filenames.pickle"
filenames_file_path_test = test_dir + "/filenames.pickle"

class_info_file_path_train = train_dir + "/class_info.pickle"
class_info_file_path_test = test_dir + "/class_info.pickle"

cub_dataset_dir = data_dir + "/CUB_200_2011"
```

Loading the dataset

Use the methods defined in the *Loading the dataset* section when we created the Stage-I
StackGAN. Load the high- and low-resolution datasets separately. Also, load the training
and test datasets separately:

```
X_hr_train, y_hr_train, embeddings_train =
load_dataset(filenames_file_path=filenames_file_path_train,
class_info_file_path=class_info_file_path_train,
cub_dataset_dir=cub_dataset_dir,
embeddings_file_path=embeddings_file_path_train,
                                                    image_size=(256,
256))

X_hr_test, y_hr_test, embeddings_test =
load_dataset(filenames_file_path=filenames_file_path_test,
class_info_file_path=class_info_file_path_test,
cub_dataset_dir=cub_dataset_dir,
embeddings_file_path=embeddings_file_path_test,
                                                image_size=(256, 256))

X_lr_train, y_lr_train, _ =
load_dataset(filenames_file_path=filenames_file_path_train,
class_info_file_path=class_info_file_path_train,
                                    cub_dataset_dir=cub_dataset_dir,
embeddings_file_path=embeddings_file_path_train,
                                        image_size=(64, 64))

X_lr_test, y_lr_test, _ =
load_dataset(filenames_file_path=filenames_file_path_test,
class_info_file_path=class_info_file_path_test,
                                    cub_dataset_dir=cub_dataset_dir,
embeddings_file_path=embeddings_file_path_test,
                                        image_size=(64, 64))
```

Creating models

Create the Keras models as we did previously, which are specified in the *Stage-I StackGAN* section under *A Keras implementation of StackGAN*:

Start by defining the optimizers required for the training:

```
dis_optimizer = Adam(lr=stage1_discriminator_lr, beta_1=0.5, beta_2=0.999)
gen_optimizer = Adam(lr=stage1_generator_lr, beta_1=0.5, beta_2=0.999)
```

We will use the `Adam` optimizer with the learning rate equal to `0.0002` and the `beta_1` value equal to `0.5` and `beta_2` equal to `0.999`.

Now build and create models:

```
stage2_dis = build_stage2_discriminator()
stage2_dis.compile(loss='binary_crossentropy', optimizer=dis_optimizer)

stage1_gen = build_stage1_generator()
stage1_gen.compile(loss="binary_crossentropy", optimizer=gen_optimizer)

stage1_gen.load_weights("stage1_gen.h5")

stage2_gen = build_stage2_generator()
stage2_gen.compile(loss="binary_crossentropy", optimizer=gen_optimizer)

embedding_compressor_model = build_embedding_compressor_model()
embedding_compressor_model.compile(loss='binary_crossentropy',
optimizer='adam')

adversarial_model = build_adversarial_model(stage2_gen, stage2_dis,
stage1_gen)
adversarial_model.compile(loss=['binary_crossentropy', KL_loss],
loss_weights=[1.0, 2.0],
                        optimizer=gen_optimizer, metrics=None)
```

`KL_loss` is the custom loss function, which is specified in the *Training the Stage-I StackGAN* section.

We now have the dataset and models ready for the Stage-II StackGAN. Let's train the model.

Training the model

Let's go through this process step by step.

1. Start by adding TensorBoard to store losses:

```
tensorboard = TensorBoard(log_dir="logs/".format(time.time()))
tensorboard.set_model(stage2_gen)
tensorboard.set_model(stage2_dis)
```

2. Then, create two tensors with the labels `real` and `fake`. These will be required during the training of the generator and the discriminator. Use label smoothing, which is covered in Chapter 1, *Introduction to Generative Adversarial Networks*:

```
real_labels = np.ones((batch_size, 1), dtype=float) * 0.9
fake_labels = np.zeros((batch_size, 1), dtype=float) * 0.1
```

3. Next, create a `for` loop, which should run for the number of times specified by the number of epochs, as follows:

```
for epoch in range(epochs):
    print("=========================================")
    print("Epoch is:", epoch)

    gen_losses = []
    dis_losses = []
```

4. Create another loop inside the epochs loop, which will run for a specified number of batches:

```
print("Number of batches:{}".format(number_of_batches))
for index in range(number_of_batches):
    print("Batch:{}".format(index))
```

5. Sample the data required for the training:

```
        # Create a mini-batch of noise vectors
        z_noise = np.random.normal(0, 1, size=(batch_size, z_dim))
        X_hr_train_batch = X_hr_train[index * batch_size:(index +
1) * batch_size]
        embedding_batch = embeddings_train[index *
batch_size:(index + 1) * batch_size]

        # Normalize images
        X_hr_train_batch = (X_hr_train_batch - 127.5) / 127.5
```

6. Next, use the generator network to generate fake images with dimensions of `256x256x2`. In this step, we first use the generator network from Stage-I to generate low-resolution fake images. Then, we use the generator network in Stage-II to generate high-resolution images conditioned on the low-resolution images.

```
        lr_fake_images, _ = stage1_gen.predict([embedding_batch,
z_noise], verbose=3)
        hr_fake_images, _ = stage2_gen.predict([embedding_batch,
lr_fake_images], verbose=3)
```

7. Use the compressor model to compress the embedding. Spatially replicate it to convert it to a tensor of a shape of (batch_size, 4, 4, 128)

```
        compressed_embedding =
embedding_compressor_model.predict_on_batch(embedding_batch)
        compressed_embedding = np.reshape(compressed_embedding,
(-1, 1, 1, condition_dim))
        compressed_embedding = np.tile(compressed_embedding, (1, 4,
4, 1))
```

8. After that, train the discriminator model on the fake images, the real images, and the wrong images:

```
        dis_loss_real =
stage2_dis.train_on_batch([X_hr_train_batch, compressed_embedding],
                                    np.reshape(real_labels,
(batch_size, 1)))
        dis_loss_fake = stage2_dis.train_on_batch([hr_fake_images,
compressed_embedding],
                                    np.reshape(fake_labels,
(batch_size, 1)))
        dis_loss_wrong =
stage2_dis.train_on_batch([X_hr_train_batch[:(batch_size - 1)],
compressed_embedding[1:]],
np.reshape(fake_labels[1:], (batch_size-1, 1)))
```

9. Next, train the adversarial model. This is a combination of the generator model and the discriminator model. We provide it with three inputs and the corresponding truth values:

```
        g_loss = adversarial_model.train_on_batch([embedding_batch,
z_noise, compressed_embedding],[K.ones((batch_size, 1)) * 0.9,
K.ones((batch_size, 256)) * 0.9])
```

10. Compute the losses and save them for evaluation purposes:

```
        d_loss = 0.5 * np.add(dis_loss_real, 0.5 *
np.add(dis_loss_wrong,  dis_loss_fake))
        print("d_loss:{}".format(d_loss))

    print("g_loss:{}".format(g_loss))
```

After each epoch, save losses to TensorBoard:

```
    write_log(tensorboard, 'discriminator_loss',
np.mean(dis_losses), epoch)
    write_log(tensorboard, 'generator_loss',
np.mean(gen_losses)[0], epoch)
```

11. After each epoch, to evaluate the progress, generate images and save them in the results directory. In the following code, we save only the first generated image. Change this accordingly to save the images as appropriate.

```
    # Generate and save images after every 2nd epoch
    if epoch % 2 == 0:
        # z_noise2 = np.random.uniform(-1, 1, size=(batch_size,
    z_dim))
        z_noise2 = np.random.normal(0, 1, size=(batch_size, z_dim))
        embedding_batch = embeddings_test[0:batch_size]

        lr_fake_images, _ = stage1_gen.predict([embedding_batch,
    z_noise2], verbose=3)
        hr_fake_images, _ = stage2_gen.predict([embedding_batch,
    lr_fake_images], verbose=3)

        # Save images
        for i, img in enumerate(hr_fake_images[:10]):
            save_rgb_img(img,
    "results2/gen_{}_{}.png".format(epoch, i))
```

Here, `save_rgb_img()` is a utility function, which is defined in the *Training the Stage-I StackGAN* section.

12. Finally, save the models or their weight values:

```
    # Saving the models
    stage2_gen.save_weights("stage2_gen.h5")
    stage2_dis.save_weights("stage2_dis.h5")
```

Congratulations, we have now successfully completed the training of a Stage-II StackGAN. We now have a generator network that can generate realistic-looking images of dimensions 256x256x3. If you provide the generator network with a text embedding and a noise variable, it will generate a 256x256x3 resolution image. Let's visualize losses plots for the networks.

Visualizing the generated images

After training the network for 500 epochs, the network will start generating decent images as shown as follows.

Images generated by Stage-I and Stage-II of the StackGAN network

I suggest that you train the network for 1,000 epochs. If everything goes well, after 1,000 epochs, the generator networks will start generating realistic images.

Visualizing losses

To visualize the losses for the training, start the TensorBoard server as follows:

```
tensorboard --logdir=logs
```

Now, open `localhost:6006` in your browser. The **SCALARS** section
of TensorBoard contains plots for both losses as shown here:

The loss plot for the discriminator network for Stage-I is shown as follows:

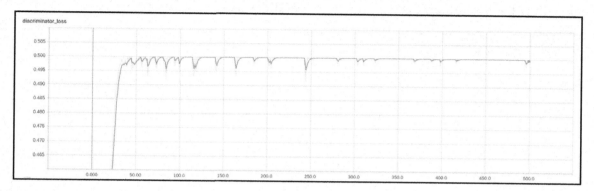

The loss plot for the generator network for Stage-I is shown as follows:

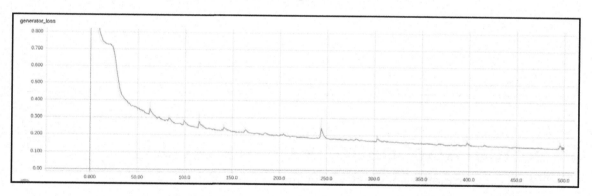

Loss plots for the generator network and the discriminator network for Stage-II can be
similarly obtained from Tensorboard.

These plots will help you to decide whether to continue or to stop the training. If the losses
are not decreasing anymore, you can stop the training, as there is no chance of
improvement. If the losses keep increasing, you must stop the training. Play with the
hyperparameters and select a set of hyperparameters which you think can provide better
results. If the losses are decreasing gradually, keep training the model.

Visualizing the graphs

The **GRAPHS** section of TensorBoard contains the graphs for both networks. If the networks are not performing well, these graphs can help you debug the networks. They also show the flow of tensors and different operations inside each graph:

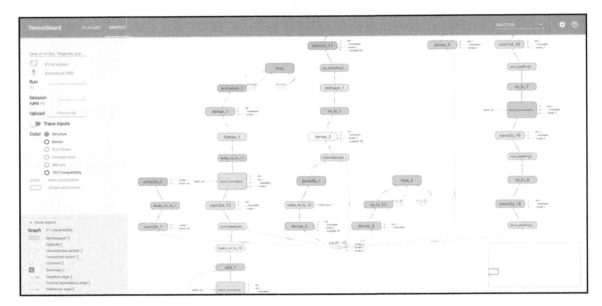

Practical applications of StackGAN

The industry applications of a StackGAN include the following:

- Generating high-resolution images automatically for entertainment purposes or educational purposes
- **Creating comics**: With the use of a StackGAN, the process of creating comics can be reduced to days as the StackGAN can generate comics automatically and assist in the creative process
- **Movie creation**: A StackGAN can assist a movie creator by generating frames from text descriptions
- **Art creation**: A StackGAN can assist an artist by generating sketches from text descriptions

Summary

In this chapter, we have learned about and implemented a StackGAN network to generate high-resolution images from text descriptions. We started with a basic introduction to StackGAN, in which we explored the architectural details of a StackGAN and discovered the losses used for the training of StackGAN. Then, we downloaded and prepared the dataset. After that, we started implementing the StackGAN in the Keras framework. After the implementation, we trained the Stage-I and Stage-II StackGANS sequentially. After successfully training the network, we evaluated the model and saved it for further use.

In the next chapter, we will work with CycleGAN, a network that can convert paintings into photos.

7
CycleGAN - Turn Paintings into Photos

CycleGAN is a type of **Generative Adversarial Network (GAN)** for cross-domain transfer tasks, such as changing the style of an image, turning paintings into photos, and vice versa, photo enhancement, changing the season of a photo, and many more. CycleGANs were introduced by Jun-Yan Zhu, Taesung Park, Phillip Isola, and Alexei A. Efros in a paper entitled: *Unpaired Image-to-Image Translation using Cycle-Consistent Adversarial Networks*. This was produced in February 2018 at the **Berkeley AI Research (BAIR)** laboratory, UC Berkeley, which is available at the following link: `https://arxiv.org/pdf/1703.10593.pdf`. CycleGANs caused a stir in the GAN community because of their widespread use cases. In this chapter, we will be working with CycleGANs and, specifically, using them to turn paintings into photos.

In this chapter, we will cover the following topics:

- An introduction to CycleGANs
- The architecture of a CycleGAN
- Data gathering and preparation
- A Keras implementation of a CycleGAN
- The objective functions
- Training the CycleGAN
- Practical applications of CycleGANs

An introduction to CycleGANs

To turn photos into paintings or paintings, into photos, normal GANs require a pair of images. A CycleGAN is a type of GAN network that can translate an image from one domain X, to another domain Y, without the need for paired images. A CycleGAN tries to learn a generator network, which, in turn, learns two mappings. Instead of training a single generator network used in most of the GANs, CycleGANs train two generator and two discriminator networks.

There are two generator networks in a CycleGAN, which are as follows:

1. **Generator A**: Learns a mapping $G : X \rightarrow Y$, where X is the source domain and Y is the target domain. It takes an image from the source domain A, and converts it into an image that is similar to an image from the target domain B. Basically, the aim of the network is to learn a mapping so that $G(X)$ is similar to Y.
2. **Generator B**: Learns a mapping $F : Y \rightarrow X$, and then takes an image from the target domain B, and converts it into an image that is similar to an image from the source domain A. Similarly, the aim of the network is to learn another mapping, so that $F(G(X)$ is similar to X.

The architecture of both networks is the same, but we train them separately.

There are two discriminator networks in a CycleGAN, which are as follows:

1. **Discriminator A**: The job of discriminator A is to discriminate between the images generated by the generator network A, which are represented as $G(X)$, and the real images from the source domain A, which are represented as X.
2. **Discriminator B**: The job of discriminator B is to discriminate between the images generated by the generator network B, which are represented as $F(Y)$, and the real images from the source domain B, which are represented as Y.

The architecture of both networks is the same. Similar to the generator networks, we train the discriminator networks separately. This is shown in the following diagram:

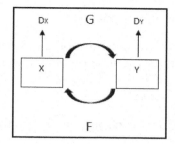

Illustration of a CycleGAN with two generator and two adversarial discriminator networks. Source: https://arxiv.org/pdf/1703.10593.pdf

Let's look at the architecture of a CycleGAN in detail in the following section.

The architecture of a CycleGAN

A CycleGAN is made up overall of two architectures: a generator and a discriminator. The generator architecture is used to create two models, Generator A and Generator B. The discriminator architecture is used to create another two models, Discriminator A, and Discriminator B. We will now go through the architecture of both networks in the next two sections.

The architecture of the generator

The generator network is an auto-encoder type of network. It takes an image as an input and outputs another image. It has two parts: an encoder and a decoder. The encoder contains convolutional layers with downsampling capabilities and transforms an input of a shape of `128x128x3` to an internal representation. The decoder contains two upsampling blocks and a final convolution layer, which transforms the internal representation to an output of a shape of `128x128x3`.

The generator network contains the following blocks:

- The convolution block
- The residual block
- The upsampling block
- The final convolution layer

Let's go through each component one by one:

- **The convolution block**: The convolution block contains a 2D convolution layer, followed by an instance normalization layer and relu as the activation function. Refer to `Chapter 1`, *Introduction to Generative Adversarial Networks*, to learn more about *Instance Normalization*.

The generator network contains three convolution blocks, the configuration of which is as follows:

Layer name	Hyperparameters	Input shape	Output shape
2D convolution layer	`filters=32, kernel_size=7, strides=1, padding='same'`	(128, 128, 3)	(128, 128, 32)
Instance normalization layer	`axis=1`	(128, 128, 32)	(128, 128, 32)
Activation layer	`activation='relu'`	(128, 128, 32)	(128, 128, 32)
2D convolution layer	`filters=64, kernel_size=3, strides=2, padding='same'`	(128, 128, 32)	(64, 64, 64)
Instance normalization layer	`axis=1`	(64, 64, 64)	(64, 64, 64)
Activation layer	`activation='relu'`	(64, 64, 64)	(64, 64, 64)
2D convolution layer	`filters=128, kernel_size=3, strides=2, padding='same'`	(64, 64, 64)	(32, 32, 128)
Instance normalization layer	`axis=1`	(32, 32, 128)	(32, 32, 128)
Activation layer	`activation='relu'`	(32, 32, 128)	(32, 32, 128)

- **The residual block**: The residual block contains two 2D convolution layers. Both layers are followed by a batch normalization layer with a value of momentum equal to 0.8. The generator network contains six residual blocks, the configuration of which is as follows:

Layer name	Hyperparameters	Input shape	Output shape

2D convolution layer	`filters=128,`
	`kernel_size=3,`
	`strides=1,`
	`padding='same'`
		(32, 32, 128)	(32, 32, 128)

Batch normalization Layer	`axis=3, momentum=0.9,` `epsilon=1e-5`	(32, 32, 128)	(32, 32, 128)

2D convolution layer	`filters=138,`
	`kernel_size=3,`
	`strides=1,`
	`padding='same'`
		(32, 32, 128)	((32, 32, 128)

Batch normalization layer	`axis=3, momentum=0.9,` `epsilon=1e-5`	(32, 32, 128)	(32, 32, 128)
Addition layer	None	(32, 32, 128)	(32, 32, 128)

The addition layer calculates the sum of the input tensor to the block and the output of the last batch normalization layer.

- **The upsampling block**: The upsampling block contains a transpose 2D convolution layer and uses `relu` as the activation function. There are two upsampling blocks in the generator network. The configuration of the first upsampling block is as follows:

Layer name	Hyperparameters	Input shape	Output shape

Transpose 2D convolution layer	`filters=64, kernel_size=3,`
	`strides=2, padding='same',`
	`use_bias=False`
		(32, 32, 128)	(64, 64, 64)

Instance normalization layer	`axis=1`	(64, 64, 64)	(64, 64, 64)
Activation layer	`activation='relu'`	(64, 64, 64)	(64, 64, 64)

The configuration of the second upsampling block is as follows:

Layer name	Hyperparameters	Input shape	Output shape
Transpose 2D convolution layer	`filters=32, kernel_size=3, strides=2, padding='same', use_bias=False`	(64, 64, 64)	(128, 128, 32)
Instance normalization layer	`axis=1`	(128, 128, 32)	(128, 128, 32)
Activation layer	`activation='relu'`	(128, 128, 32)	(128, 128, 32)

- **The last convolution layer**: The last layer is a 2D convolution layer that uses `tanh` as the activation function. It generates an image of a shape of (256, 256, 3). The configuration of the last layer is as follows:

Layer name	Hyperparameters	Input shape	Output shape
2D convolution layer	`filters=3, kernel_size=7, strides=1, padding='same', activation='tanh'`	(128, 128, 32)	(128, 128, 3)

These hyperparameters are best suited for the Keras framework. If you are using any other framework, modify accordingly.

The architecture of the discriminator

The architecture of the discriminator network is similar to the architecture of the discriminator in a PatchGAN network. It is a deep convolutional neural network and contains several convolution blocks. Basically, it takes an image of a shape of (128, 128, 3) and predicts whether the image is real or fake. It contains several ZeroPadding2D layers, the documentation for which is available at the following link: `https://keras.io/layers/convolutional/#zeropadding2d`. The following table shows the architecture of the discriminator network in detail:

Layer name	Hyperparameters	Input shape	Output shape
Input layer	`none`	(128, 128, 3)	(128, 128, 3)
ZeroPadding2D layer	`padding(1, 1)`	(128, 128, 3)	(130, 130, 3)

2D convolution layer	`filters=64, kernel_size=4, strides=2, padding='valid'`	(130, 130, 3)	(64, 64, 64)
Activation layer	`activation='leakyrelu', alpha=0.2`	(64, 64, 64)	(64, 64, 64)
ZeroPadding2D layer	`padding(1, 1)`	(64, 64, 64)	(66, 66, 64)
2D convolution layer	`filters=128, kernel_size=4, strides=2, padding='valid'`	(66, 66, 64)	(32, 32, 128)
Instance normalization layer	`axis=1`	(32, 32, 128)	(32, 32, 128)
Activation layer	`activation='leakyrelu', alpha=0.2`	(32, 32, 128)	(32, 32, 128)
ZeroPadding2D layer	`padding(1, 1)`	(32, 32, 128)	(34, 34, 128)
2D convolution layer	`filters=256, kernel_size=4, strides=2, padding='valid'`	(34, 34, 128)	(16, 16, 256)
Instance normalization layer	`axis=1`	(16, 16, 256)	(16, 16, 256)
Activation layer	`activation='leakyrelu', alpha=0.2`	(16, 16, 256)	(16, 16, 256)
ZeroPadding2D layer	`padding(1, 1)`	(16, 16, 256)	(18, 18, 256)
2D convolution layer	`filters=512, kernel_size=4, strides=2, padding='valid'`	(18, 18, 256)	(8, 8, 512)
Instance normalization layer	`axis=1`	(8, 8, 512)	(8, 8, 512)
Activation layer	`activation='leakyrelu', alpha=0.2`	(8, 8, 512)	(8, 8, 512)
ZeroPadding2D layer	`padding(1, 1)`	(8, 8, 512)	(10, 10, 512)
2D convolution layer	`filters=1, kernel_size=4, strides=1, padding='valid', activation='sigmoid'`	(10, 10, 512)	(7, 7, 1)

The discriminator network returns a tensor with a shape of (7, 7, 1). We have now covered the detailed architecture of both networks. In the next section, we'll take a look at the objective function required to train CycleGANs.

 The ZeroPadding2D layer adds rows and columns of zeros at the top, bottom, left, and right of an image tensor.

The training objective function

Similar to other GANs, CycleGANs have a training objective function, which we need to minimize in order to train the model. The loss function is a weighted sum of the following losses:

1. Adversarial loss
2. Cycle consistency loss

Let's explore the adversarial loss and the cycle consistency loss in detail in the following sections.

Adversarial loss

The adversarial loss is the loss between the image from the real distribution A or B, and the images generated by the generator networks. We have two mapping functions and we will be applying adversarial loss to both of the mappings.

The adversarial loss for the mapping $G : X \rightarrow Y$ is written as follows:

$$
\begin{aligned}
\mathcal{L}_{\text{GAN}}(G, D_Y, X, Y) = & \mathbb{E}_{y \sim p_{\text{data}}(y)}[\log D_Y(y)] \\
& + \mathbb{E}_{x \sim p_{\text{data}}(x)}[\log(1 - D_Y(G(x)))],
\end{aligned}
\tag{1}
$$

Here, x is an image from one domain from distribution A, and y is an image from another domain from distribution B. The discriminator D_y tries to distinguish between the image generated by the G mapping ($G(x)$), and the real image y from a different distribution B. The discriminator D_x tries to distinguish between the image generated by the F mapping ($F(y)$) and the real image x from the distribution A. The objective of G is to minimize the adversarial loss function against an adversary D, which constantly tries to maximize it.

Cycle consistency loss

The problem with only using adversarial loss is that the network can map the same set of input images to any random permutation of images in the target domain. Any of the learned mappings can, therefore, learn an output distribution that is similar to the target distribution. There can be many possible mapping functions between x_i and y_i. Cycle consistency loss overcomes this problem by reducing the number of possible mappings. A cycle consistent mapping function is a function that can translate an image x from domain A to another image y in domain B, and generate back the original image.

A forward cycle consistent mapping function appears as follows:

$$x \to G(x) \to F(G(x)) \approx x$$

A backward cycle consistent mapping function looks as follows:

$$y \to F(y) \to G(F(y)) \approx y$$

The formula for cycle consistency loss is as follows:

$$\mathcal{L}_{cyc}(G, F) = \mathbb{E}_{x \sim p_{data}(x)}[\|F(G(x)) - x\|_1] \\ + \mathbb{E}_{y \sim p_{data}(y)}[\|G(F(y)) - y\|_1].$$

With cycle consistency loss, the images reconstructed by $F(G(x))$ and $G(F(y))$ will be similar to x and y, respectively.

Full objective function

The full objective function is a weighted sum of both the adversarial loss and the cycle consistency loss, which is represented as follows:

$$\mathcal{L}(G, F, D_X, D_Y) = \mathcal{L}_{\text{GAN}}(G, D_Y, X, Y)$$
$$+ \mathcal{L}_{\text{GAN}}(F, D_X, Y, X)$$
$$+ \lambda \mathcal{L}_{\text{cyc}}(G, F),$$

Here, $\mathcal{L}_{GAN}(G, D_Y, X, Y)$ is the first adversarial loss and $\mathcal{L}_{GAN}(F, D_X, Y, X)$ is the second adversarial loss. The first adversarial loss is calculated on the generator A, and the discriminator B. The second adversarial loss is calculated on the generator B, and the discriminator A.

To train a CycleGAN, we need to optimize the following function:

$$G^*, F^* = \arg\min_{G,F} \max_{D_x, D_Y} \mathcal{L}(G, F, D_X, D_Y).$$

The previous equation shows that, to train a CycleGAN, you need to minimize the losses of the generator networks and maximize the losses of the discriminator networks. After the optimization, we will get a set of trained networks that are capable of generating photos from paintings.

Setting up the project

If you haven't already cloned the repository with the complete code for all chapters, clone the repository now. The downloaded code has a directory called `Chapter07`, which contains the entire code for this chapter. Execute the following commands to set up the project:

1. Start by navigating to the parent directory as follows:

```
cd Generative-Adversarial-Networks-Projects
```

2. Now, change the directory from the current directory to `Chapter07`, as shown in the following example:

```
cd Chapter07
```

3. Next, create a Python virtual environment for this project, as shown in the following code:

```
virtualenv venv
virtualenv venv -p python3 # Create a virtual environment using
          python3 interpreter
virtualenv venv -p python2 # Create a virtual environment using
          python2 interpreter
```

We will be using this newly created virtual environment for this project. Each chapter has its own separate virtual environment.

4. Activate the newly created virtual environment, as shown in the following code:

```
source venv/bin/activate
```

After you have activated the virtual environment, all further commands will be executed in this virtual environment.

5. Install all libraries given in the `requirements.txt` file by executing the following command:

```
pip install -r requirements.txt
```

You can refer to the `README.md` file for further instructions on how to set up the project. Very often, developers face the problem of mismatching dependencies. Creating a separate virtual environment for each project will take care of this problem.

In this section, we have successfully set up the project and installed the requisite dependencies. In the next section, we'll work on the dataset.

Downloading the dataset

In this chapter, we will be working with the `monet2photo` dataset. This dataset is open source and is made available by the **Berkeley AI Research (BAIR)** laboratory, UC Berkeley. You can choose to download the dataset manually from the following link: `https://people.eecs.berkeley.edu/~taesung_park/CycleGAN/datasets/monet2photo.zip`.

After downloading it, unzip it in the root directory.

Alternatively, to automatically download the dataset, execute the following commands:

```
wget
https://people.eecs.berkeley.edu/~taesung_park/CycleGAN/datasets/monet2phot
o.zip
upzip monet2photo.zip
```

These commands will download the dataset and unzip it in the project's root directory.

 The monet2photo dataset is available for educational purposes only. To use it in commercial projects, you have to get permission from the BAIR laboratory, UC Berkeley. We don't hold the copyright for the images available in the dataset.

Keras implementation of CycleGAN

As discussed earlier in this chapter in the *An Introduction to CycleGANs* section, CycleGANs have two network architectures, a generator and a discriminator network. In this section, we will write the implementation for all the networks.

Before starting to write the implementations, however, create a Python file, main.py, and import the essential modules, as follows:

```
from glob import glob
import matplotlib.pyplot as plt
import numpy as np
import tensorflow as tf
from keras import Input, Model
from keras.layers import Conv2D, BatchNormalization, Activation, Add,
Conv2DTranspose, \
    ZeroPadding2D, LeakyReLU
from keras.optimizers import Adam
from keras_contrib.layers import InstanceNormalization
from scipy.misc import imread, imresize
```

The generator network

We have already explored the architecture of the generator network earlier in this chapter in the *The architecture of the generator network* section. Let's start by writing the layers for the generator network in the Keras framework and then create a Keras model, using the functional API of the Keras framework.

Perform the following steps to implement the generator network in Keras:

1. Start by defining the hyperparameters required for the generator network, as follows:

```
input_shape = (128, 128, 3)
residual_blocks = 6
```

2. Next, create an input layer to feed the input to the network, as follows:

```
input_layer = Input(shape=input_shape)
```

3. Add the first convolution block with the hyperparameters specified previously in the *The architecture of the generator network* section, as follows:

```
x = Conv2D(filters=32, kernel_size=7, strides=1,
padding="same")(input_layer)
x = InstanceNormalization(axis=1)(x)
x = Activation("relu")(x)
```

4. Add the second convolution block, as follows:

```
x = Conv2D(filters=64, kernel_size=3, strides=2, padding="same")(x)
x = InstanceNormalization(axis=1)(x)
x = Activation("relu")(x)
```

5. Add the third convolution block, as follows:

```
x = Conv2D(filters=128, kernel_size=3, strides=2,
padding="same")(x)
x = InstanceNormalization(axis=1)(x)
x = Activation("relu")(x)
```

6. Define a residual block, as follows:

```
def residual_block(x):
    """
    Residual block
    """
    res = Conv2D(filters=128, kernel_size=3, strides=1,
padding="same")(x)
    res = BatchNormalization(axis=3, momentum=0.9,
epsilon=1e-5)(res)
    res = Activation('relu')(res)

    res = Conv2D(filters=128, kernel_size=3, strides=1,
padding="same")(res)
    res = BatchNormalization(axis=3, momentum=0.9,
```

```
        epsilon=1e-5)(res)

    return Add()([res, x])
```

Now, use the `residual_block()` function to add six residual blocks to the model, as shown in the following example:

```
for _ in range(residual_blocks):
    x = residual_block(x)
```

7. Next, add an upsampling block, as follows:

```
x = Conv2DTranspose(filters=64, kernel_size=3, strides=2,
padding='same', use_bias=False)(x)
x = InstanceNormalization(axis=1)(x)
x = Activation("relu")(x)
```

8. Add another upsampling block, as follows:

```
x = Conv2DTranspose(filters=32, kernel_size=3, strides=2,
padding='same', use_bias=False)(x)
x = InstanceNormalization(axis=1)(x)
x = Activation("relu")(x)
```

9. Finally, add the output convolution layer, as follows:

```
x = Conv2D(filters=3, kernel_size=7, strides=1, padding="same")(x)
output = Activation('tanh')(x)
```

This is the last layer of the generator network. It generates an image with a shape of (128, 128, 3).

10. Now, create a Keras model by specifying the `inputs` and `outputs` for the network, as follows:

```
model = Model(inputs=[input_layer], outputs=[output])
```

The entire code for the generator network appears as follows:

```
def build_generator():
    """
    Create a generator network using the hyperparameter values defined
below
    """
    input_shape = (128, 128, 3)
    residual_blocks = 6
    input_layer = Input(shape=input_shape)
```

```
    # First Convolution block
    x = Conv2D(filters=32, kernel_size=7, strides=1,
padding="same")(input_layer)
    x = InstanceNormalization(axis=1)(x)
    x = Activation("relu")(x)

    # 2nd Convolution block
    x = Conv2D(filters=64, kernel_size=3, strides=2, padding="same")(x)
    x = InstanceNormalization(axis=1)(x)
    x = Activation("relu")(x)

    # 3rd Convolution block
    x = Conv2D(filters=128, kernel_size=3, strides=2, padding="same")(x)
    x = InstanceNormalization(axis=1)(x)
    x = Activation("relu")(x)

    # Residual blocks
    for _ in range(residual_blocks):
        x = residual_block(x)

    # Upsampling blocks
    # 1st Upsampling block
    x = Conv2DTranspose(filters=64, kernel_size=3, strides=2,
padding='same', use_bias=False)(x)
    x = InstanceNormalization(axis=1)(x)
    x = Activation("relu")(x)

    # 2nd Upsampling block
    x = Conv2DTranspose(filters=32, kernel_size=3, strides=2,
padding='same', use_bias=False)(x)
    x = InstanceNormalization(axis=1)(x)
    x = Activation("relu")(x)

    # Last Convolution layer
    x = Conv2D(filters=3, kernel_size=7, strides=1, padding="same")(x)
    output = Activation('tanh')(x)

    model = Model(inputs=[input_layer], outputs=[output])
    return model
```

We have successfully created a Keras model for the generator network. In the next section, we will create a Keras model for the discriminator network.

The discriminator network

We have already explored the architecture of the discriminator network in the *The architecture of the discriminator network* section. Let's start by writing the layers for the discriminator network in the Keras framework and then create a Keras model, using the functional API of the Keras framework.

Perform the following steps to implement the discriminator network in Keras:

1. Start by defining the hyperparameters required for the discriminator network, as follows:

```
input_shape = (128, 128, 3)
hidden_layers = 3
```

2. Next, add an input layer to feed the input to the network, as follows:

```
input_layer = Input(shape=input_shape)
```

3. Next, add a 2D zero padding layer, as follows:

```
x = ZeroPadding2D(padding=(1, 1))(input_layer)
```

This layer will add padding to the input tensor on both the *x* and *y* axes.

4. Next, add a convolution block using the hyperparameters specified previously in the *The architecture of the discriminator network* section, as follows:

```
x = Conv2D(filters=64, kernel_size=4, strides=2,
padding="valid")(x)
x = LeakyReLU(alpha=0.2)(x)
```

5. Next, add another 2D zero padding layer, as follows:

```
x = ZeroPadding2D(padding=(1, 1))(x)
```

6. Next, add three convolution blocks using the hyperparameters specified previously in the *The architecture of the discriminator network* section, as follows:

```
for i in range(1, hidden_layers + 1):
    x = Conv2D(filters=2 ** i * 64, kernel_size=4, strides=2,
padding="valid")(x)
    x = InstanceNormalization(axis=1)(x)
    x = LeakyReLU(alpha=0.2)(x)
    x = ZeroPadding2D(padding=(1, 1))(x)
```

Each convolution block has two convolution layers, an instance normalization layer, an activation layer, and a 2D zero padding layer.

7. Now, add the final (output) convolution layer to the network, as follows:

```
output = Conv2D(filters=1, kernel_size=4, strides=1,
activation="sigmoid")(x)
```

8. Finally, create a Keras model by specifying inputs and outputs for the network, as follows:

```
model = Model(inputs=[input_layer], outputs=[output])
```

The entire code for the discriminator network appears as follows:

```
def build_discriminator():
    """
    Create a discriminator network using the hyperparameter values defined
below
    """
    input_shape = (128, 128, 3)
    hidden_layers = 3

    input_layer = Input(shape=input_shape)

    x = ZeroPadding2D(padding=(1, 1))(input_layer)

    # 1st Convolutional block
    x = Conv2D(filters=64, kernel_size=4, strides=2, padding="valid")(x)
    x = LeakyReLU(alpha=0.2)(x)

    x = ZeroPadding2D(padding=(1, 1))(x)

    # 3 Hidden Convolution blocks
    for i in range(1, hidden_layers + 1):
        x = Conv2D(filters=2 ** i * 64, kernel_size=4, strides=2,
padding="valid")(x)
        x = InstanceNormalization(axis=1)(x)
        x = LeakyReLU(alpha=0.2)(x)

        x = ZeroPadding2D(padding=(1, 1))(x)

    # Last Convolution layer
    output = Conv2D(filters=1, kernel_size=4, strides=1,
activation="sigmoid")(x)

    model = Model(inputs=[input_layer], outputs=[output])
    return model
```

We have successfully created a Keras model for the discriminator network too. In the next section, we'll train the network.

Training the CycleGAN

We have already covered the training objective function in the *An Introduction to CycleGANs* section. We have also created the respective Keras models for both networks. Training the CycleGAN is a multi-step process. We will perform the following steps to train the network:

1. Loading the dataset
2. Creating the generator and the discriminator networks
3. Training the network for a specified number of epochs
4. Plotting the losses
5. Generating new images

Let's define the essential variables before starting to train the network, as follows:

```
data_dir = "/Path/to/dataset/directory/*.*"
batch_size = 1
epochs = 500
```

Loading the dataset

Before doing anything else, load the dataset by performing the following steps:

1. Start by creating a list of image paths, using the `glob` module as follows:

   ```
   imagesA = glob(data_dir + '/testA/*.*')
   imagesB = glob(data_dir + '/testB/*.*')
   ```

   We have data from two domains, A and B, which is why we have created two lists.

2. Next, iterate over the lists. Load, resize, and horizontally flip the images inside the loop, as follows:

   ```
   allImagesA = []
   allImagesB = []

   # Iterate over the lists
   for index, filename in enumerate(imagesA):
   ```

```
# Load images
imgA = imread(filename, mode='RGB')
imgB = imread(imagesB[index], mode='RGB')
# Resize images
imgA = imresize(imgA, (128, 128))
imgB = imresize(imgB, (128, 128))
# Randomly horizontally flip images
if np.random.random() > 0.5:
    imgA = np.fliplr(imgA)
    imgB = np.fliplr(imgB)

allImagesA.append(imgA)
allImagesB.append(imgB)
```

3. Now, normalize the images to bring the pixel values to a range between -1 and 1, as follows:

```
# Normalize images
allImagesA = np.array(allImagesA) / 127.5 - 1.
allImagesB = np.array(allImagesB) / 127.5 - 1.
```

The entire code to load the dataset appears as follows:

```
def load_images(data_dir):
    imagesA = glob(data_dir + '/testA/*.*')
    imagesB = glob(data_dir + '/testB/*.*')

    allImagesA = []
    allImagesB = []

    for index, filename in enumerate(imagesA):
        # Load images
        imgA = imread(filename, mode='RGB')
        imgB = imread(imagesB[index], mode='RGB')
        # Resize images
        imgA = imresize(imgA, (128, 128))
        imgB = imresize(imgB, (128, 128))
        # Randomly horizontally flip images
        if np.random.random() > 0.5:
            imgA = np.fliplr(imgA)
            imgB = np.fliplr(imgB)

        allImagesA.append(imgA)
        allImagesB.append(imgB)

    # Normalize images
    allImagesA = np.array(allImagesA) / 127.5 - 1.
```

```
allImagesB = np.array(allImagesB) / 127.5 - 1.

return allImagesA, allImagesB
```

The preceding function will return two Numpy ndarrays. We will use it to load and preprocess the images before we start the training.

Building and compiling the networks

In this section, let's build the essential networks and prepare them for training. Perform the steps as follows:

1. Start by defining the optimizer required for the training, as shown in the following code:

   ```
   # Define the common optimizer
   common_optimizer = Adam(0.0002, 0.5)
   ```

   We will use the Adam optimizer with the learning_rate equal to 0.0002, and the beta_1 value equal to 0.5.

2. Start by creating the discriminator networks, as shown in the following code:

   ```
   discriminatorA = build_discriminator()
   discriminatorB = build_discriminator()
   ```

   As mentioned in the *The Architecture of the discriminator network* section, a CycleGAN has two discriminator networks.

3. Next, compile the networks, as follows:

   ```
   discriminatorA.compile(loss='mse', optimizer=common_optimizer,
   metrics=['accuracy'])
   discriminatorB.compile(loss='mse', optimizer=common_optimizer,
   metrics=['accuracy'])
   ```

   Use mse as the loss function and accuracy as the metric to compile the networks.

4. Next, create the generator networks A (generatorAToB) and B (generatorBToA). The input to the generator network A is a real image (realA) from the dataset A, and the output will be a reconstructed image (fakeB). The input to the generator network B is a real image (realB) from the dataset B, and the output will be a reconstructed image (fakeA), as follows:

```
generatorAToB = build_generator()
generatorBToA = build_generator()
```

As mentioned in the *The Architecture of a CycleGAN* section, CycleGAN has two generator networks. generatorAToB will translate an image from domain A to domain B. Similarly, generatorBToA will translate an image from domain B to domain A.

We have now created two generator and two discriminator networks. In the next subsection, we will create and compile an adversarial network.

Creating and compiling an adversarial network

The adversarial network is a combined network. It uses all four networks in a single Keras model. The main purpose of creating an adversarial network is to train the generator networks. When we train the adversarial network, it only trains the generator networks, but freezes the training of the discriminator networks. Let's create an adversarial model with the desired functionality.

1. Start by creating two input layers to the network, as follows:

```
inputA = Input(shape=(128, 128, 3))
inputB = Input(shape=(128, 128, 3))
```

Both inputs will take images of a dimension of (128, 128, 3). These are symbolic input variables and don't hold actual values. They are used to create a Keras model (TensorFlow graph).

2. Next, use the generator networks to generate fake images, as follows:

```
generatedB = generatorAToB(inputA)
generatedA = generatorBToA(inputB)
```

Use the symbolic input layers to generate images.

3. Now, reconstruct the original images using the generator networks again, as follows:

```
reconstructedA = generatorBToA(generatedB)
reconstructedB = generatorAToB(generatedA)
```

4. Use the generator networks to generate fake images, as follows:

```
generatedAId = generatorBToA(inputA)
generatedBId = generatorAToB(inputB)
```

The generator network A (`generatorAToB`) will translate an image from domain A to domain B. Similarly, the generator network B (`generatorBToA`) will translate an image from domain B to domain A.

5. Next, make both of the discriminator networks non-trainable, as follows:

```
discriminatorA.trainable = False
discriminatorB.trainable = False
```

We don't want to train the discriminator networks in our adversarial network.

6. Use the discriminator networks to predict whether each generated image is real or fake, as follows:

```
probsA = discriminatorA(generatedA)
probsB = discriminatorB(generatedB)
```

7. Create a Keras model and specify the inputs and outputs for the network, as follows:

```
adversarial_model = Model(inputs=[inputA, inputB],outputs=[probsA,
probsB, reconstructedA, reconstructedB, generatedAId,
generatedBId])
```

Our adversarial network will take two input values, which are Tensors, and return six output values, which are also Tensors.

8. Next, compile the adversarial network, as follows:

```
adversarial_model.compile(loss=['mse', 'mse', 'mae', 'mae', 'mae',
'mae'],
                          loss_weights=[1, 1, 10.0, 10.0, 1.0,
1.0],
                          optimizer=common_optimizer)
```

The adversarial network returns six values and we need to specify the loss function for each output value. For the first two values, we are using **mean squared error** loss, as this is part of the **adversarial loss**. For the next four values, we are using **mean absolute error** loss, which is part of the cycle-consistency loss. The weight values for six different losses are 1, 1, 10.0, 10.0, 1.0, 1.0. We are using `common_optimizer` to train the network.

We have now successfully created a Keras model for the adversarial network. If you have difficulty in understanding how a Keras model works, have a look at the documentation of the TensorFlow graph and its functionality.

Before embarking on the training, perform the following two essential steps. TensorBoard will be used in the later sections:

Add TensorBoard to store the losses and the graphs for visualization purposes, as follows:

```
tensorboard = TensorBoard(log_dir="logs/{}".format(time.time()),
write_images=True, write_grads=True,
                          write_graph=True)
tensorboard.set_model(generatorAToB)
tensorboard.set_model(generatorBToA)
tensorboard.set_model(discriminatorA)
tensorboard.set_model(discriminatorB)
```

Create a four-dimensional array containing all values equal to one, which represents the real label. Similarly, create another four-dimensional array with all values equal to zero, which represents the fake label, as follows:

```
real_labels = np.ones((batch_size, 7, 7, 1))
fake_labels = np.zeros((batch_size, 7, 7, 1))
```

Use numpy's `ones()` and `zeros()` functions to create the desired ndarrays. Now that we have the essential components ready, let's start the training.

Starting the training

To train the network for a specified number of epochs, perform the following steps:

1. Start by loading the dataset for both domains, as follows:

   ```
   imagesA, imagesB = load_images(data_dir=data_dir)
   ```

   We have already defined the `load_images` function in the *Loading the data* subsection in the *Training a CycleGAN* section.

2. Next, create a `for` loop, which should run for the number of times specified by the number of epochs, as follows:

```
for epoch in range(epochs):
    print("Epoch:{}".format(epoch))
```

3. Create two lists to store the losses for all mini-batches, as follows:

```
dis_losses = []
gen_losses = []
```

4. Calculate the number of mini-batches inside the `epochs` loop, as follows:

```
num_batches = int(min(imagesA.shape[0], imagesB.shape[0]) /
                  batch_size)
print("Number of batches:{}".format(num_batches))
```

5. Next, create another loop inside the epochs loop and make it run for the number of times that is specified by `num_batches`, as follows:

```
for index in range(num_batches):
    print("Batch:{}".format(index))
```

Our entire code for the training of the discriminator networks and the adversarial network will be inside this loop.

Training the discriminator networks

The code inside this sub-section is a continuation of the code in the last section. Here, you will see how to train the discriminator networks:

1. Start by sampling a mini-batch of images for both domains, as shown in the following code:

```
batchA = imagesA[index * batch_size:(index + 1) * batch_size]
batchB = imagesB[index * batch_size:(index + 1) * batch_size]
```

2. Next, generate fake images using the generator networks, as follows:

```
generatedB = generatorAToB.predict(batchA)
generatedA = generatorBToA.predict(batchB)
```

3. After that, train the discriminator network A on both real and fake images (generated by the generator network), as follows:

```
        dALoss1 = discriminatorA.train_on_batch(batchA,
real_labels)
        dALoss2 = discriminatorB.train_on_batch(generatedA,
fake_labels)
```

This step will train the discriminator A on a mini-batch of real images and fake images and will improve the network slightly.

4. Next, train the discriminator B on the real and fake images, as follows:

```
    dBLoss1 = discriminatorB.train_on_batch(batchB, real_labels)
    dbLoss2 = discriminatorB.train_on_batch(generatedB, fake_labels)
```

5. Now, calculate the total loss value for the discriminator networks, as follows:

```
    d_loss = 0.5 * np.add(0.5 * np.add(dALoss1, dALoss2), 0.5 *
             np.add(dBLoss1, dbLoss2))
```

Up until now, we have been adding code to train the discriminator networks. In the next sub-section, we'll train the adversarial network to train the generator networks.

Training the adversarial network

To train the adversarial network, we need both input values and ground truth values. The input values to the network are batchA and batchB. The ground truth values are real_labels, real_labels, batchA, batchB, batchA, batchB, as follows:

```
    g_loss = adversarial_model.train_on_batch([batchA, batchB],
                                    [real_labels, real_labels,
    batchA, batchB, batchA, batchB])
```

This step will train the generator network without training the generating networks.

After the completion of a single iteration (loop) over each mini-batch, store the losses in lists called dis_losses and gen_losses, as follows:

```
        dis_losses.append(d_loss)
        gen_losses.append(g_loss)
```

After every 10 epochs, use the generator networks to generate a set of images:

```
# Sample and save images after every 10 epochs
if epoch % 10 == 0:
    # Get a batch of test data
    batchA, batchB = load_test_batch(data_dir=data_dir, batch_size=2)
    # Generate images
    generatedB = generatorAToB.predict(batchA)
    generatedA = generatorBToA.predict(batchB)
    # Get reconstructed images
    reconsA = generatorBToA.predict(generatedB)
    reconsB = generatorAToB.predict(generatedA)
    # Save original, generated and reconstructed images
    for i in range(len(generatedA)):
        save_images(originalA=batchA[i], generatedB=generatedB[i],
recosntructedA=reconsA[i],
                    originalB=batchB[i], generatedA=generatedA[i],
reconstructedB=reconsB[i],
                    path="results/gen_{}_{}".format(epoch, i))
```

Put the preceding code block inside the `epochs` loop. After every 10 epochs, it will generate a batch of fake images and save them to the results directory.

Next, store the average losses to TensorBoard for visualization. Store both losses: the average loss for the generator network, and the average loss for the discriminator network, as shown in the following example:

```
write_log(tensorboard, 'discriminator_loss', np.mean(dis_losses),
          epoch)
write_log(tensorboard, 'generator_loss', np.mean(gen_losses), epoch)
```

Put the preceding code block inside the `epochs` loop.

Saving the model

Saving a model in Keras requires just one line of code. To save the generator models, add the following lines:

```
# Specify the path for the generator A model
generatorAToB.save("directory/for/the/generatorAToB/model.h5")

# Specify the path for the generator B model
generatorBToA.save("directory/for/the/generatorBToA/model.h5")
```

Similarly, save the discriminator models by adding the following lines:

```
# Specify the path for the discriminator A model
discriminatorA.save("directory/for/the/discriminatorA/model.h5")

# Specify the path for the discriminator B model
discriminatorB.save("directory/for/the/discriminatorB/model.h5")
```

Visualizing the images generated

After training the network for 100 epochs, the network will start generating decent images. Let's have a look at the images generated by the generator networks.

After 10 epochs, the images appear as follows:

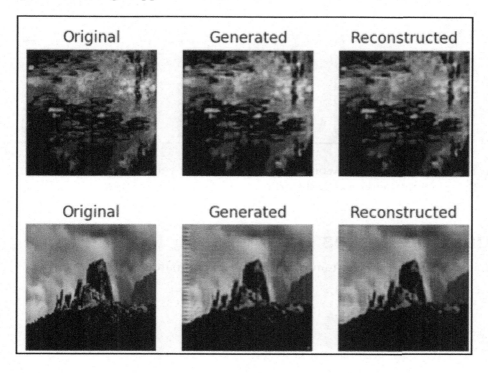

After 20 epochs, the images appear as follows:

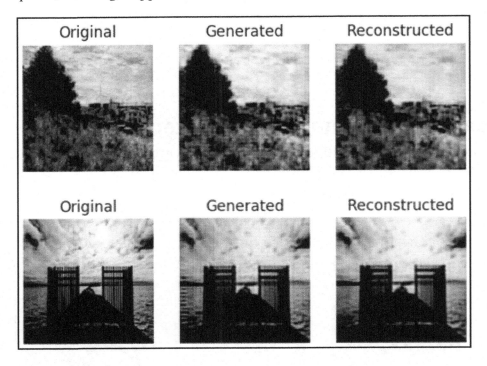

I suggest that you train the network for 1,000 epochs. If everything goes well, after 1,000 epochs, the generator networks will start generating realistic images.

Visualizing losses

To visualize the losses for the training, start the TensorBoard server as follows:

```
tensorboard --logdir=logs
```

Now, open `localhost:6006` in your browser. The **SCALARS** section of TensorBoard contains plots for both losses, as shown in the following examples:

The loss plot for the discriminator network is shown as follows:

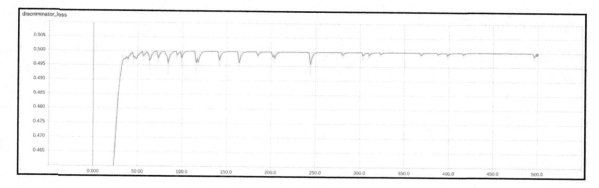

The loss plot for the generator network is shown as follows:

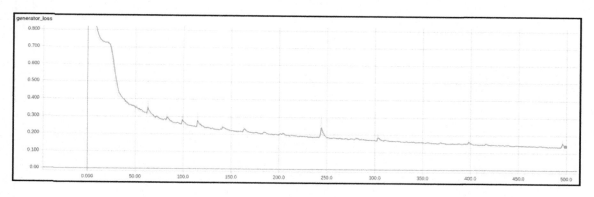

These plots will help you to decide whether to continue or stop the training. If the losses are no longer decreasing, you can stop the training, as there is no chance of improvement. If the losses keep increasing, you must stop the training. Play with the hyperparameters and select a set of hyperparameters that you think can provide better results. If the losses are decreasing gradually, keep training the model.

Visualizing the graphs

The **GRAPHS** section of TensorBoard contains the graphs for both networks. If the networks are not performing well, these graphs can help you debug the networks. They also show the flow of tensors and different operations inside each graph, as shown in the following example:

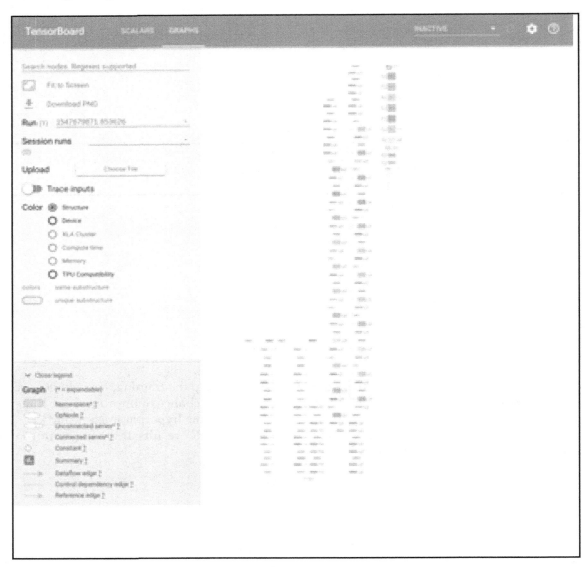

Practical applications of CycleGANs

There are many applications of CycleGANs. In this chapter, we have used a CycleGAN to turn paintings into photos. They can also be used in the following cases:

- **Style transfer**: For example, turning photos into paintings and vice versa, turning pictures of horses into zebras and vice versa, and turning pictures of oranges into pictures of apples and vice versa
- **Photo enhancement**: CycleGANs can be used to enhance the quality of pictures
- **Season transfer**: For example, turning a picture of winter into a picture of summer and vice versa
- **Game style transfer**: CycleGANs can be used to transfer the style of Game A to Game B

Summary

In this chapter, we have learned how to turn paintings into photos using a CycleGAN. We started with an introduction to CyleGANs and explored the architectures of networks involved in CycleGANs. We also explored the different loss functions required to train CycleGANs. This was followed by an implementation of CycleGAN in the Keras framework. We trained the CycleGAN on the `monet2photo` dataset and visualized the generated images, the losses, and the graphs for different networks. Before concluding the chapter, we explored the real-world use cases of CycleGANs.

In the next chapter, we will work on the pix2pix network for image-to-image translation. In pix2pix, we will explore conditional GANs for image translation.

Further reading

CycleGAN has many known use cases. Try to explore new uses using the following articles for assistance:

- *Turning Fortnite into PUBG with Deep Learning (CycleGAN):* https://towardsdatascience.com/turning-fortnite-into-pubg-with-deep-learning-cyclegan-2f9d339dcdb0
- *GAN — CycleGAN (Playing magic with pictures):* https://medium.com/@jonathan_hui/gan-cyclegan-6a50e7600d7

- *Introduction to CycleGANs:* `https://medium.com/coding-blocks/introduction-to-cyclegans-1dbdb8fbe781`
- *Understanding and Implementing CycleGAN in TensorFlow:* `https://hardikbansal.github.io/CycleGANBlog/`

8

Conditional GAN - Image-to-Image Translation Using Conditional Adversarial Networks

Pix2pix is a type of **Generative Adversarial Network (GAN)** that is used for image-to-image translation. Image-to-image translation is a method for translating one representation of an image into another representation. Pix2pix learns a mapping from input images into output images. It can be used to convert black and white images to color images, sketches to photographs, day images to night images, and satellite images to map images. The pix2pix network was first introduced in the paper titled *Image-to-Image Translation with Conditional Adversarial Networks*, by Phillip Isola, Jun-Yan Zhu, Tinghui Zhou, Alexei A. Efros; which can be found at the following link: `https://arxiv.org/pdf/1611.07004.pdf`.

In this chapter, we will cover the following topics:

- Introducing the Pix2pix network
- The architecture of the Pix2pix network
- Data gathering and preparation
- The Keras implementation of Pix2pix
- Objective functions
- Training Pix2pix
- Evaluating the trained model
- Practical applications of the Pix2pix network

Introducing Pix2pix

Pix2pix is a variant of the conditional GAN. We have already covered conditional GANs in Chapter 3, *Face-Aging Using Conditional GAN (cGAN)*. Before moving forward, make sure you take a look at what cGANs are. Once you are comfortable with cGANs, you can continue with this chapter. Pix2pix is a type of GAN that is capable of performing image-to-image translation using the unsupervised method of **machine learning** (ML). Once trained, pix2pix can translate an image from domain A to domain B. Vanilla CNNs can also be used for image-to-image translation, but they don't generate realistic and sharp images. On the other hand, pix2pix has shown immense potential to be able to generate realistic and sharp images. We will be training pix2pix to translate labels of facades to images of facade. Let's start by understanding the architecture of pix2pix.

The architecture of pix2pix

Similar to other GANs, pix2pix is made up of two networks: a generator and a discriminator network. The architecture of the generator network is inspired by the architecture of U-Net (https://arxiv.org/pdf/1505.04597.pdf). Similarly, the architecture of the discriminator network is inspired by the architecture of PatchGAN (https://arxiv.org/pdf/1604.04382.pdf). Both networks are deep convolutional neural networks. In this section, we will be exploring pix2pix in detail.

The generator network

As we mentioned in the previous section, the generator network is heavily inspired by the architecture of U-Net. The architecture of U-Net is almost the same as that of an auto-encoder network. One major difference between them is that the U-Net network has skip connections between the layers in the encoder, and the decoder parts of the generator network and auto-encoder doesn't have skip connections. The U-Net network consists of two networks: the encoder network and the decoder network. The following diagram illustrates the architecture of U-Net at a basic level:

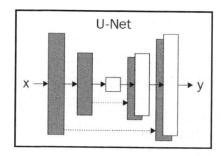

The previous diagram should give you an understanding of the architecture of a U-Net. As you can see, the output of the first layer is directly merged with the last layer. The output of the second layer is merged with the second last layer and so on. If n is the total number of layers, there are skip connections between the ith layer in the encoder network and the $(n-i)$th layer in the decoder network. The ith layer can be any layer among these layers. Let's take a closer look at both of the networks one by one.

The encoder network

The encoder network is the initial network of the generator network and contains eight **convolutional blocks** with the following configuration:

Layer Name	Hyperparameters	Input Shape	Output Shape
1st 2D Convolution Layer	filters=64, kernel_size=4, strides=2, padding='same',	(256, 256, 1)	(128, 128, 64)
Activation Layer	activation='leakyrelu', alpha=0.2	(128, 128, 64)	(128, 128, 64)
2nd 2D Convolution Layer	filters=128, kernel_size=4, strides=2, padding='same',	(128, 128, 64)	(64, 64, 128)
Batch Normalization Layer	None	(64, 64, 128)	(64, 64, 128)
Activation Layer	activation='leakyrelu', alpha=0.2	(64, 64, 128)	(64, 64, 128)
3rd 2D Convolution Layer	filters=256, kernel_size=4, strides=2, padding='same',	(64, 64, 128)	(32, 32, 256)

Batch Normalization Layer	None	(32, 32, 256)	(32, 32, 256)
Activation Layer	activation='leakyrelu', alpha=0.2	(32, 32, 256)	(32, 32, 256)
4th 2D Convolution Layer	filters=512, kernel_size=4, strides=2, padding='same',	(32, 32, 256)	(16, 16, 512)
Batch Normalization Layer	None	(16, 16, 512)	(16, 16, 512)
Activation Layer	activation='leakyrelu', alpha=0.2	(16, 16, 512)	(16, 16, 512)
5th 2D Convolution Layer	filters=512, kernel_size=4, strides=2, padding='same',	(16, 16, 512)	(8, 8, 512)
Batch Normalization Layer	None	(8, 8, 512)	(8, 8, 512)
Activation Layer	activation='leakyrelu', alpha=0.2	(8, 8, 512)	(8, 8, 512)
6th 2D Convolution Layer	filters=512, kernel_size=4, strides=2, padding='same',	(8, 8, 512)	(4, 4, 512)
Batch Normalization Layer	None	(4, 4, 512)	(4, 4, 512)
Activation Layer	activation='leakyrelu', alpha=0.2	(4, 4, 512)	(4, 4, 512)
7th 2D Convolution Layer	filters=512, kernel_size=4, strides=2, padding='same',	(4, 4, 512)	(2, 2, 512)
Batch Normalization Layer	None	(2, 2, 512)	(2, 2, 512)
Activation Layer	activation='leakyrelu', alpha=0.2	(2, 2, 512)	(2, 2, 512)

8th 2D Convolution Layer	filters=512, kernel_size=4, strides=2, padding='same',	(2, 2, 512)	(1, 1, 512)
Batch Normalization Layer	None	(1, 1, 512)	(1, 1, 512)
Activation Layer	activation='leakyrelu', alpha=0.2	(1, 1, 512)	(1, 1, 512)

The encoder network is followed by a decoder network. We'll have a look at the architecture of the decoder network in the following section.

The decoder network

The decoder network in the generator network also consists of eight **upsampling convolutional blocks**. The configuration for the eight upsampling convolutional blocks is as follows:

Layer Name	Hyperparameters	Input Shape	Output Shape
1st 2D Upsampling Layer	size=(2, 2)	(1, 1, 512)	(2, 2, 512)
2D Convolution Layer	filters=512, kernel_size=4, strides=1, padding='same',	(2, 2, 512)	(2, 2, 512)
Batch Normalization Layer	None	(2, 2, 512)	(2, 2, 512)
Dropout Layer	dropout=0.5	(2, 2, 512)	(2, 2, 512)
Concatenation Layer (7th Conv layer from the encoder network)	axis=3	(2, 2, 512)	(2, 2, 1024)
Activation Layer	activation='relu'	(2, 2, 1024)	(2, 2, 1024)
2nd 2D Upsampling Layer	size=(2, 2)	(2, 2, 1024)	(4, 4, 1024)
2D Convolution Layer	filters=1024, kernel_size=4, strides=1, padding='same',	(4, 4, 1024)	(4, 4, 1024)

Batch Normalization Layer	None	(4, 4, 1024)	(4, 4, 1024)
Dropout Layer	dropout=0.5	(4, 4, 1024)	(4, 4, 1024)
Concatenation Layer (6th Conv layer from the encoder network)	axis=3	(4, 4, 1024)	(4, 4, 1536)
Activation Layer	activation='relu'	(4, 4, 1536)	(4, 4, 1536)
3rd 2D Upsampling Layer	size=(2, 2)	(4, 4, 1536)	(8, 8, 1536)
2D Convolution Layer	filters=1024, kernel_size=4, strides=1, padding='same',	(8, 8, 1536)	(8, 8, 1024)
Batch Normalization Layer	None	(8, 8, 1024)	(8, 8, 1024)
Dropout Layer	dropout=0.5	(8, 8, 1024)	(8, 8, 1024)
Concatenation Layer (5th Conv layer from the encoder network)	axis=3	(8, 8, 1024)	(8, 8, 1536)
Activation Layer	activation='relu'	(8, 8, 1536)	(8, 8, 1536)
4th 2D Upsampling Layer	size=(2, 2)	(8, 8, 1536)	(16, 16, 1536)
2D Convolution Layer	filters=1024, kernel_size=4, strides=1, padding='same',	(16, 16, 1536)	(16, 16, 1024)
Batch Normalization Layer	None	(16, 16, 1024)	(16, 16, 1024)
Concatenation Layer (4th Conv layer from the encoder network)	axis=3	(16, 16, 1024)	(16, 16, 1536)

Activation Layer	activation='relu'	(16, 16, 1536)	(16, 16, 1536)
5th 2D Upsampling Layer	size=(2, 2)	(16, 16, 1536)	(32, 32, 1536)
2D Convolution Layer	filters=1024, kernel_size=4, strides=1, padding='same',	(32, 32, 1536)	(32, 32, 1024)
Batch Normalization Layer	None	(32, 32, 1024)	(32, 32, 1024)
Concatenation Layer (3rd Conv layer from the encoder network)	axis=3	(32, 32, 1024)	(32, 32, 1280)
Activation Layer	activation='relu'	(32, 32, 1280)	(32, 32, 1280)
6th 2D Upsampling Layer	size=(2, 2)	(64, 64, 1280)	(64, 64, 1280)
2D Convolution Layer	filters=512, kernel_size=4, strides=1, padding='same',	(64, 64, 1280)	(64, 64, 512)
Batch Normalization Layer	None	(64, 64, 512)	(64, 64, 512)
Concatenation Layer (2nd Conv layer from the encoder network)	axis=3	(64, 64, 512)	(64, 64, 640)
Activation Layer	activation='relu'	(64, 64, 640)	(64, 64, 640)
7th 2D Upsampling Layer	size=(2, 2)	(64, 64, 640)	(128, 128, 640)
2D Convolution Layer	filters=256, kernel_size=4, strides=1, padding='same',	(128, 128, 640)	(128, 128, 256)
Batch Normalization Layer	None	(128, 128, 256)	(128, 128, 256)

Concatenation Layer (1st Conv layer from the encoder network)	axis=3	(128, 128, 256)	(128, 128, 320)
Activation Layer	activation='relu'	(128, 128, 320)	(128, 128, 320)
8th 2D Upsampling Layer	size=(2, 2)	(128, 128, 320)	(256, 256, 320)
2D Convolution Layer	filters=1, kernel_size=4, strides=1, padding='same',	(256, 256, 320)	(256, 256, 1)
Activation Layer	activation='tanh'	(256, 256, 1)	(256, 256, 1)

The generator network has **seven skip-connections**, which can be defined as follows:

- Concatenation of the output from the 1st encoder block to the 7th decoder block
- Concatenation of the output from the 2nd encoder block to the 6th decoder block
- Concatenation of the output from the 3rd encoder block to the 5th decoder block
- Concatenation of the output from the 4th encoder block to the 4th decoder block
- Concatenation of the output from the 5th encoder block to the 3rd decoder block
- Concatenation of the output from the 6th encoder block to the 2nd decoder block
- Concatenation of the output from the 7th encoder block to the 1st decoder block

The concatenation happens along the channel axis. The last layer of the encoder network passes the tensor to the first layer of the decoder network. There is no concatenation at the last block of the encoder network and the last block of the decoder network.

The generator network is made up of these two networks. Basically, the encoder network is a downsampler and the decoder network is an upsampler. The encoder network downsamples an image with dimensions of (256, 256, 1) to an internal representation of a dimension of (1, 1, 512). On the other hand, the decoder network upsamples the internal representation with dimensions of (1, 1, 512) to an output image of a dimension of (256, 256, 1).

We will cover more on the architecture in the *Keras implementation of pix2pix* section.

The discriminator network

The architecture of the discriminator network in pix2pix is inspired by the architecture of the PatchGAN network. The PatchGAN network contains eight convolutional blocks as follows:

Layer Name	Hyperparameters	Input Shape	Output Shape
1st 2D Convolution Layer	filters=64, kernel_size=4, strides=2, padding='same',	(256, 256, 1)	(256, 256, 64)
Activation Layer	activation='leakyrelu', alpha=0.2	(128, 128, 64)	(128, 128, 64)
2nd 2D Convolution Layer	filters=128, kernel_size=4, strides=2, padding='same',	(128, 128, 64)	(64, 64, 128)
Batch Normalization Layer	None	(64, 64, 128)	(64, 64, 128)
Activation Layer	activation='leakyrelu', alpha=0.2	(64, 64, 128)	(64, 64, 128)
3rd 2D Convolution Layer	filters=256, kernel_size=4, strides=2, padding='same',	(64, 64, 128)	(32, 32, 256)
Batch Normalization Layer	None	(32, 32, 256)	(32, 32, 256)
Activation Layer	activation='leakyrelu', alpha=0.2	(32, 32, 256)	(32, 32, 256)
4th 2D Convolution Layer	filters=512, kernel_size=4, strides=2, padding='same',	(32, 32, 256)	(16, 16, 512)
Batch Normalization Layer	None	(16, 16, 512)	(16, 16, 512)
Activation Layer	activation='leakyrelu', alpha=0.2	(16, 16, 512)	(16, 16, 512)
5th 2D Convolution Layer	filters=512, kernel_size=4, strides=2, padding='same',	(16, 16, 512)	(8, 8, 512)

Batch Normalization Layer	None	(8, 8, 512)	(8, 8, 512)
Activation Layer	activation='leakyrelu', alpha=0.2	(8, 8, 512)	(8, 8, 512)
6th 2D Convolution Layer	filters=512, kernel_size=4, strides=2, padding='same',	(8, 8, 512)	(4, 4, 512)
Batch Normalization Layer	None	(4, 4, 512)	(4, 4, 512)
Activation Layer	activation='leakyrelu', alpha=0.2	(4, 4, 512)	(4, 4, 512)
7th 2D Convolution Layer	filters=512, kernel_size=4, strides=2, padding='same',	(4, 4, 512)	(2, 2, 512)
Batch Normalization Layer	None	(2, 2, 512)	(2, 2, 512)
Activation Layer	activation='leakyrelu', alpha=0.2	(2, 2, 512)	(2, 2, 512)
8th 2D Convolution Layer	filters=512, kernel_size=4, strides=2, padding='same',	(4, 4, 512)	(1, 1, 512)
Batch Normalization Layer	None	(1, 1, 512)	(1, 1, 512)
Activation Layer	activation='leakyrelu', alpha=0.2	(1, 1, 512)	(1, 1, 512)
Flatten Layer	None	(1, 1, 512)	(512,)
Dense Layer	units=2, activation='softmax'	(1, 1, 512)	(2,)

This table highlights the architecture and the configuration of the discriminator network. A flatten layer flattens the tensor to a one-dimensional array.

> The remaining layers in the discriminator network are covered in the *The Keras implementation of pix2pix* section of this chapter.

We have now explored the architecture and configuration of both networks. We will now explore the training objective function that's required to train pix2pix.

The training objective function

Pix2pix is a conditional generative adversarial network and the objective function for conditional GANs can be expressed as follows:

$$L_{cGAN}(G, D) = E_{x,y}[log\ D(x, y) + E_{x,z}[log(1 - D(x, G(x, z))]$$

Here, network G (the generator) is trying to minimize the preceding function against an adversary D (the discriminator) and the adversary D tries to maximize the preceding function.

If we have to compare the objective function for a vanilla GAN and a conditional GAN, the objective function of a vanilla GAN is as follows:

$$L_{GAN}(G, D) = E_y[log\ D(y) + E_{x,z}[log(1 - D(G(x, z))]$$

To make the images less blurry, we can add an L1 loss function to the objective function. The L1 loss function can be expressed as follows:

$$L_{L1}(G) = E_{x,y,z}[\|y - G(x, z)\|_1]$$

In this equation, *y*, is the original image and *G(x, z)* is the image generated by the generator network. The L1 loss is calculated by the sum of the all the absolute differences between all pixel values of the original image and all pixel values of the generated image.

The final objective function for pix2pix is as follows:

$$G^* = \arg \min_G \max_D \mathcal{L}_{cGAN}(G, D) + \lambda \mathcal{L}_{L1}(G).$$

This is a weighted sum of the loss function of the conditional GANs and the L1 loss function.

Now we have a basic understanding of the pix2pix network. Before starting to implement pix2pix in Keras, let's set up the project.

Setting up the project

If you haven't already cloned the repository with the complete code for all chapters, clone the repository now. The cloned repository has a directory called Chapter09, which contains the entire code for this chapter. Execute the following commands to set up the project:

1. Start by navigating to the parent directory as follows:

   ```
   cd Generative-Adversarial-Networks-Projects
   ```

2. Now change the directory from the current directory to Chapter09:

   ```
   cd Chapter09
   ```

3. Next, create a Python virtual environment for this project:

   ```
   virtualenv venv
   virtualenv venv -p python3 # Create a virtual environment using
   python3 interpreter
   virtualenv venv -p python2 # Create a virtual environment using
   python2 interpreter
   ```

   We will be using this newly created virtual environment for this project. Each chapter has its own separate virtual environment.

4. Next, activate the newly created virtual environment:

   ```
   source venv/bin/activate
   ```

   After you activate the virtual environment, all further commands will be executed in this virtual environment.

5. Next, install all libraries given in the requirements.txt file by executing the following command:

   ```
   pip install -r requirements.txt
   ```

You can refer to the README.md file for further instructions on how to set up the project. Very often, developers face the problem of mismatching dependencies. Creating a separate virtual environment for each project will take care of this problem.

In this section, we have successfully set up the project and installed the required dependencies. In the next section, we will work on the dataset. We will now explore the various steps required to download and format the dataset.

Preparing the data

In this chapter, we will be working with the Facades dataset, which is available at the following link:

`http://efrosgans.eecs.berkeley.edu/pix2pix/datasets/facades.tar.gz.`

This dataset contains facade labels and ground truth facade images. A facade is generally the front side of a building, and facade labels are architectural labels of a facade image. We will learn more about facades after we download the dataset. Perform the following commands to download and extract the dataset:

1. Download the dataset by executing the following commands:

    ```
    # Before downloading the dataset navigate to data directory
    cd data

    # Download the dataset
    wget
    http://efrosgans.eecs.berkeley.edu/pix2pix/datasets/facades.tar.gz
    ```

2. After downloading the dataset, extract the dataset using the following command:

    ```
    tar -xvzf facades.tar.gz
    ```

The file structure of the downloaded dataset is as follows:

The dataset is divided into training, testing, and validation datasets. Let's work on extracting the images.

Perform the following steps to load the dataset:

1. Start by creating a list of `.h5` files containing facade labels and another list of `.h5` containing facade images as follows:

```
data_dir_path = os.path.join(data_dir, data_type)

# Get all .h5 files containing training images
facade_photos_h5 = [f for f in
os.listdir(os.path.join(data_dir_path, 'images')) if '.h5' in f]
facade_labels_h5 = [f for f in
os.listdir(os.path.join(data_dir_path, 'facades')) if '.h5' in f]
```

2. Next, iterate (loop) over the lists to load each image sequentially:

```
final_facade_photos = None
final_facade_labels = None

for index in range(len(facade_photos_h5)):
```

All code, following this step, will be inside the preceding `for` loop.

3. Next, load the `h5` files containing images and retrieve the Numpy NDArrays of the actual images:

```
facade_photos_path = data_dir_path + '/images/' +
                     facade_photos_h5[index]
facade_labels_path = data_dir_path + '/facades/' +
                     facade_labels_h5[index]

facade_photos = h5py.File(facade_photos_path, 'r')
facade_labels = h5py.File(facade_labels_path, 'r')
```

4. Next, resize the images to the desired image size as follows:

```
# Resize and normalize images
num_photos = facade_photos['data'].shape[0]
num_labels = facade_labels['data'].shape[0]

all_facades_photos = np.array(facade_photos['data'],
dtype=np.float32)
all_facades_photos = all_facades_photos.reshape((num_photos,
img_width, img_height, 1)) / 255.0

all_facades_labels = np.array(facade_labels['data'],
dtype=np.float32)
all_facades_labels = all_facades_labels.reshape((num_labels,
img_width, img_height, 1)) / 255.0
```

5. Next, add the resized images to the final NDArrays:

```
if final_facade_photos is not None and final_facade_labels is not
None:
final_facade_photos = np.concatenate([final_facade_photos,
                                all_facades_photos], axis=0)
final_facade_labels = np.concatenate([final_facade_labels,
all_facades_labels], axis=0)
    else:
        final_facade_photos = all_facades_photos
        final_facade_labels = all_facades_labels
```

The entire code to load and resize images looks as follows:

```
def load_dataset(data_dir, data_type, img_width, img_height):
    data_dir_path = os.path.join(data_dir, data_type)

    # Get all .h5 files containing training images
    facade_photos_h5 = [f for f in os.listdir(os.path.join(data_dir_path,
'images')) if '.h5' in f]
    facade_labels_h5 = [f for f in os.listdir(os.path.join(data_dir_path,
'facades')) if '.h5' in f]

    final_facade_photos = None
    final_facade_labels = None

    for index in range(len(facade_photos_h5)):
        facade_photos_path = data_dir_path + '/images/' +
facade_photos_h5[index]
        facade_labels_path = data_dir_path + '/facades/' +
facade_labels_h5[index]

        facade_photos = h5py.File(facade_photos_path, 'r')
        facade_labels = h5py.File(facade_labels_path, 'r')

        # Resize and normalize images
        num_photos = facade_photos['data'].shape[0]
        num_labels = facade_labels['data'].shape[0]

        all_facades_photos = np.array(facade_photos['data'],
dtype=np.float32)
        all_facades_photos = all_facades_photos.reshape((num_photos,
img_width, img_height, 1)) / 255.0

        all_facades_labels = np.array(facade_labels['data'],
dtype=np.float32)
        all_facades_labels = all_facades_labels.reshape((num_labels,
img_width, img_height, 1)) / 255.0
```

```
        if final_facade_photos is not None and final_facade_labels is not
None:
            final_facade_photos = np.concatenate([final_facade_photos,
all_facades_photos], axis=0)
            final_facade_labels = np.concatenate([final_facade_labels,
all_facades_labels], axis=0)
        else:
            final_facade_photos = all_facades_photos
            final_facade_labels = all_facades_labels

    return final_facade_photos, final_facade_labels
```

The previous function will load images from the `.h5` files inside the training, testing, and validation directories.

Visualizing images

A Python function to visualize the facade labels and the images of facades looks as follows:

```
def visualize_bw_image(img):
    """
    Visualize a black and white image
    """
    fig = plt.figure()
    ax = fig.add_subplot(1, 1, 1)
    ax.imshow(img, cmap='gray', interpolation='nearest')
    ax.axis("off")
    ax.set_title("Image")
    plt.show()
```

Use the preceding function to visualize the facade labels or the photos of facades, as follows:

```
visualize_bw_image(image)
visualize_bw_image(image)
```

An example of an image of the facade of a building is as follows:

The following image represents the architectural labels for the preceding facade image:

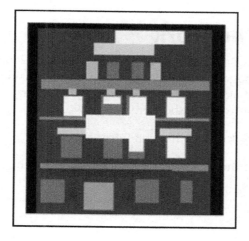

We will train a pix2pix network that is capable of generating an image of a facade from a facade label. Let's start working with the Keras implementations for the generator and the discriminator.

A Keras implementation of pix2pix

As mentioned, pix2pix has two networks: a generator and a discriminator. The generator is inspired by the architecture of U-Net. Similarly, the discriminator network is inspired by the architecture of PatchGAN. We will implement both networks in the following sections.

Before starting to write the implementations, create a Python file `main.py` and import the essential modules as follows:

```
import os
import time

import h5py
import keras.backend as K
import matplotlib.pyplot as plt
import numpy as np
from cv2 import imwrite
from keras import Input, Model
from keras.layers import Convolution2D, LeakyReLU, BatchNormalization,
UpSampling2D, Dropout,     Activation, Flatten, Dense, Lambda, Reshape,
concatenate
from keras.optimizers import Adam
```

The generator network

The generator network takes an image of a dimension of (256, 256, 1) from a source domain A and translates it to an image in target domain B, with dimensions of (256, 256, 1). Basically, it translates an image from a source domain A to a target domain B. Let's implement the generator network in the Keras framework.

Perform the following steps to create the generator network:

1. Start by defining the hyperparameters required for the generator network:

```
kernel_size = 4
strides = 2
leakyrelu_alpha = 0.2
upsampling_size = 2
dropout = 0.5
output_channels = 1
input_shape = (256, 256, 1)
```

2. Now create an input layer to feed input to the network as follows:

```
input_layer = Input(shape=input_shape)
```

The input layer takes an input image of a shape of (256, 256, 1) and passes it to the next layer in the network.

As mentioned, the generator network has two parts: an encoder and decoder. In the next few steps, we will write the code of the encoder part.

3. Add the first convolutional block to the generator network with parameters indicated previously in the *The architecture of pix2pix* section:

```
# 1st Convolutional block in the encoder network
encoder1 = Convolution2D(filters=64, kernel_size=kernel_size,
padding='same', strides=strides)(input_layer)
encoder1 = LeakyReLU(alpha=leakyrelu_alpha)(encoder1)
```

The first convolutional block contains a 2D convolution layer with an activation function. Unlike the other seven convolutional blocks, it doesn't have a batch normalization layer.

4. Add the other seven convolutional blocks to the generator network:

```
# 2nd Convolutional block in the encoder network
encoder2 = Convolution2D(filters=128, kernel_size=kernel_size,
padding='same',
                              strides=strides)(encoder1)
encoder2 = BatchNormalization()(encoder2)
encoder2 = LeakyReLU(alpha=leakyrelu_alpha)(encoder2)

# 3rd Convolutional block in the encoder network
encoder3 = Convolution2D(filters=256, kernel_size=kernel_size,
padding='same',
                              strides=strides)(encoder2)
encoder3 = BatchNormalization()(encoder3)
encoder3 = LeakyReLU(alpha=leakyrelu_alpha)(encoder3)

# 4th Convolutional block in the encoder network
encoder4 = Convolution2D(filters=512, kernel_size=kernel_size,
padding='same',
                              strides=strides)(encoder3)
encoder4 = BatchNormalization()(encoder4)
encoder4 = LeakyReLU(alpha=leakyrelu_alpha)(encoder4)

# 5th Convolutional block in the encoder network
encoder5 = Convolution2D(filters=512, kernel_size=kernel_size,
padding='same',
                              strides=strides)(encoder4)
encoder5 = BatchNormalization()(encoder5)
encoder5 = LeakyReLU(alpha=leakyrelu_alpha)(encoder5)

# 6th Convolutional block in the encoder network
encoder6 = Convolution2D(filters=512, kernel_size=kernel_size,
padding='same',
                              strides=strides)(encoder5)
```

```
encoder6 = BatchNormalization()(encoder6)
encoder6 = LeakyReLU(alpha=leakyrelu_alpha)(encoder6)

# 7th Convolutional block in the encoder network
encoder7 = Convolution2D(filters=512, kernel_size=kernel_size,
padding='same',
                              strides=strides)(encoder6)
encoder7 = BatchNormalization()(encoder7)
encoder7 = LeakyReLU(alpha=leakyrelu_alpha)(encoder7)

# 8th Convolutional block in the encoder network
encoder8 = Convolution2D(filters=512, kernel_size=kernel_size,
padding='same',
                              strides=strides)(encoder7)
encoder8 = BatchNormalization()(encoder8)
encoder8 = LeakyReLU(alpha=leakyrelu_alpha)(encoder8)
```

This is the end of the encoder part in the generator network. The second part in the generator network is the decoder. In the next few steps, let's write the code for the decoder.

5. Add the first upsampling convolutional block to the parameters indicated previously in the *The architecture of pix2pix* section:

```
# 1st Upsampling Convolutional Block in the decoder network
decoder1 = UpSampling2D(size=upsampling_size)(encoder8)
decoder1 = Convolution2D(filters=512, kernel_size=kernel_size,
padding='same')(decoder1)
decoder1 = BatchNormalization()(decoder1)
decoder1 = Dropout(dropout)(decoder1)
decoder1 = concatenate([decoder1, encoder7], axis=3)
decoder1 = Activation('relu')(decoder1)
```

The first upsampling block takes an input from the last layer of the encoder part. It has a 2D upsampling layer, a 2D convolution layer, a batch normalization layer, a dropout layer, a concatenation operation, and an activation function. Refer to the Keras documentation to find out more about these layers, which is available at https://keras.io/.

6. Similarly, add the next seven convolutional blocks as follows:

```
# 2nd Upsampling Convolutional block in the decoder network
decoder2 = UpSampling2D(size=upsampling_size)(decoder1)
decoder2 = Convolution2D(filters=1024, kernel_size=kernel_size,
padding='same')(decoder2)
decoder2 = BatchNormalization()(decoder2)
decoder2 = Dropout(dropout)(decoder2)
decoder2 = concatenate([decoder2, encoder6])
decoder2 = Activation('relu')(decoder2)
```

```
# 3rd Upsampling Convolutional block in the decoder network
decoder3 = UpSampling2D(size=upsampling_size)(decoder2)
decoder3 = Convolution2D(filters=1024, kernel_size=kernel_size,
padding='same')(decoder3)
decoder3 = BatchNormalization()(decoder3)
decoder3 = Dropout(dropout)(decoder3)
decoder3 = concatenate([decoder3, encoder5])
decoder3 = Activation('relu')(decoder3)

# 4th Upsampling Convolutional block in the decoder network
decoder4 = UpSampling2D(size=upsampling_size)(decoder3)
decoder4 = Convolution2D(filters=1024, kernel_size=kernel_size,
padding='same')(decoder4)
decoder4 = BatchNormalization()(decoder4)
decoder4 = concatenate([decoder4, encoder4])
decoder4 = Activation('relu')(decoder4)

# 5th Upsampling Convolutional block in the decoder network
decoder5 = UpSampling2D(size=upsampling_size)(decoder4)
decoder5 = Convolution2D(filters=1024, kernel_size=kernel_size,
padding='same')(decoder5)
decoder5 = BatchNormalization()(decoder5)
decoder5 = concatenate([decoder5, encoder3])
decoder5 = Activation('relu')(decoder5)

# 6th Upsampling Convolutional block in the decoder network
decoder6 = UpSampling2D(size=upsampling_size)(decoder5)
decoder6 = Convolution2D(filters=512, kernel_size=kernel_size,
padding='same')(decoder6)
decoder6 = BatchNormalization()(decoder6)
decoder6 = concatenate([decoder6, encoder2])
decoder6 = Activation('relu')(decoder6)

# 7th Upsampling Convolutional block in the decoder network
decoder7 = UpSampling2D(size=upsampling_size)(decoder6)
decoder7 = Convolution2D(filters=256, kernel_size=kernel_size,
padding='same')(decoder7)
decoder7 = BatchNormalization()(decoder7)
decoder7 = concatenate([decoder7, encoder1])
decoder7 = Activation('relu')(decoder7)

# Last Convolutional layer
decoder8 = UpSampling2D(size=upsampling_size)(decoder7)
decoder8 = Convolution2D(filters=output_channels,
kernel_size=kernel_size, padding='same')(decoder8)
decoder8 = Activation('tanh')(decoder8)
```

The activation function for the last layer is `'tanh'` because we intend our generator to generate values in a range between -1 to 1. The `'concatenate'` layer is used to add skip-connections. The last layer will generate a tensor of a dimension of (256, 256, 1).

 The 'concatenate' layer concatenates tensors along the channel dimension. You can provide a value for the axis, along which you want your tensors to be concatenated.

7. Finally, create a Keras model by specifying the inputs and outputs for the generator network:

```
# Create a Keras model
model = Model(inputs=[input_layer], outputs=[decoder8])
```

The entire code for the generator network inside a Python function looks as follows:

```python
def build_unet_generator():
    """
    Create U-Net Generator using the hyperparameter values defined
    below
    """

    kernel_size = 4
    strides = 2
    leakyrelu_alpha = 0.2
    upsampling_size = 2
    dropout = 0.5
    output_channels = 1
    input_shape = (256, 256, 1)

    input_layer = Input(shape=input_shape)

    # Encoder Network

    # 1st Convolutional block in the encoder network
    encoder1 = Convolution2D(filters=64, kernel_size=kernel_size,
                             padding='same',
                             strides=strides)(input_layer)
    encoder1 = LeakyReLU(alpha=leakyrelu_alpha)(encoder1)

    # 2nd Convolutional block in the encoder network
    encoder2 = Convolution2D(filters=128, kernel_size=kernel_size,
                             padding='same',
                             strides=strides)(encoder1)
    encoder2 = BatchNormalization()(encoder2)
    encoder2 = LeakyReLU(alpha=leakyrelu_alpha)(encoder2)
```

```
# 3rd Convolutional block in the encoder network
encoder3 = Convolution2D(filters=256, kernel_size=kernel_size,
                         padding='same',
                         strides=strides)(encoder2)
encoder3 = BatchNormalization()(encoder3)
encoder3 = LeakyReLU(alpha=leakyrelu_alpha)(encoder3)

# 4th Convolutional block in the encoder network
encoder4 = Convolution2D(filters=512, kernel_size=kernel_size,
                         padding='same',
                         strides=strides)(encoder3)
encoder4 = BatchNormalization()(encoder4)
encoder4 = LeakyReLU(alpha=leakyrelu_alpha)(encoder4)

# 5th Convolutional block in the encoder network
encoder5 = Convolution2D(filters=512, kernel_size=kernel_size,
                         padding='same',
                         strides=strides)(encoder4)
encoder5 = BatchNormalization()(encoder5)
encoder5 = LeakyReLU(alpha=leakyrelu_alpha)(encoder5)

# 6th Convolutional block in the encoder network
encoder6 = Convolution2D(filters=512, kernel_size=kernel_size,
                         padding='same',
                         strides=strides)(encoder5)
encoder6 = BatchNormalization()(encoder6)
encoder6 = LeakyReLU(alpha=leakyrelu_alpha)(encoder6)

# 7th Convolutional block in the encoder network
encoder7 = Convolution2D(filters=512, kernel_size=kernel_size,
                         padding='same',
                         strides=strides)(encoder6)
encoder7 = BatchNormalization()(encoder7)
encoder7 = LeakyReLU(alpha=leakyrelu_alpha)(encoder7)

# 8th Convolutional block in the encoder network
encoder8 = Convolution2D(filters=512, kernel_size=kernel_size,
                         padding='same',
                         strides=strides)(encoder7)
encoder8 = BatchNormalization()(encoder8)
encoder8 = LeakyReLU(alpha=leakyrelu_alpha)(encoder8)

# Decoder Network

# 1st Upsampling Convolutional Block in the decoder network
decoder1 = UpSampling2D(size=upsampling_size)(encoder8)
decoder1 = Convolution2D(filters=512, kernel_size=kernel_size,
                         padding='same')(decoder1)
```

```
decoder1 = BatchNormalization()(decoder1)
decoder1 = Dropout(dropout)(decoder1)
decoder1 = concatenate([decoder1, encoder7], axis=3)
decoder1 = Activation('relu')(decoder1)

# 2nd Upsampling Convolutional block in the decoder network
decoder2 = UpSampling2D(size=upsampling_size)(decoder1)
decoder2 = Convolution2D(filters=1024, kernel_size=kernel_size,
                         padding='same')(decoder2)
decoder2 = BatchNormalization()(decoder2)
decoder2 = Dropout(dropout)(decoder2)
decoder2 = concatenate([decoder2, encoder6])
decoder2 = Activation('relu')(decoder2)

# 3rd Upsampling Convolutional block in the decoder network
decoder3 = UpSampling2D(size=upsampling_size)(decoder2)
decoder3 = Convolution2D(filters=1024, kernel_size=kernel_size,
                         padding='same')(decoder3)
decoder3 = BatchNormalization()(decoder3)
decoder3 = Dropout(dropout)(decoder3)
decoder3 = concatenate([decoder3, encoder5])
decoder3 = Activation('relu')(decoder3)

# 4th Upsampling Convolutional block in the decoder network
decoder4 = UpSampling2D(size=upsampling_size)(decoder3)
decoder4 = Convolution2D(filters=1024, kernel_size=kernel_size,
                         padding='same')(decoder4)
decoder4 = BatchNormalization()(decoder4)
decoder4 = concatenate([decoder4, encoder4])
decoder4 = Activation('relu')(decoder4)

# 5th Upsampling Convolutional block in the decoder network
decoder5 = UpSampling2D(size=upsampling_size)(decoder4)
decoder5 = Convolution2D(filters=1024, kernel_size=kernel_size,
                         padding='same')(decoder5)
decoder5 = BatchNormalization()(decoder5)
decoder5 = concatenate([decoder5, encoder3])
decoder5 = Activation('relu')(decoder5)

# 6th Upsampling Convolutional block in the decoder network
decoder6 = UpSampling2D(size=upsampling_size)(decoder5)
decoder6 = Convolution2D(filters=512, kernel_size=kernel_size,
                         padding='same')(decoder6)
decoder6 = BatchNormalization()(decoder6)
decoder6 = concatenate([decoder6, encoder2])
decoder6 = Activation('relu')(decoder6)

# 7th Upsampling Convolutional block in the decoder network
```

```
decoder7 = UpSampling2D(size=upsampling_size)(decoder6)
decoder7 = Convolution2D(filters=256, kernel_size=kernel_size,
                         padding='same')(decoder7)
decoder7 = BatchNormalization()(decoder7)
decoder7 = concatenate([decoder7, encoder1])
decoder7 = Activation('relu')(decoder7)

# Last Convolutional layer
decoder8 = UpSampling2D(size=upsampling_size)(decoder7)
decoder8 = Convolution2D(filters=output_channels,
            kernel_size=kernel_size, padding='same')(decoder8)
decoder8 = Activation('tanh')(decoder8)

model = Model(inputs=[input_layer], outputs=[decoder8])
return model
```

We have now successfully created a Keras model for the generator network. In the next section, we will create a Keras model for the discriminator network.

The discriminator network

The discriminator network is inspired by the architecture of PatchGAN. It contains eight convolutional blocks, a dense layer, and a flatten layer. The discriminator network takes a set of patches extracted from an image of a dimension of (256, 256, 1) and predicts the probability of the given patches. Let's implement the discriminator in Keras.

1. Start by initializing the hyperparameters required for the generator network:

```
kernel_size = 4
strides = 2
leakyrelu_alpha = 0.2
padding = 'same'
num_filters_start = 64   # Number of filters to start with
num_kernels = 100
kernel_dim = 5
patchgan_output_dim = (256, 256, 1)
patchgan_patch_dim = (256, 256, 1)

# Calculate number of patches
number_patches = int((patchgan_output_dim[0] /
patchgan_patch_dim[0]) * (patchgan_output_dim[1] /
patchgan_patch_dim[1]))
```

2. Let's add an input layer to the network. This takes a patch that is a tensor of dimensions `patchgan_patch_dim`:

```
input_layer = Input(shape=patchgan_patch_dim)
```

3. Next, add a convolutional layer to the network as follows. The configuration for the block is given in the *The architecture of pix2pix* section:

```
des = Convolution2D(filters=64, kernel_size=kernel_size,
padding=padding, strides=strides)(input_layer)
des = LeakyReLU(alpha=leakyrelu_alpha)(des)
```

4. Next, calculate the number of convolutional blocks using the following code:

```
# Calculate the number of convolutional layers
total_conv_layers = int(np.floor(np.log(patchgan_output_dim[1]) /
                    np.log(2)))
list_filters = [num_filters_start * min(total_conv_layers, (2 **
i)) for i in range(total_conv_layers)]
```

5. Next, add another seven convolutional blocks using the hyper-parameters values indicated previously in the *The architecture of pix2pix* section as follows:

```
# Next 7 Convolutional blocks
for filters in list_filters[1:]:
    des = Convolution2D(filters=filters, kernel_size=kernel_size,
padding=padding, strides=strides)(des)
    des = BatchNormalization()(des)
    des = LeakyReLU(alpha=leakyrelu_alpha)(des)
```

6. Next, add a flatten layer to the network, shown as follows:

```
flatten_layer = Flatten()(des)
```

A flatten layer transforms an n-dimensional tensor into a one-dimensional tensor.

7. Similarly, add a dense layer with two nodes/neurons and `softmax` as the activation function. This takes a tensor coming from the `Flatten` layer and converts it into a tensor of a dimension of (`batch_size, 2`):

```
dense_layer = Dense(units=2, activation='softmax')(flatten_layer)
```

The `softmax` function converts a vector to a probability distribution.

8. Next, create a Keras model for the PatchGAN network as follows:

```
model_patch_gan = Model(inputs=[input_layer], outputs=[dense_layer,
flatten_layer])
```

The PatchGAN model will take the input tensor as input and outputs two tensors, one from the dense layer and one from the flatten layer. Our PatchGAN network is now ready. It cannot, however, be used as a discriminator by itself; instead, it classifies a single patch into the categories of real or fake. To create the complete discriminator, follow these steps:

1. We will be extracting patches from the input image and feeding them to the PatchGAN one by one. Create a list of input layers equal to the number of patches as follows:

```
# Create a list of input layers equal to number of patches
list_input_layers = [Input(shape=patchgan_patch_dim) for _ in
range(number_patches)]
```

2. Next, pass the patches to the PatchGAN network and get the probability distributions:

```
# Pass the patches to the PatchGAN and get probability distribution
output1 = [model_patch_gan(patch)[0] for patch in
list_input_layers]
output2 = [model_patch_gan(patch)[1] for patch in
list_input_layers]
```

If we have multiple patches, both `output1` and `output2` will be a list of tensors. We should now have two lists of tensors.

3. If you have multiple patches, concatenate them along the channel dimension to calculate the perpetual loss:

```
# In case of multiple patches, concatenate them along the channel
dimension to calculate perceptual loss
if len(output1) > 1:
    output1 = concatenate(output1)
else:
    output1 = output1[0]

# In case of multiple patches, merge output2 as well
if len(output2) > 1:
    output2 = concatenate(output2)
else:
    output2 = output2[0]
```

4. Next, create a dense layer, as follows:

```
dense_layer2 = Dense(num_kernels * kernel_dim, use_bias=False,
activation=None)
```

5. Next, add a custom loss layer. This layer calculates the mini-batch discrimination for the tensor fed to the layer:

```
custom_loss_layer = Lambda(lambda x: K.sum(
    K.exp(-K.sum(K.abs(K.expand_dims(x, 3) -
K.expand_dims(K.permute_dimensions(x, pattern=(1, 2, 0)), 0)), 2)), 2))
```

6. Next, pass the output2 tensor through dense_layer2:

```
output2 = dense_layer2(output2)
```

7. Next, reshape output2 to a tensor of dimensions of (num_kernels, kernel_dim):

```
output2 = Reshape((num_kernels, kernel_dim))(output2)
```

8. Next, pass the output2 tensor to the custom_loss_layer:

```
output2 = custom_loss_layer(output2)
```

9. Next, concatenate output1 and output2 to create a tensor and pass this through a dense layer:

```
output1 = concatenate([output1, output2])
final_output = Dense(2, activation="softmax")(output1)
```

Use "softmax" as the activation function for the last dense layer. This returns a probability distribution.

10. Finally, create the discriminator model by specifying the inputs and outputs for the network as follows:

```
discriminator = Model(inputs=list_input_layers,
outputs=[final_output])
```

The entire code for the discriminator network is as follows:

```
def build_patchgan_discriminator():
    """
    Create PatchGAN discriminator using the hyperparameter values defined
below
    """
    kernel_size = 4
```

```
    strides = 2
    leakyrelu_alpha = 0.2
    padding = 'same'
    num_filters_start = 64   # Number of filters to start with
    num_kernels = 100
    kernel_dim = 5
    patchgan_output_dim = (256, 256, 1)
    patchgan_patch_dim = (256, 256, 1)
    number_patches = int(
        (patchgan_output_dim[0] / patchgan_patch_dim[0]) *
(patchgan_output_dim[1] / patchgan_patch_dim[1]))

    input_layer = Input(shape=patchgan_patch_dim)

    des = Convolution2D(filters=64, kernel_size=kernel_size,
padding=padding, strides=strides)(input_layer)
    des = LeakyReLU(alpha=leakyrelu_alpha)(des)

    # Calculate the number of convolutional layers
    total_conv_layers = int(np.floor(np.log(patchgan_output_dim[1]) /
np.log(2)))
    list_filters = [num_filters_start * min(total_conv_layers, (2 ** i))
for i in range(total_conv_layers)]

    # Next 7 Convolutional blocks
    for filters in list_filters[1:]:
        des = Convolution2D(filters=filters, kernel_size=kernel_size,
padding=padding, strides=strides)(des)
        des = BatchNormalization()(des)
        des = LeakyReLU(alpha=leakyrelu_alpha)(des)

    # Add a flatten layer
    flatten_layer = Flatten()(des)

    # Add the final dense layer
    dense_layer = Dense(units=2, activation='softmax')(flatten_layer)

    # Create the PatchGAN model
    model_patch_gan = Model(inputs=[input_layer], outputs=[dense_layer,
flatten_layer])

    # Create a list of input layers equal to the number of patches
    list_input_layers = [Input(shape=patchgan_patch_dim) for _ in
range(number_patches)]

    # Pass the patches through the PatchGAN network
    output1 = [model_patch_gan(patch)[0] for patch in list_input_layers]
    output2 = [model_patch_gan(patch)[1] for patch in list_input_layers]
```

```
    # In case of multiple patches, concatenate outputs to calculate
perceptual loss
    if len(output1) > 1:
        output1 = concatenate(output1)
    else:
        output1 = output1[0]

    # In case of multiple patches, merge output2 as well
    if len(output2) > 1:
        output2 = concatenate(output2)
    else:
        output2 = output2[0]

    # Add a dense layer
    dense_layer2 = Dense(num_kernels * kernel_dim, use_bias=False,
activation=None)

    # Add a lambda layer
    custom_loss_layer = Lambda(lambda x: K.sum(
        K.exp(-K.sum(K.abs(K.expand_dims(x, 3) -
K.expand_dims(K.permute_dimensions(x, pattern=(1, 2, 0)), 0)), 2)), 2))

    # Pass the output2 tensor through dense_layer2
    output2 = dense_layer2(output2)

    # Reshape the output2 tensor
    output2 = Reshape((num_kernels, kernel_dim))(output2)

    # Pass the output2 tensor through the custom_loss_layer
    output2 = custom_loss_layer(output2)

    # Finally concatenate output1 and output2
    output1 = concatenate([output1, output2])
    final_output = Dense(2, activation="softmax")(output1)

    # Create a discriminator model
    discriminator = Model(inputs=list_input_layers, outputs=[final_output])
    return discriminator
```

We have now successfully created the discriminator network. Next, let's create an adversarial network.

The adversarial network

In this section, we will create an **adversarial network** containing the U-Net generator network and the PatchGAN discriminator network. Perform the following steps to create an adversarial network:

1. Start by initializing the hyperparameters:

```
input_image_dim = (256, 256, 1)
patch_dim = (256, 256)
```

2. Next, create an input layer to feed the input to the network, as follows:

```
input_layer = Input(shape=input_image_dim)
```

3. Next, use the generator network to generate a fake image:

```
generated_images = generator(input_layer)
```

4. Next, extract patches from the generated image:

```
# Chop the generated images into patches
img_height, img_width = input_img_dim[:2]
patch_height, patch_width = patch_dim

row_idx_list = [(i * patch_height, (i + 1) * patch_height) for i in
range(int(img_height / patch_height))]
column_idx_list = [(i * patch_width, (i + 1) * patch_width) for i
in range(int(img_width / patch_width))]

generated_patches_list = []
for row_idx in row_idx_list:
    for column_idx in column_idx_list:
        generated_patches_list.append(Lambda(lambda z: z[:,
column_idx[0]:column_idx[1], row_idx[0]:row_idx[1], :],
output_shape=input_img_dim)(generated_images))
```

5. Freeze the training of the discriminator network, as we don't want to train the discriminator network:

```
discriminator.trainable = False
```

6. We should now have a list of patches. Pass these through the PatchGAN discriminator network:

```
dis_output = discriminator(generated_patches_list)
```

7. Finally, create a Keras model by specifying the inputs and outputs for the network as follows:

```
model = Model(inputs=[input_layer], outputs=[generated_images,
                 dis_output])
```

These steps create an adversarial model using both networks: the generator network and the discriminator network. The entire code for the adversarial model looks as follows:

```
def build_adversarial_model(generator, discriminator):
    """
    Create an adversarial model
    """
    input_image_dim = (256, 256, 1)
    patch_dim = (256, 256)

    # Create an input layer
    input_layer = Input(shape=input_image_dim)

    # Use the generator network to generate images
    generated_images = generator(input_layer)

    # Extract patches from the generated images
    img_height, img_width = input_img_dim[:2]
    patch_height, patch_width = patch_dim

    row_idx_list = [(i * patch_height, (i + 1) * patch_height) for i in
range(int(img_height / patch_height))]
    column_idx_list = [(i * patch_width, (i + 1) * patch_width) for i in
range(int(img_width / patch_width))]

    generated_patches_list = []
    for row_idx in row_idx_list:
        for column_idx in column_idx_list:
            generated_patches_list.append(Lambda(lambda z: z[:,
column_idx[0]:column_idx[1], row_idx[0]:row_idx[1], :],
output_shape=input_img_dim)(generated_images))

    discriminator.trainable = False

    # Pass the generated patches through the discriminator network
    dis_output = discriminator(generated_patches_list)
    # Create a model
    model = Model(inputs=[input_layer], outputs=[generated_images,
dis_output])
    return model
```

We have now successfully created models for the generator network, the discriminator network, and an adversarial model. We are ready to train pix2pix. In the next section, we will train the pix2pix network on the facades dataset.

Training the pix2pix network

Like any other GAN, training the pix2pix network is a two-step process. In the first step, we train the discriminator network. In the second step, we train the adversarial network, which eventually trains the generator network. Let's start training the network.

Perform the following steps to train an SRGAN network:

1. Start by defining the hyperparameters that are required for training:

```
epochs = 500
num_images_per_epoch = 400
batch_size = 1
img_width = 256
img_height = 256
num_channels = 1
input_img_dim = (256, 256, 1)
patch_dim = (256, 256)

# Specify dataset directory path
dataset_dir = "pix2pix-keras/pix2pix/data/facades_bw"
```

2. Next, define the common optimizer, shown as follows:

```
common_optimizer = Adam(lr=1E-4, beta_1=0.9, beta_2=0.999,
                        epsilon=1e-08)
```

For all networks, we will use the Adam optimizer with the learning rate equal to 1e-4, beta_1 equal to 0.9, beta_2 equal to 0.999, and epsilon equal to 1e-08.

3. Next, build and compile the PatchGAN discriminator network, as follows:

```
patchgan_discriminator = build_patchgan_discriminator()
patchgan_discriminator.compile(loss='binary_crossentropy',
optimizer=common_optimizer)
```

To compile the discriminator model, use binary_crossentropy as the loss function and common_optimizer as the training optimizer.

4. Now build and compile the generator network, as follows:

```
unet_generator = build_unet_generator()
unet_generator.compile(loss='mae', optimizer=common_optimizer)
```

To compile the discriminator model, use mse as the loss function and common_optimizer as the training optimizer.

5. Next, build and compile the adversarial model, as follows:

```
adversarial_model = build_adversarial_model(unet_generator,
patchgan_discriminator)
adversarial_model.compile(loss=['mae', 'binary_crossentropy'],
loss_weights=[1E2, 1], optimizer=common_optimizer)
```

To compile the adversarial model, use a list of losses ['mse', 'binary_crossentropy'] and common_optimizer as the training optimizer.

6. Now load the training, validation, and test datasets, as follows:

```
training_facade_photos, training_facade_labels =
load_dataset(data_dir=dataset_dir,
data_type='training',img_width=img_width, img_height=img_height)

test_facade_photos, test_facade_labels =
load_dataset(data_dir=dataset_dir,
data_type='testing',img_width=img_width, img_height=img_height)

validation_facade_photos, validation_facade_labels =
load_dataset(data_dir=dataset_dir,
data_type='validation',img_width=img_width, img_height=img_height)
```

The load_dataset function was defined in the *Data preparation* section. Each set contains a set of ndarrays of all images. The dimension of each set will be (#total_images, 256, 256, 1).

7. Add tensorboard to visualize the training losses and to visualize the network graphs:

```
tensorboard = TensorBoard(log_dir="logs/".format(time.time()))
tensorboard.set_model(unet_generator)
tensorboard.set_model(patchgan_discriminator)
```

8. Next, create a for loop, which should run for the number of times specified by the number of epochs, as follows:

```
for epoch in range(epochs):
    print("Epoch:{}".format(epoch))
```

9. Create two lists to store the losses for all mini-batches:

```
dis_losses = []
gen_losses = []
# Initialize a variable
batch_counter = 1
```

10. Next, create another loop inside the epochs loop, and make it run for the number of times that is specified by num_batches, as follows:

```
num_batches = int(training_facade_photos.shape[0] / batch_size)
for index in range(int(training_facade_photos.shape[0] /
batch_size)):
    print("Batch:{}".format(index))
```

Our entire code for the training of the discriminator networks and the adversarial network will be inside this loop.

11. Next, sample a mini-batch of training and validation data, shown as follows:

```
        train_facades_batch = training_facade_labels[index *
batch_size:(index + 1) * batch_size]
        train_images_batch = training_facade_photos[index *
batch_size:(index + 1) * batch_size]

        val_facades_batch = validation_facade_labels[index *
batch_size:(index + 1) * batch_size]
        val_images_batch = validation_facade_photos[index *
batch_size:(index + 1) * batch_size]
```

12. Next, generate a batch of fake images and extract patches from them. Use the generate_and_extract_patches function as follows:

```
patches, labels = generate_and_extract_patches(train_images_batch,
train_facades_batch, unet_generator,batch_counter, patch_dim)
```

The generate_and_extract_patches function is defined as follows:

```
def generate_and_extract_patches(images, facades, generator_model,
batch_counter, patch_dim):
    # Alternatively, train the discriminator network on real and
generated images
```

```
     if batch_counter % 2 == 0:
         # Generate fake images
         output_images = generator_model.predict(facades)

         # Create a batch of ground truth labels
         labels = np.zeros((output_images.shape[0], 2),
dtype=np.uint8)
         labels[:, 0] = 1

     else:
         # Take real images
         output_images = images

         # Create a batch of ground truth labels
         labels = np.zeros((output_images.shape[0], 2),
dtype=np.uint8)
         labels[:, 1] = 1

     patches = []
     for y in range(0, output_images.shape[0], patch_dim[0]):
         for x in range(0, output_images.shape[1], patch_dim[1]):
             image_patches = output_images[:, y: y + patch_dim[0],
x: x + patch_dim[1], :]
             patches.append(np.asarray(image_patches,
dtype=np.float32))

     return patches, labels
```

The preceding function uses the generator network to generate fake images and then extracts patches from the generated images. Now we should have a list of patches and their ground truth values.

13. Now, train the discriminator network on the generated patches:

    ```
    d_loss = patchgan_discriminator.train_on_batch(patches, labels)
    ```

This will train the discriminator network on the extracted patches and the ground truth labels.

14. Next, train the adversarial model. The adversarial model will train the generator network but freezes the training of the discriminator network. Use the following code:

    ```
    labels = np.zeros((train_images_batch.shape[0], 2), dtype=np.uint8)
         labels[:, 1] = 1

         # Train the adversarial model
    ```

```
                    g_loss =
adversarial_model.train_on_batch(train_facades_batch,
[train_images_batch, labels])
```

15. Increase the batch counter after the completion of each mini-batch:

    ```
    batch_counter += 1
    ```

16. After the completion of a single iteration (loop) over each mini-batch, store the losses in lists called `dis_losses` and `gen_losses`:

    ```
    dis_losses.append(d_loss)
    gen_losses.append(g_loss)
    ```

17. Also, store the average losses to TensorBoard for visualization. Store both losses: the average loss for the generator network and the average loss for the discriminator network:

    ```
    write_log(tensorboard, 'discriminator_loss', np.mean(dis_losses),
            epoch)
    write_log(tensorboard, 'generator_loss', np.mean(gen_losses),
    epoch)
    ```

18. After every 10 epochs, use the generator networks to generate a set of images:

    ```
    # After every 10th epoch, generate and save images for visualization
    if epoch % 10 == 0:
        # Sample a batch of validation datasets
        val_facades_batch = validation_facade_labels[0:5]
        val_images_batch = validation_facade_photos[0:5]

        # Generate images
        validation_generated_images =
    unet_generator.predict(val_facades_batch)

        # Save images
        save_images(val_images_batch, val_facades_batch,
    validation_generated_images, epoch, 'validation', limit=5)
    ```

Put the preceding code block inside the epochs loop. After every 10 epochs, it will generate a batch of fake images and save them to the results directory. Here, `save_images()` is a utility function defined as follows:

```
def save_images(real_images, real_sketches, generated_images, num_epoch,
dataset_name, limit):
    real_sketches = real_sketches * 255.0
    real_images = real_images * 255.0
    generated_images = generated_images * 255.0
```

```
    # Save some images only
    real_sketches = real_sketches[:limit]
    generated_images = generated_images[:limit]
    real_images = real_images[:limit]

    # Create a stack of images
    X = np.hstack((real_sketches, generated_images, real_images))

    # Save stack of images
    imwrite('results/X_full_{}_{}.png'.format(dataset_name, num_epoch),
X[0])
```

Now we have successfully trained the pix2pix network on the facades dataset. Train the network for 1,000 epochs to get a generator network with good quality.

Saving the models

Saving a model in Keras requires just one line of code. To save the generator model, add the following line:

```
    # Specify the path for the generator model
    unet_generator.save_weights("generator.h5")
```

Similarly, save the discriminator model by adding the following line:

```
    # Specify the path for the discriminator model
    patchgan_discriminator.save_weights("discriminator.h5")
```

Visualizing the generated images

After training the network for 20 epochs, the network will start generating decent images: Let's have a look at the images generated by the generator network.

After 20, 50, 150, and 200 epochs (from left to right), the images look as follows:

Each block contains a facade label, the generated photo, and the actual image, which are vertically stacked. I suggest that you train the network for 1,000 epochs. If everything goes well, after 1,000 epochs, the generator networks will start generating realistic images.

Visualizing the losses

To visualize the losses for the training, start the TensorBoard server, as follows:

```
tensorboard --logdir=logs
```

Now, open `localhost:6006` in your browser. The **SCALARS** section
of TensorBoard contains plots for both losses, as shown in the following screenshot:

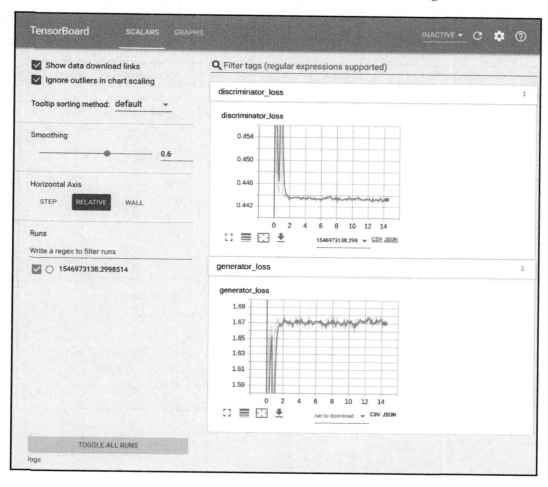

SCALARS section of TensorBoard

These plots will help you to decide whether to continue or stop the training. If the losses are
not decreasing anymore, you can stop the training, as there is no chance of improvement. If
the losses keep increasing, you must stop the training. Play with the hyperparameters, and
select a set of hyperparameters that you think can provide better results. If the losses are
decreasing gradually, keep training the model.

Visualizing the graphs

The **GRAPHS** section of TensorBoard contains the graphs for both networks. If the networks are not performing well, these graphs can help you debug the networks. They also show the flow of tensors and different operations inside each graph:

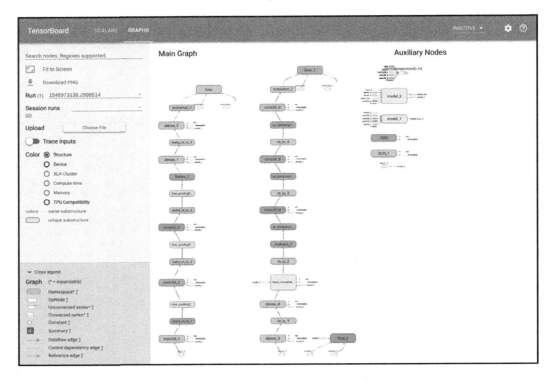

Flow of tensors and different operations inside each graph

Practical applications of a pix2pix network

There are many applications of a pix2pix network. These include the following:

- To convert pixel level segmentation into real images
- To convert day images into night images and vice versa
- To convert satellite areal images into map images
- To convert sketches into photos
- To convert black and white images into colored images and vice versa

The following is an image that was taken from the official paper indicated. It shows the different use cases of a pix2pix network:

Source: Image-to-Image Translation with Conditional Adversarial Networks:

Source: arXiv:1611.07004 [cs.CV]

Summary

In this chapter, we have learned what a pix2pix network is and explored its architecture. We started by downloading and preparing the dataset for training, and then prepared the project and looked at a Keras implementation of a pix2pix network. After that, we looked at the objective function for the training of a pix2pix network. We then trained the pix2pix network on the facades dataset and explored some practical applications of a pix2pix network.

In the next chapter, we will be predicting the future of GANs. We are going to be looking at what might happen in the GAN domain in the near future and how it might change our industries and our daily lives.

Predicting the Future of GANs 9

If you have completed all of the exercises in the chapters of this book, you have come a long way in your quest to learn and code **Generative adversarial networks (GANs)** for various real-world applications. GANs have the potential to cause disruption in a number of different industries. Scientists and researchers have developed various GANs that can be used to build commercial applications. Throughout this book, we have explored and implemented some of the most famous GAN architectures.

So, let's recap what we have learned thus far:

- We started with a gentle introduction to GANs, and learned various important concepts.
- We then explored a 3D-GAN, which is a type of GAN than can generate 3D images. We trained the 3D-GAN to generate 3D models of real-world objects such as an *airplane* or a *table.*
- In the third chapter, we explored conditional GANs for face aging. We learned how to use conditional GANs to translate an image of a face into an image of the same face at a different age. We also discussed various real-world applications of Age-cGANs.
- After that, we explored **Deep Convolutional generative adversarial networks (DCGANs)**, which we used to generate the faces of anime characters.
- In the fifth chapter, we explored **Super-Resolution generative adversarial networks (SRGANs)**, which we can use to generate high-resolution images from low-resolution images. After that, we discussed how SRGANs can solve some very interesting real-world problems.
- We then explored StackGANs, which we used to carry out a text-to-image synthesis task. We explored a dataset before training a StackGAN, and then we concluded the chapter by discussing the practical applications of StackGANs.

- In the seventh chapter, we explored CycleGANs, this time for an image-to-image translation task. Our objective here was to turn paintings into photos. We also discussed real-world applications of CycleGANs
- Finally, in the eighth chapter, we explored the pix2pix network, a type of conditional GAN. We trained the pix2pix network to generate images of facades from architectural labels. Like the other chapters, we concluded this chapter by discussing the real-world applications of the pix2pix network.

In this chapter, we will cover the following topics:

- Our predictions about the future of GANs
- The potential future applications of GANs
- Further areas where GANs can be explored

Our predictions about the future of GANs

In my opinion, the future of GANs will be characterized by the following:

- Open acceptance of GANs and their applications by the research community.
- Impressive results—GANs have so far shown very impressive results on tasks that were difficult to perform using conventional methods. Transforming low-resolution images to high-resolution images, for example, was previously quite a challenging task and was generally carried out using CNNs. GAN architectures, such as SRGANs or pix2pix, have shown the potential of GANs for this application, while the StackGAN network has proved useful for text-to-image synthesis tasks. Nowadays, anyone can create an SRGAN network and train it on their own images.
- Advancements in deep learning techniques.
- GANs being used in commercial applications.
- Maturation of the training process of GANs.

Improving existing deep learning methods

Supervised deep learning methods require a huge amount of data to train models. Acquiring this data is costly and time-consuming. Sometimes, it is impossible to acquire data, as it is not publicly available, or if it is publicly available, the dataset might be very small in size. This is where GANs can come to the rescue. Once trained with a reasonably small dataset, GANs can be deployed to generate new data from the same domain. For example, let's say you are working on an image classification task. You have a dataset, but it is not big enough for your task. We can train a GAN on existing images, and it can then be deployed to generate new images in the same domain. Although GANs currently have training instability problems, several researchers have shown that it is possible to generate realistic images.

The evolution of the commercial applications of GANs

We will see a lot more commercial applications of GANs in the coming years. Many commercial applications of GANs have already been developed and have made a positive impression. The mobile application Prisma, for example, was one of the first widely successful applications of GANs. We are likely to see the democratization of GANs in the near future, and once we do, we will start to see GANs improving our day-to-day life.

Maturation of the GAN training process

After four years since its inception in 2014, GANs still suffer from training instability problems. Sometimes, the GAN doesn't converge at all, as both networks diverge from their training paths. While writing this book, I suffered from this problem many times. Many efforts have been made by researchers to stabilize the training of the GANs. I predict that this process will mature with the advancements in the field of deep learning, and we will soon be able to train models without any problems.

Potential future applications of GANs

The future of GANs is bright! There are several areas in which I think it is likely that GANs will be used in the near future:

- Creating infographics from text
- Generating website designs
- Compressing data
- Drug discovery and development
- Generating text
- Generating music

Creating infographics from text

Designing infographics is a lengthy process. It takes hours of labor and requires specific skills. In marketing and social promotions, infographics work like a charm; they are the main ingredient of social media marketing. Sometimes, due to the lengthy process of creation, companies have to settle with a less effective strategy. AI and GANs can help designers in the creative process.

Generating website designs

Again, designing websites is a manual, creative process that requires skilled, manual work and takes a long time. GANs can assist designers by coming up with an initial design that can be used as inspiration, therefore saving a lot of money and time.

Compressing data

The internet allows us to transfer a huge amount of data to any location, but this comes at a price. GANs enable us to increase the resolution of image and videos. We can transfer low-resolution images and videos to their desired location, then GANs can be used to enhance the quality of the data, which requires less bandwidth. This opens up a whole host of possibilities.

Drug discovery and development

Using GANs for drug development might sound like a dream, but GANs have already been used for generating molecular architectures, given a desired set of chemical and biological properties. Pharmaceutical companies spend billions in the research and development of new drugs. GANs for drug development can reduce this cost significantly.

GANs for generating text

GANs have already proved useful for image generation tasks. Most of the research in GANs is currently focused on high-resolution image generation, text-to-image synthesis, style transfer, image-to-image translation, and other similar tasks. There is not as much research at the moment into using GANs for text generation. This is because GANs were designed to generate continuous values, so training GANs for discrete values is really challenging. In the future, it is predicted that more research will be undertaken in text generation tasks.

GANs for generating music

Music generation using GANs is another area that hasn't been explored sufficiently. The process of music creation is creative and very complex. GANs have the potential to transform the music industry, and if this happens, we might soon be listening to tracks created by GANs.

Exploring GANs

Other GAN architectures that you can explore include the following:

- **BigGAN**: *LARGE SCALE GAN TRAINING FOR HIGH FIDELITY NATURAL IMAGE SYNTHESIS* (https://arxiv.org/pdf/1809.11096.pdf)
- **WaveGAN**: Synthesizing Audio with Generative Adversarial Networks (https://arxiv.org/abs/1802.04208)
- **BEGAN**: *BEGAN: Boundary Equilibrium Generative Adversarial Networks* (https://arxiv.org/abs/1703.10717)
- **AC-GAN**: *Conditional Image Synthesis With Auxiliary Classifier GANs* (https://arxiv.org/abs/1610.09585)

- **AdaGAN**: *AdaGAN: Boosting Generative Models* (`https://arxiv.org/abs/1701.02386v1`)
- **ArtGAN**: *ArtGAN: Artwork Synthesis with Conditional Categorial GANs* (`https://arxiv.org/abs/1702.03410`)
- **BAGAN**: *BAGAN: Data Augmentation with Balancing GAN* (`https://arxiv.org/abs/1803.09655`)
- **BicycleGAN**: *Toward Multimodal Image-to-Image Translation* (`https://arxiv.org/abs/1711.11586`)
- **CapsGAN**: *CapsGAN: Using Dynamic Routing for Generative Adversarial Networks* (`https://arxiv.org/abs/1806.03968`)
- **E-GAN**: *Evolutionary Generative Adversarial Networks* (`https://arxiv.org/abs/1803.00657`)
- **WGAN**: *Wasserstein GAN* (`https://arxiv.org/abs/1701.07875v2`)

There are hundreds of other GAN architectures that have been developed by researchers.

Summary

In this book, my intention was to give you a taste of GANs and their applications in the world. The only limit is your imagination. There is an enormous list of different GAN architectures available, and they are becoming increasingly mature. GANs still have a fair way to go, because they still have problems, such as training instability and mode collapse, but various solutions have now been proposed, including label smoothing, instance normalization, and mini-batch discrimination. I hope that this book has helped you in the implementation of GANs for your own purposes. If you have any queries, drop me an email at `ahikailash1@gmail.com`.

Other Books You May Enjoy

If you enjoyed this book, you may be interested in these other books by Packt:

Generative Adversarial Networks Cookbook
Josh Kalin

ISBN: 9781789139907

- Structure a GAN architecture in pseudocode
- Understand the common architecture for each of the GAN models you will build
- Implement different GAN architectures in TensorFlow and Keras
- Use different datasets to enable neural network functionality in GAN models
- Combine different GAN models and learn how to fine-tune them
- Produce a model that can take 2D images and produce 3D models
- Develop a GAN to do style transfer with Pix2Pix

Python Deep Learning - Second Edition
Ivan Vasilev et al.

ISBN: 9781789348460

- Grasp the mathematical theory behind neural networks and deep learning processes
- Investigate and resolve computer vision challenges using convolutional networks and capsule networks
- Solve generative tasks using variational autoencoders and Generative Adversarial Networks
- Implement complex NLP tasks using recurrent networks (LSTM and GRU) and attention models
- Explore reinforcement learning and understand how agents behave in a complex environment
- Get up to date with applications of deep learning in autonomous vehicles

Leave a review - let other readers know what you think

Please share your thoughts on this book with others by leaving a review on the site that you bought it from. If you purchased the book from Amazon, please leave us an honest review on this book's Amazon page. This is vital so that other potential readers can see and use your unbiased opinion to make purchasing decisions, we can understand what our customers think about our products, and our authors can see your feedback on the title that they have worked with Packt to create. It will only take a few minutes of your time, but is valuable to other potential customers, our authors, and Packt. Thank you!

Index